# The Practical Guide to
# CONTRACTS
## & Other Essential
# KNOWLEDGE

What They Are Not Teaching Executives
and Project Managers

*2nd Edition*

**Dr. Dondi M. Day**

Emerald Isle Publishing

The Practical Guide to Contracts & Other Essential Knowledge, 2nd Ed.

Copyright © 2024 by Dondi M. Day. All rights reserved.

No part of this publication may be reproduced, distributed, or transmitted in any form or by any means, including photocopying, recording, or other electronic or mechanical methods, without the prior written permission of the author, except in the case of brief quotations embodied in critical reviews and certain other noncommercial uses permitted by copyright law. The scenarios and examples in this guidebook are fictional and intended only for illustrative purposes. Any resemblance to real persons, organizations, or events is purely coincidental.

ISBN: 979-8-218-50277-5 (Paperback, 2nd Ed.)
ISBN: 979-8-218-31886-4 (Paperback, 1st Ed. Obsolete)
ISBN: 979-8-330-29050-5 (Companion Workshop and Study Guide
(for sale at an additional cost))

Printed in the United States
Published by Emerald Isle Publishing, LLC.

https://islepublishing.com
P.O. Box 5041
Emerald Isle, NC 28594-5041

For information about our workshops, coaching, training, or to book a training event, please contact the author at https://islepublishing.com or dondi.day@emeraldislepublishing.com

**DISCLAIMER: THIS GUIDEBOOK IS FOR INFORMATIONAL PURPOSES ONLY AND DOES NOT CONSTITUTE LEGAL ADVICE. THE AUTHOR IS NOT A LAWYER AND DOES NOT PROVIDE LEGAL SERVICES. CONSULT WITH A QUALIFIED ATTORNEY FOR ANY LEGAL QUESTIONS OR CONCERNS RELATED TO CONTRACT NEGOTIATION, EXECUTION, TERMINATION, OR DISPUTES.**

This guidebook does not discuss the many types of contracts available in the commercial marketplace, and it is not intended to be a guide to any contract form. Instead, it is meant to give the readers a general and broad understanding of the various terms and conditions and how they may present risks to an organization.

## Dedication and Acknowledgements

To my guiding light, Almighty God,
my loving wife, Tracey,
and our precious boys, Brayden and Logan—this book is for you.

---

With heartfelt gratitude to Dr. Gerald and
the esteemed faculty at Liberty University,
whose collective mentorship and unwavering encouragement
made this journey not only possible but also profoundly enriching.

# TABLE OF CONTENTS

**Preface** ............................................................................................................. 1
    Target Audience ................................................................................................ 2
    Complete Your Learning with the Workshop and Study Guide ........................ 2
    Unique Features And Approach ......................................................................... 3
    How This Book May Enhance Your Exam Preparation .................................... 3
    What This Book Is Not ...................................................................................... 5

**1 Contractual Cornerstones** ................................................................ 7
    Getting Started in the Business of Contracts ..................................................... 8
    What is a Contract? ........................................................................................... 9
    What is the Purpose of a Contract? ................................................................... 9
    Why Do We Need Written Contracts? ............................................................ 12
    Insight Story: A Handshake and a Promise ..................................................... 12
    Discussion: A Handshake & Promise .............................................................. 13
    Conclusion ....................................................................................................... 14

**2 Elements of Contract Formation** ............................................... 15
    The Essential Elements of a Valid Contract .................................................... 15
    Why It Matters ................................................................................................ 16
    Insight Story: We Are Liable for Unpaid Change Orders ................................ 18
    Acceptance by Actions ..................................................................................... 19
    Insight Story: Isn't My Customer's Silence Considered Acceptance? ............... 20
    Privity of Contract: Understanding Your Legal Connections .......................... 22
    How Privity Impacts You: A Hypothetical Scenario ....................................... 22
    The Importance of Flow-Down Clauses ......................................................... 22
    Protecting Your Interests ................................................................................. 23
    Conclusion ....................................................................................................... 23

**3 The Anatomy of a Contract** ........................................................... 25
    Contractual Elements ...................................................................................... 26
    Preamble .......................................................................................................... 26

Contract Recitals .................................................................................27
Interpretation Clause ..........................................................................27
Definitions...........................................................................................27
Main Body of the Contract ................................................................28
Headings..............................................................................................28
Understanding the Contract ..............................................................29
Terms and Conditions: Understanding the Difference ....................30
Legality of Purpose.............................................................................31
The Parties ..........................................................................................31
Competent Parties ..............................................................................31
Conditional Acceptance and Counteroffers.....................................32
Time and Delivery ..............................................................................33
Enforceability .....................................................................................34
Importance of Thoroughly Reviewing Contract Terms and Conditions.................34
Common Mistakes..............................................................................35
Determining When a Contract is Complete.....................................36
Conclusion .........................................................................................37

## 4  Drafting Clear and Unambiguous Contract Documents .....................39
Where it all Begins..............................................................................41
Insight Story: I Need the Equipment Now! ......................................42
Insight Story: I Want My Grass to be Green! ...................................45
Recycling Contracts is Bad!................................................................47
Getting it Together: Project Requirements and Scopes of Work ....48
Specifications ......................................................................................50
General Drafting Guidelines..............................................................51
Your Choice of Words........................................................................52
Shall, Will, May, and Should .............................................................54
Summary .............................................................................................55

## 5  Terms and Conditions....................................................................57
Acceptance of Products and Services ................................................58
Insight Story: Defective Equipment ..................................................60
Audit ....................................................................................................62
Assignment .........................................................................................64
Changes...............................................................................................65
Compliance with Laws and Regulations...........................................70
Confidentiality ...................................................................................74
Contract Documents .........................................................................77
Contractor Responsibilities ...............................................................79
Coordination with Others.................................................................81
Default .................................................................................................86

Default: Handling Subcontractor Disputes and Termination ........................... 88
Insight Story: The Project From Hell ........................................................ 88
Notice Letter ............................................................................................... 93
John's Subcontractor Dilemma .................................................................. 96
Additional Thoughts .................................................................................. 99
Differing Site Conditions ............................................................................ 99
Delays ....................................................................................................... 103
The No Damages for Delay Clause: A Double-Edged Sword ................... 103
Damages for Delay Clause: The Flip Side ................................................ 104
Delivery Milestones .................................................................................. 105
Milestone Clauses: Essential Strategies .................................................... 106
Dispute Resolution ................................................................................... 108
The Importance of Dispute Resolution Clauses ....................................... 108
Entire Agreement ..................................................................................... 111
Insight Story: Updated Equipment List ................................................... 111
Error or Inconsistency in Contract Documents ....................................... 116
Insight Story: Is Anyone up for a Quick Swim? ...................................... 117
Expediting ................................................................................................ 120
The Risk of Expediting ............................................................................. 121
Flow-down (or Flow-through) and Incorporated by Reference ............... 122
Mitigating the Risks ................................................................................. 123
Force Majeure ........................................................................................... 124
Termination Rights: A Critical Consideration ......................................... 125
Governing Law (or Choice of Law) and Venue ........................................ 127
Headings ................................................................................................... 129
Indemnification ........................................................................................ 131
Understanding Damages .......................................................................... 131
Indemnification: Taking on the Responsibility of Others ....................... 132
Beware of Ambiguous Language .............................................................. 132
Three Key Obligations: Indemnifying, Defending, and Holding Harmless ......... 132
Types of Indemnification and Example Clauses ...................................... 133
Word Placement is Critical ....................................................................... 134
Seek Mutual Indemnification ................................................................... 134
Limit Your Liability ................................................................................. 134
Key Takeaway ........................................................................................... 134
Inspection ................................................................................................. 134
Limitation of Liability .............................................................................. 136
Why is a Limitation of Liability Clause Important? ................................ 136
Types of Damages and the Need for Limitation ...................................... 136
What a Limitation of Liability Clause Does ............................................ 136
Enforceability and Carveouts ................................................................... 137

Example Carveout Language ........................................................... 138
Insight Story: The Project that We Could Not Complete .................. 138
Liquidated Damages ...................................................................... 140
What Are Liquidated Damages? ..................................................... 140
Example Clauses ............................................................................ 140
Advantages for You (the Contractor) .............................................. 142
Example Cap Language ................................................................. 142
Advantages for Your Customer ...................................................... 142
Weighing the Pros and Cons .......................................................... 143
Enforceability and Additional Considerations ................................ 143
Key Takeaways for Subcontracts .................................................... 143
No Damages by Contractor ........................................................... 145
No Damages for Delay ................................................................... 148
Notices ........................................................................................... 150
Order of Precedence ...................................................................... 157
Pay–If–Paid and Pay–When–Paid (Contingent Payment Clauses) .. 159
Price and Payment ......................................................................... 162
Records Retention ......................................................................... 164
Scope of Work ............................................................................... 165
Set-off ............................................................................................ 166
Severability .................................................................................... 167
Survival .......................................................................................... 169
Special Terms and Conditions ....................................................... 169
Suspension ..................................................................................... 170
Insight Story: Unanticipated Suspension ....................................... 171
Term of Contract ........................................................................... 173
Termination for Convenience ....................................................... 173
Insight Story: New Flooring .......................................................... 175
Time is of the Essence ................................................................... 177
Title and Risk of Loss .................................................................... 179
Warranty ........................................................................................ 181
Insight Story: Who is to Blame? .................................................... 185
Waiver and Release forms and Contract Language ........................ 193
Insight Story: Getting Paid! ........................................................... 193
Commentary .................................................................................. 198
Lien Waivers and Claim Release Forms ......................................... 199
Conclusion .................................................................................... 200

# 6 Risk Management Through Project Documentation .............. 201
What Exactly is Project Documentation? ...................................... 202
The Power of Documentation ....................................................... 203

Insight Story: The Crooked Subcontractor ........................................................... 204
Commentary ...................................................................................................... 209
The Agenda: A Small Document with Big Impact ............................................. 210
Insight Story: We are Having Problems Now ..................................................... 210
Commentary ...................................................................................................... 212
Effective Meeting Facilitation: ............................................................................ 212
Important Note for General Contractors: .......................................................... 212
The Project Management Plan .......................................................................... 213
The Value of Meeting Minutes: ......................................................................... 215
Discrepancies in Meeting Minutes: .................................................................... 215
Insight Story: That's Your Interpretation! .......................................................... 216
Commentary ...................................................................................................... 216
Project Review Meetings ................................................................................... 217
Insight Story: The ICW Project Kick-off Meeting ............................................. 218
The Critical Role of Letters and Correspondence: ............................................. 225
Responding to Correspondence: ........................................................................ 225
Strategic Use of Notice Letters: ......................................................................... 226
Journals: The Unsung Heroes of Project Documentation .................................. 226
Key Takeaway: ................................................................................................... 227
Daily Site Reports: The Backbone of Project Tracking ...................................... 228
RACI Matrix: A Powerful Tool for Defining Roles and Responsibilities ............ 229
Insight Story: A Case of the Missing Requirements ........................................... 229
Commentary ...................................................................................................... 237
Change Order Logs ............................................................................................ 239
Insight Story: The Ghosting General Contractor ............................................... 240
Risk Register ...................................................................................................... 242
Lessons Learned ................................................................................................. 243
Conclusion ........................................................................................................ 244

# 7 Claims Management: Drafting Notice Letters and Electronic Mail ..... 245
How to Write an Effective Letter ....................................................................... 246
Parts of a Notice Letter ...................................................................................... 246
The Manner of Sending the Letter .................................................................... 246
Sent by e-mail and Courier Service ................................................................... 247
The Body of the Letter ...................................................................................... 248
Closing .............................................................................................................. 249
Navigating Authority in Project Management ................................................... 250
Understanding Authority: The Key to Avoiding Costly Mistakes ....................... 251
Protect Yourself: Verify Authority Before You Proceed ...................................... 251
Miscommunication ............................................................................................ 252
Best Practices for Managing Change Orders ..................................................... 252

Insight Story: Where is the Scope Creep? ..................................................... 254
Communication Skills that Aren't Taught but Learned ................................... 256
Insight Story: The Message in the e-Mail ........................................................ 256
Commentary ................................................................................................. 263
Other Considerations about e-Mail ............................................................... 264
Other Considerations about Letters ............................................................... 264
Summary ...................................................................................................... 265

# 8 Project-Specific Subcontract Management ............................................. 267
Vetting Your Subcontractors .......................................................................... 267
Recommendations ........................................................................................ 268
Insight Story: I've Had It. Let's Terminate Them Today! ................................. 270
Synopsis ....................................................................................................... 271
Exhibit A – Scope of Work ........................................................................... 281
Commentary ................................................................................................ 299
Summary ..................................................................................................... 300
Attachment Six ............................................................................................ 300
Attachment Eight ........................................................................................ 302
Attachment Nine ......................................................................................... 306
Attachment Ten ........................................................................................... 308
Conclusion .................................................................................................. 311

# 9 Bonds and Insurance ............................................................................... 313
Safeguarding Project Success ....................................................................... 313
Bid Bonds: Ensuring Serious Contenders .................................................... 314
Performance Bonds: Guaranteeing Completion .......................................... 314
Payment Bonds: Protecting the Workforce .................................................. 314
Maintenance Bonds: Assuring Post-Completion Quality ............................. 315
How Construction Bonds Reduce Risk ....................................................... 315
Insurance for Construction and Engineering Firms ..................................... 315
Types of Insurance for Construction and Engineering Firms ....................... 316
Owner's Insurance Policy (OIP) .................................................................. 317
How the Owner's Insurance Policy Works: ................................................. 318
Importance of Obtaining Insurance ............................................................ 318
Verifying a Certificate of Insurance ............................................................. 319
Understanding a Certificate of Insurance .................................................... 319
The Growing Challenge of Fraudulent COIs .............................................. 321
Identifying Fraudulent COIs: Key Indicators .............................................. 322
Insight Story: Bridge Over Troubled Waters ............................................... 323
Drawbacks and Limitations of Bonds and Insurance .................................. 324
Conclusion ................................................................................................. 325

## 10 The New Landscape of Contracts .................................................. 327
Key Principles of Relational Contracting ........................................... 328
The Vested Methodology ................................................................ 329
Innovative Contracting Models ........................................................ 329
Benefits and Challenges of Innovative Contracting ........................... 330
Embracing a New Era of Contracting ............................................... 330
Insight Story: The Collaborative Build .............................................. 331
Collaborative Agreement ................................................................. 334
Conclusion ..................................................................................... 336

## 11 Leading the Way in Project Management .................................... 337
The New Paradigm in Project Management: The Rise of Leadership ... 338
The Human Factor: A Game Changer .............................................. 339
Leadership Styles: A Multifaceted Landscape ................................... 342
Beyond Theory: Leadership Styles in Action .................................... 345
The Quest for the "Right" Leadership Style ...................................... 347
The Journey Continues: Your Leadership Evolution ......................... 348
Conclusion ..................................................................................... 348

## Final Thoughts ................................................................................ 351
## Additional Research ....................................................................... 353
## Glossary ......................................................................................... 354
## Index ............................................................................................. 367
## Bibliography ................................................................................... 373
## About The Author .......................................................................... 376
## Let's Stay In Touch! ........................................................................ 377
## Buy the Companion Study Guide ................................................... 378

# PREFACE

I initially developed this guidebook for my workshops, aiming to introduce contract terms, conditions, and construction claims management. While researching and reviewing similar introductory books, I discovered a recurring issue: most were thorough but overly complicated and legalistic. They provided plenty of information but lacked the practical tools needed for success in contract and project management. Many relied heavily on citing case law studies, offering little in the way of actionable, practical, hands-on knowledge. This approach fell short of guiding readers through the essential tasks they face daily.

I saw the potential for a guidebook and study guide that addressed the practical aspects of contracts, specifically tailored for those working in project management. I envisioned a book that offered unambiguous, straightforward recommendations on accomplishing key tasks in the field. How can you potentially avoid or limit risks associated with specific contract terms and conditions? How do you draft an effective notice letter? What are the crucial considerations when terminating a subcontract or drafting a scope of work?

This guidebook is designed to answer these questions and much more. It provides a series of user-friendly, approachable how-to guides that were noticeably absent from many other introductory resources. My goal is to equip you with fundamental, pragmatic ideas and solutions that can be implemented immediately.

Drawing from my extensive experience as a Contract and Claims Manager, I've compiled procedures and techniques that have proven effective in real-world scenarios. While the approaches outlined here are not the only way to do things, they represent tried-and-tested methods that have worked for me and many others. This guidebook distills knowledge gained from my experience, countless courses, field experiences, and teaching sessions.

I aim to help you avoid common pitfalls, better understand the intricacies of contract terms and conditions, and manage contractual obligations more effectively. You'll find unique features in this guidebook, such as examples of various notice letters and detailed explanations of the circumstances for which each is appropriate.

I invite you to explore and apply the strategies presented here. As you embark on your contract or project management journey, remember that knowledge is most powerful when shared. I welcome your feedback, questions, and insights as we work together to elevate the practice of contract and project management. My contact information is at the back of this guidebook.

## Target Audience

Beyond project teams, "The Practical Guide to Contracts and Other Essential Knowledge" is equally beneficial for executives, business owners, and individuals seeking a concise yet comprehensive understanding of contract terms and conditions. Whether you're reviewing a vendor agreement, negotiating a partnership deal, or simply need a quick reference for deciphering legal jargon, this guidebook provides the clarity and confidence to make informed decisions. Its accessible language and practical tips empower readers to protect their interests, avoid common pitfalls, and build stronger business relationships through well-crafted contracts.

## Complete Your Learning with the Workshop and Study Guide

This comprehensive workshop and study guide is the ideal companion to "The Practical Guide to Contracts and Other Essential Knowledge." Designed to deepen professionals' grasp of contract principles and their practical application in contract and project management, this resource is indispensable for anyone seeking to master and achieve project success across all industries. Follow the QR code to IngramSpark or purchase it off of Amazon at https://a.co/d/cA4v2Ei.

## Unique Features And Approach

The Practical Guide to Contracts and Other Essential Knowledge offers a unique approach to understanding contract terms and conditions, focusing on real-world scenarios and practical application. It includes full-text examples of notice letters and explanations of their appropriate use, making it a valuable resource for project managers and executives. The guidebook also emphasizes risk management, helping readers identify and mitigate potential risks in contracts. It uses simplified language, avoiding excessive legal jargon, and provides actionable insights for immediate implementation. Additionally, it aims to enhance exam preparation by offering practical insights and real-world examples.

## How This Book May Enhance Your Exam Preparation

This guidebook aims to provide practical insights and real-world examples to supplement your exam preparation. It delves into the practical application of contract and project management principles, equipping you with the knowledge to navigate the complex world of contracts and claims management.

DISCLAIMER: Please note that while this guide is not an official study resource or endorsed by any certifying body, it can be a valuable supplementary tool for those preparing for such exams, offering insights and practical advice. Readers are strongly encouraged to consult with the certifying organizations for the most up-to-date and comprehensive information regarding their official exam preparation materials and requirements; this guide should not be used as the sole source of preparation.

Key areas covered in this guide that may be beneficial for exam preparation include:

- Project Procurement and Contract Management: The book provides detailed explanations of various contract clauses and their implications, which can help project managers navigate complex procurement and contract scenarios.
- Contract Administration: The book offers practical guidance on managing contracts throughout their lifecycle, including change management, dispute resolution, and performance monitoring. These skills are essential for effective contract administration.
- Risk Management: The book emphasizes risk management throughout the project lifecycle, including identifying, assessing, and mitigating risks associated with contracts and project execution.
- Stakeholder Management: The book highlights the importance of effective stakeholder management, including communication, collaboration, and addressing stakeholder concerns. These skills are crucial for successful project management.
- Legal and Regulatory Compliance: Identify and address legal and regulatory requirements, ensuring compliance and mitigating risks.
- Leadership: The book underscores the importance of leadership in project management, discussing various leadership styles and their impact on team performance and project outcomes.

By studying the concepts and techniques presented in this guide, alongside official exam materials and resources, you'll enhance your understanding of contract management, strengthen your professional expertise, and can enhance your preparedness on relevant project and contract management exams.

Remember, this guide is a valuable tool to complement your exam preparation, not a replacement for official resources provided by the certifying organizations. While this guide can enhance your understanding and potentially improve your performance, it should not be considered a comprehensive source of exam information. Exam success ultimately depends on your individual effort and preparation using a variety of resources.

## What This Book Is Not

This book isn't a comprehensive dissertation on critical path planning, scheduling activities, or resource leveling. While these topics are undeniably crucial for managing construction projects, they are not the focus here. Instead, this guide zeroes in on contract formation, terms and conditions, change orders, disputes, and claims management—key areas that are essential for anyone involved in project management.

However, it's important to recognize that this book is not a magic solution. I won't promise instant competence or success just by reading these pages. Achieving mastery requires significant time, effort, and hands-on experience. This guide provides a blueprint for success, but it's up to you to actively engage with the material and apply the concepts in your daily work.

Remember, like any other plan for success, this one demands action. The ideas and wisdom shared here will only be effective if you put them into practice and continuously broaden your knowledge base.

# 1

# CONTRACTUAL CORNERSTONES

Welcome to the world of contracts! If you're anything like most project managers, you might be thinking, "Contracts? Ugh, legal stuff. Not my area of expertise." But here's the thing: contracts are the backbone of every project you manage. They're not just legal documents; they're your roadmap to success, your shield against risk, and your key to getting paid[1].

In this foundational chapter of "The Practical Guide to Contracts & Other Essential Knowledge, 2nd Edition," we'll demystify the world of contracts and equip you with the essential knowledge you need to navigate them confidently. Whether you are an executive, a project manager, or someone interested in the nuances of contractual obligations, this chapter is designed to provide you with a solid grounding in the basics of contracts.

We'll start with the fundamentals: what exactly is a contract, and why are they so crucial for every business transaction? Contracts are not mere formalities; they are strategic tools that formalize agreements, manage risk, and define

---

1 Tomáš Hanák and Eva Vítková, "Causes and Effects of Contract Management Problems: Case Study of Road Construction," *Frontiers in Built Environment* 8 (2022), https://doi.org/10.3389/fbuil.2022.1009944.

relationships. Throughout the next few chapters, we'll explore how contracts can become a valuable asset in your professional toolkit.

Our goal is to empower you to navigate the complexities of contracts with confidence, allowing you to protect your interests as well as those of your organization. Prepare to transform your approach to contracts from viewing them as mere formalities to recognizing them as essential components of successful business management.

## Getting Started in the Business of Contracts

You may be one of the countless people who believe working in contract management requires a law degree. That's simply not true! While understanding contracts is undoubtedly important for everyone involved, from boots on the ground to the C-suite, you don't need to be a legal expert.

Think of it like this: You don't have to be a master chef to cook a delicious meal, but understanding basic recipes and kitchen safety is crucial. Similarly, everyone involved in a project should have working knowledge of contract fundamentals, how to interpret them, and the potential risks involved. This knowledge will empower you to make informed decisions and contribute effectively to the project's success.

So, let's roll up our sleeves and demystify the world of contracts together, equipping you with the practical knowledge you need to navigate projects with confidence.

To establish a solid foundation, let's address three fundamental questions about contracts:

1. What is a contract?

2. What's the purpose of a contract?

3. Why do we need written contracts??

As we delve deeper into the following sections, you might wonder why each question is essential. Each question serves as a building block in your understanding of contracts. Just as a strong foundation is essential for a building to stand tall, a solid understanding of these fundamental questions will help you navigate the complexities of contracts throughout your career. Let's continue our journey into the world of contracts!

## What is a Contract?

A contract is more than just a piece of paper with signatures; it's a promise, a commitment, and a roadmap for a successful partnership. Think of it as a handshake with legal teeth—it spells out the rights and responsibilities of each party, ensuring everyone knows what's expected of them. In essence, a contract is a legally binding agreement that outlines the terms and conditions of a relationship, whether it's between two businesses, an employer and employee, or a buyer and seller. It's like a recipe for a successful venture, with each ingredient carefully measured and documented to avoid any unpleasant surprises.

## What is the Purpose of a Contract?

While contracts serve as a formal agreement outlining the understanding and responsibilities of all parties involved, their purpose extends far beyond that. Contracts are, in essence, powerful tools for risk management. They allow parties to strategically shift known and unknown risks, safeguarding their interests in a project.

In today's litigious business environment, projects are riddled with potential hazards. A well-crafted contract enables you to transfer these risks to other parties, creating a safety net for your organization. This risk transference isn't a one-way street, however. Once the contract is signed, you can employ specific contract language, such as flow-down clauses, to pass those same risks further downstream to your subcontractors or suppliers. It's a strategic dance of risk allocation.

Of course, contracts also serve the traditional purpose of clarifying expectations, defining roles and responsibilities, and establishing a framework for dispute resolution. But it's essential to recognize their broader function as risk management instruments.

Let's take a brief look at some specific contract terms and conditions (in alphabetical order) that facilitate risk transference. We'll delve into each of these in more detail in the following chapters, exploring their nuances and implications for project success.

- Acceptance (Substantial/Final): A formal acknowledgment that work has been completed satisfactorily.
- Compliance with Laws and Regulations: It is required that parties comply with applicable laws and regulations.
- Damages Caused by Owner's Delay: Compensation for losses incurred due to delays caused by the owner.
- Damages for Contractor's Delay: Compensation for losses incurred due to delays caused by the contractor.
- Differing Site Conditions: Provisions for addressing unexpected conditions at a construction site and allocating responsibility for related costs.
- Dispute Resolution: Procedures for resolving disagreements or disputes between the parties.
- Extended Warranty: A longer warranty period than the standard warranty.
- Force Majeure: A clause excusing parties from performance due to unforeseeable events like natural disasters or pandemics.
- Indemnification: An agreement by one party to compensate the other for losses or damages arising from specified events or circumstances.
- Inspection: The process of examining a work to ensure it meets specified standards.
- Late Payments by the Owner: Provisions addressing the consequences of late payments by the owner.

- Limitation of Liability and Cap: A provision limiting the amount of damages one party can recover from the other.
- Liquidated Damages: A predetermined amount of money agreed upon by contract parties to be paid as compensation for a specific breach of contract.
- Milestones: Specific points in a project timeline used to measure progress and ensure timely completion.
- No Damages for Delay: A clause waiving certain delay-related claims, limiting liability for delays.
- Paid When/If Paid: A clause making subcontractor payment contingent on the owner's payment to the general contractor.
- Price and Payment: Terms outlining the agreed-upon price for goods or services, as well as the payment schedule.
- Price Escalation: A mechanism for adjusting prices due to inflation or changes in market conditions.
- Termination (Convenience/Default): Provisions for ending the contract, either for convenience or due to a breach.
- Waiver and Liens: An agreement to give up certain rights or remedies, such as the right to file a lien.
- Warranty: A guarantee of the quality of goods or services provided, along with a promise to repair or replace defective items.

By understanding these and other contract provisions, you'll be empowered to negotiate more favorable terms, allocate risks strategically, and protect your organization from potential liabilities. Remember, a well-crafted contract isn't just about documenting an agreement; it's about managing risk and ensuring project success.

## Why Do We Need Written Contracts?

It's common for some people to think, "Why can't we shake on it and get on with the project?" or "Why do we need contracts?" In one of my philosophy classes, a professor shared an ancient parable that helps to address these questions. In the story, a group of blind men encounters an elephant. Each man touches a different part and describes the elephant based on his limited experience, leading to conflicting descriptions between them. We all perceive things differently! This parable highlights the subjective nature of individual perspectives and the need for clear communication.

Written contracts are essential because they provide a tangible record of the agreement between parties. Moreover, they may be required in certain states and in certain circumstances. They outline commercial terms, pricing, work to be done, and other key provisions. In the event of a dispute, a written contract serves as a reference to determine each party's duties and responsibilities. If the dispute escalates to arbitration or court, the contract becomes crucial evidence for the arbitrator, judge, or jury to make an informed decision. Having a written document ensures that all parties have a shared understanding and a solid basis for resolving conflicts.

### *Insight Story: A Handshake and a Promise*

Ron, the proprietor of a reputable auto restoration shop, was immediately struck by the classic allure of the Cadillac that Emma drove in. "She's a beauty, Emma!" he exclaimed, his eyes tracing the elegant curves of the car. "I'd be honored to bring her back to pristine condition." He handed Emma an estimate: "$4,000 for a comprehensive restoration, including dent removal and a full repaint."

Emma, recognizing the fair price for such specialized work from a trusted shop, readily agreed. They shook hands to seal their agreement: Emma would pay $4,000, and Ron would restore the Cadillac to its former glory. This exchange of promises—Ron's offer to restore the car and Emma's acceptance by agreeing to pay the stated price—formed a legally binding contract, supported by the payment, or "consideration," which is something of value exchanged by both parties.

Let's examine this agreement. The "offer" was Ron's proposal to restore the car for $4,000. Emma's "acceptance" was her agreement to this proposal, confirmed by their handshake. The "consideration" was the $4,000 Emma promised, which matched the value of Ron's restoration services. This mutual exchange of value is crucial for the enforceability of their contract, transforming a simple promise into a legally binding obligation.

Imagine if Ron had merely said, "I'll restore your Cadillac for free." While generous, this would not constitute a contract since there's no consideration from Emma's side—it would be a unilateral promise, akin to a gift, which isn't legally enforceable if Ron later decided not to proceed.

By ensuring a clear mutual obligation through the exchange of money for services, both parties in this scenario are protected and incentivized to fulfill their commitments, showcasing the fundamental nature of a legally binding contract.

## Discussion: A Handshake & Promise

Let's take a moment and discuss verbal agreements. What if there was a disagreement over the quality of the work? Verbal agreements are common in business, but they can be a recipe for disaster. Memories fade, details get lost, and disagreements arise over what was actually agreed upon. That's where written contracts come in, providing a clear and reliable record of the agreement.

Think of a written contract as a project roadmap, outlining the scope of work, payment terms, timelines, and other key details. This clarity prevents misunderstandings and ensures everyone knows their role. It's like having a referee on hand to resolve any disputes that may arise.

But written contracts offer more than just clarity. They also hold people accountable. A written commitment carries more weight than a casual conversation, making it more likely that both parties will fulfill their obligations. And if a dispute does arise, a written contract is your best defense in court, providing solid evidence of the agreed-upon terms.

In short, written contracts are essential for any business dealing. They offer clarity, enforceability, and peace of mind. So, next time you're tempted to rely on a handshake and a verbal agreement, remember the risks and consider putting it in writing. It could save you a lot of trouble in the long run. If you can't get a contract in place quickly, consider drafting a memorandum of understanding (MoU) to document each party's understanding. While it may not be enforceable in court, it can provide the necessary background to help the parties come to some type of dispute resolution.

## Conclusion

Congratulations on completing the first chapter of your journey to mastering contracts! You now have a solid understanding of what a contract is and why it's important. It's fundamentally an agreement between two or more parties, but there's more to it than meets the eye. A contract is a legally binding agreement that outlines specific actions or non-actions that parties are obligated to take. While oral contracts can be binding in some cases, certain contracts, like those involving real estate, must be in writing to be enforceable.

In the next chapter, we'll explore the essential elements required for a contract to be legally binding, emphasizing that these agreements, whether verbal or written, create rights and obligations for each party. Remember, a contract isn't just a formality; it's a powerful tool for managing risk, setting clear expectations, and ensuring smooth project execution. By grasping the fundamentals of contract formation, you're well on your way to protecting your interests, avoiding costly disputes, and building stronger relationships with your clients and partners.

# ELEMENTS OF CONTRACT FORMATION

Let's delve deeper into the legal definition of a contract. While it's essentially an agreement between two or more parties, there's more to it than meets the eye. A contract is a legally binding agreement that outlines specific actions or non-actions that parties are obligated to take. It's enforceable by law, provided it includes certain essential elements.

## The Essential Elements of a Valid Contract

To be legally enforceable, a contract must satisfy these core elements[2]:

1. **Offer:** An offer is a clear and unambiguous proposal made by one party (the offeror) to another (the offeree), expressing a willingness to enter into a contract on specific terms. For example, a company might offer to purchase a certain quantity of goods from a supplier at a specified price.

2. **Acceptance**: The offeree's unequivocal agreement to the offer's terms. This acceptance must mirror the terms of the offer exactly; any changes

---

2 Karra Greenberg et al., "Analyzing Contracts: State of the Field, Mixed-Methods Guiding Steps, and an Illustrative Example," *Law and Social Inquiry* 49, no. 1 (2023), https://doi.org/10.1017/lsi.2022.82.

constitute a counteroffer. For instance, the supplier agrees to provide the goods at the price stated by the company.

3. **Consideration**: The exchange of something of value between the parties. This is the mutual benefit that each party receives from the contract. Consideration can take many forms, such as money, goods, services, or even a promise to do something or refrain from doing something. For example, the company provides payment to the supplier in exchange for the goods.

4. **Capacity**: The legal ability of both parties to enter into a contract. This means they must be of legal age and mentally competent to understand the terms of the agreement.

5. **Legality**: The purpose of the contract must be legal and not violate any laws. For instance, a contract for the sale of illegal drugs would not be enforceable.

It's important to note that while oral contracts can be binding in some cases, certain contracts, such as those involving real estate, must be in writing to be enforceable.

When all these elements—offer, acceptance, consideration, capacity, and legality—are present, a legally binding contract is formed. This agreement, whether verbal or written, creates rights and obligations for each party, ensuring that their expectations are clearly defined and enforceable by law.

## Why It Matters

Understanding the distinction between terms and conditions is vital for anyone involved in contracts. These seemingly small details can significantly impact your project if not carefully considered. For instance, "pay-if-paid" and "pay-when-paid" clauses are examples of condition precedents that can have serious financial consequences for subcontractors if the project owner fails to pay the general contractor.

Over the next few chapters, we'll delve deeper into the intricacies of "pay-if-paid" and "pay-when-paid" clauses, exploring their implications and how to navigate them effectively. For now, understand that these are just two examples of conditions that can significantly impact your rights and obligations under a contract. By grasping these nuances, you'll be better equipped to protect your interests and ensure the success of your projects.

To illustrate, let's consider a scenario where you are a subcontractor reviewing a subcontract given to you by the contractor. You encounter the following "pay-if-paid" clause:

> **Paid if Paid**: Subcontractor's entitlement to payment for work is dependent on payment from Owner to Contractor, as long as it is allowed by law.

Here's another, even more concerning example of a condition precedent becoming common in commercial contracts:

> **Paid if Paid**: Contractor's obligation to make payment to Subcontractor is dependent on Contractor receiving payment from Owner, and Subcontractor assumes the risk of Owner not making payment.

Is the risk of non-payment under these clauses acceptable to you and your executive team, even if you have a good relationship with the contractor? What if you perform extra work on the project, either through formal change orders or written directives, substantially increasing the original contract value? These example clauses present significant risks, and their potentially destructive nature shouldn't be taken lightly. If you find this language in your signed contract, be cautious about doing any extra work.

As a negotiator, you should attempt to redline these clauses or add mitigating language to reduce the risks, such as [text bolded here for emphasis]:

**Paid if Paid**: Subcontractor's entitlement to payment for work is dependent on payment from Owner to Contractor, **only if Subcontractor's breach of this Agreement or deficient or delayed work is the cause of Owner's failure or refusal to pay Contractor for Subcontractor's work.**

If you are the project manager and these clauses (or similar language) appear in your signed contract, be aware of the potential risks. Push for prompt payment of your change orders and resolve any disputes as soon as possible. Do not allow unpaid change orders to accumulate. The last thing you want when the project ends is a change order log full of unpaid claims. If this is the case, and you decide to wait, be prepared to negotiate pennies on the dollar for your hard work.

## Insight Story: We Are Liable for Unpaid Change Orders

John's hands were rough and lined from years spent on construction sites. He was known for his precision in his work. Now, his latest project, a vast commercial complex, promised to challenge his seasoned skills more than any before.

The general contractor for the site was a titan of the industry, notorious for their aggressive handling of contracts. As the work progressed, John found himself inundated with requests for additional work—requests that came verbally at first, with assurances that formal change orders would soon follow.

"John, we need you to add another section to the East wing. We'll sort out the paperwork later," the project manager would say, clapping him on the shoulder with a reassuring smile.

Skeptical from past experiences, John made it a point to secure everything in writing. "I'll need that in a change order, signed and dated, before my crew starts on it," he'd reply each time, his voice firm yet polite.

By the time the project was nearing its end, John's desk was buried under a mountain of these documented requests. He spent long nights reviewing each one against his meticulous records, ensuring every penny spent was accounted for. Confident in his calculations, he awaited the final payment, only to be met with a staggering blow—the check was far less than what he had calculated.

Dismayed, John combed through the payment details and discovered that numerous change orders, which represented a significant portion of his work, were absent from the final settlement. He confronted the general contractor, his frustration palpable.

"I don't understand—these change orders were approved and completed. Why haven't they been included in the final payment?" John demanded, spreading the documents across the table.

The response was cold and nonchalant. "John, you know our contract has a 'paid-if-paid' clause. We only pay out what we receive from the owner. It's out of our hands."

"But that's not fair—look at the work my team has done. It's all documented, right here!" John argued, pointing to the stack of papers.

The contractor shrugged, unmoved. "I suggest you take it up with the owner if you have an issue with the payment."

Staring at the remnants of the project—blueprints, change orders, and unpaid invoices—John felt a profound sense of betrayal. His hard work and diligence, it seemed, were no match for the harsh realities of the construction business. The industry was a battlefield of contracts, power plays, and survival, and despite his best efforts, John had become yet another casualty.

## Acceptance by Actions

Acceptance isn't always communicated through words but can be inferred from actions. For example, if you offer to buy a product at a specific price, and the seller responds by shipping the goods, their action indicates acceptance of the offer. However, silence, on the other hand, is not typically considered acceptance.

In legal terms, silence does not provide clear and explicit consent or agreement to the terms of a proposal or offer, which are essential for forming a valid contract. The law recognizes the importance of clear communication in establishing legally binding agreements.

There are a few exceptions to this general rule. For instance, if a specific agreement exists between the parties stating that silence will be considered acceptance, or if there's an established practice within a particular industry where silence is understood as acceptance, then it may be valid.

If a party remains silent in response to a proposal, it's unclear whether they have accepted, rejected, or simply failed to respond. In such cases, it's essential to seek clarification or obtain a more explicit expression of acceptance to ensure a contract's validity. Remember that silence rarely constitutes acceptance, but this issue is prevalent, and misunderstandings often occur on projects.

To illustrate this point, let's explore another problem John encountered that highlights the potential pitfalls of relying on silence as acceptance.

## *Insight Story:*
## *Isn't My Customer's Silence Considered Acceptance?*

John, thriving in the fast-paced environment of a major construction project, was no stranger to change. This week, however, brought a new challenge. Logan, the client's project manager, had emailed him requesting pricing and schedule impacts for some proposed changes, reminding him of the project's tight deadline.

Change orders were a common occurrence on this project, often due to evolving specifications or unforeseen site conditions. John understood their necessity but found himself in a bind when Logan went radio silent after receiving his proposal. With a looming equipment order deadline, John began to wonder if Logan's silence could be interpreted as approval. Unsure, he decided to ask for my thoughts.

"So, let me get this straight," I began. "You received a request for proposal, submitted your pricing, but haven't heard back. Now you're wondering if it's safe to proceed with the changes?"

"Exactly," John confirmed, a hint of worry in his voice.

"John, I strongly advise you to review your subcontract. It likely requires written authorization for any changes. Assuming acceptance from silence is a risky gamble," I explained.

"But my client has always paid me for similar situations in the past," John countered.

"Past behavior isn't a guarantee," I cautioned. "Silence doesn't equal acceptance, and your contract might even forbid proceeding without a written change order. You don't want to end up doing a ton of extra work for free."

I'd heard this argument before from countless project managers, each relying on a history of informal approvals. But it was crucial for John to understand the potential consequences.

"John, it's imperative you understand the changes clause in your contract before making any assumptions," I stressed. "Without a signed change order, you could be left high and dry, with no payment for the additional work."

I continued, "Think of a change order as a safety net. It clearly defines the scope of the changes, the associated costs, and the revised timeline. It's a legally binding agreement that protects both you and the client, preventing misunderstandings and ensuring you get paid for your work."

"I see your point," John conceded, the gravity of the situation sinking in.

"I recommend reaching out to Logan again," I advised. "Politely request a written confirmation of the changes. It's always best to have things in writing to avoid any confusion or disputes down the road."

"Thanks for the reality check," John replied, sounding relieved. "I'll get on that right away."

## Privity of Contract: Understanding Your Legal Connections

Earlier, we touched on the concept of privity, but it's worth diving deeper as it's a cornerstone of contract law with significant implications for your business.

What is Privity of Contract? Privity of contract is the legal relationship that exists between parties who have entered into a contract. It's like a direct line connecting those involved, granting them the right to enforce the contract's terms and seek remedies if the other party fails to uphold their end of the bargain. In simpler terms, it means you can only sue someone for breach of contract if you have a direct contractual relationship with them.

## How Privity Impacts You: A Hypothetical Scenario

Imagine this: You hire a subcontractor for a project, and they, in turn, hire a sub-subcontractor to handle a specific aspect. Now, suppose the sub-subcontractor messes up, causing delays or delivering substandard work. Can you sue them directly?

The answer depends on privity. If your contract with the subcontractor doesn't include clauses that "flow down" your rights and obligations to the sub-subcontractor, you have no direct contractual relationship with them. You're not in privity. This means you cannot sue the sub-subcontractor directly, even if their actions negatively impacted your project.

## The Importance of Flow-Down Clauses

This is where flow-down clauses become crucial. These clauses essentially extend the terms of your contract with the subcontractor to their sub-subcontractors. By incorporating flow-down clauses, you create a chain of privity, allowing you to hold all parties in the chain accountable for their performance.

## Protecting Your Interests

To ensure your project's success and protect your interests, it's essential to:

- **Carefully Review Contracts**: Scrutinize your contracts to ensure they include flow-down clauses if you anticipate the involvement of sub-subcontractors.
- **Consult Legal Counsel**: If you're unsure about the implications of privity or the effectiveness of your contract clauses, seek legal advice.

By understanding the concept of privity and taking proactive steps to establish it with all relevant parties, you can avoid legal complications, streamline dispute resolution, and ultimately safeguard the success of your projects.

## Conclusion

In this chapter, we've explored the essential elements that constitute a legally binding contract: offer, acceptance, consideration, capacity, and legality. We've delved into the nuances of these elements, highlighting the importance of clear communication, mutual understanding, and adherence to legal requirements. We've also examined the distinctions between terms and conditions, emphasizing how seemingly minor details can significantly impact project outcomes. By grasping these fundamental concepts, you're equipped to navigate the complexities of contract formation and protect your interests.

In the next chapter, we'll shift our focus to the anatomy of a contract, dissecting its various components and exploring their functions. We'll examine the preamble, recitals, definitions, and the main body of the contract, shedding light on how these elements work together to create a comprehensive and enforceable agreement. We'll also discuss common drafting pitfalls and offer strategies for achieving clarity and legal compliance. By the end of this chapter, you'll have a deeper understanding of the structure and language of contracts, empowering you to confidently review, negotiate, and manage your agreements.

# THE ANATOMY OF A CONTRACT

Contracts are remarkably diverse, spanning from standardized "boilerplate" agreements to those crafted on the fly. Boilerplate clauses, often uncontroversial and pre-written, are frequently included in contracts with minimal negotiation, regardless of the specific deal. While commercial contracts offer flexibility in drafting, most adhere to a conventional structure. This typically includes a preamble, recitals (optional), definitions, the main body of the agreement, and any relevant schedules or exhibits, though the order can vary.

Some contracts retain traditional legalese, marked by archaic phrases like "Whereas" and "Witnesseth." However, there's a growing trend toward using clearer, more straightforward language. The heart of a contract often starts by stating its purpose, leading to a detailed body that specifies the terms and conditions. This body not only clarifies the reasons for the agreement, but it also incorporates boilerplate terms, which are generally standardized across different agreements. Contracts typically conclude with a closing section, including the signatures of all parties.

This chapter explores the elements of a contract. We'll examine key sections like the preamble, recitals (if present), and definitions, revealing their role in shaping a contract's objectives and enforceability. The discussion extends to the importance of both administrative and financial terms in risk management, as well as their impact on the parties involved. We'll also address common drafting pitfalls and offer strategies to achieve clarity and legal compliance. By the chapter's end, you'll gain a comprehensive understanding of the contract's basis structure.

## Contractual Elements

A contract's structure is meticulously designed to ensure clarity and enforceability. It begins with the preamble, which introduces the agreement, identifies the parties involved, and establishes the effective date. Next, the definitions section clarifies key terms, eliminating ambiguity and ensuring a shared understanding of the contract's language.

The main body of the contract details the substantive provisions, outlining each party's rights, responsibilities, and duties, which are essential for successful execution. Towards the end, boilerplate clauses offer standard legal protections, playing a crucial role in managing potential risks and disputes. Understanding each component of a contract's structure is vital for all parties. This knowledge helps navigate legal complexities, aligns expectations, and ultimately facilitates smoother contractual relationships.

## Preamble

A contract's preamble is administrative and supplies basic information. It identifies the agreement's title, the parties involved, and the date it was made. For example:

> This Consulting Agreement ("Agreement") is made and entered into this 15th day of June 2025 (the "Effective Date") by and between Jones Limited Consulting, Inc., a Delaware corporation having its principal office located at 1234 Six Forks

Road, Raleigh, NC 28616 ("Consultant"), and XYZ Communications, Inc., a New York corporation having its principal office located at 123 Main Street, New York, NY 12345 ("XYZ").

## Contract Recitals

Contracts often begin with a section named Witnesseth or Recitals after the introductory preamble. Many people gloss over this section, viewing it as boilerplate, but recitals are crucial. This section explains or introduces the nature, background, or history of the contractual relationship between the parties. Although there is no specified format, recital paragraphs often start with "Whereas" and may include numbered paragraphs. Recitals help establish the contract's fundamental objectives and can be crucial in resolving ambiguities during disputes.

## Interpretation Clause

Most commercial contracts include an interpretation clause that sets out the rules of construction. An example might be:

> **Interpretation.** The parties acknowledge that they have reviewed and revised this agreement with the help of their legal counsel. They agree that the usual rule of interpreting any ambiguities in favor of the party who did not draft the agreement will not apply.

## Definitions

The definitions section is essential for a clear, well-written contract. It ensures consistency and helps avoid misunderstandings. The keywords and phrases defined in this section are typically capitalized throughout the contract. If the contract does not include a dedicated definitions section, terms are typically defined as they are used. Most words in a contract are given their ordinary meaning unless used in a technical sense or as terms of art.

## Main Body of the Contract

The body of the contract contains the key terms governing the rights and obligations of the parties. It includes the purpose of the agreement, consideration, parties' rights and responsibilities, work to be completed, and other commercial terms and conditions. For example:

> **Services**. Subcontractor commits to supplying the services outlined in Exhibit A - Condition of Work (the "<u>Work</u>"), which is attached to this agreement and made a part of it.
>
> **Relationship of the Parties**. The relationship between Subcontractor and Contractor will be that of an independent contractor, and this agreement should not be interpreted as creating a partnership, joint venture, or employer-employee relationship.
>
> **Compensation**. In return for Subcontractor's Work, and after the conditions outlined in this agreement are met, Contractor agrees to pay Subcontractor $200,000.00 for all Work performed under this agreement. This amount includes all taxes, fees, profit, overhead, and any other costs or expenses related to the subcontractor's work."

## Headings

A contract's terms and conditions are typically numbered in paragraph form, referred to as sections. Each section usually has a heading or title to give readers an idea of the content. Some contracts, however, may lack headings or have terms and conditions merged under unrelated headings. It's essential to read the entire contract thoroughly, as headings are for reference purposes only and do not affect the interpretation of the agreement.

This guidebook covers some standard terms and conditions in construction and supply contracts, but it is not exhaustive. Contracts can include a wide range of terms and conditions, each of which should be carefully reviewed for potential risks and implications.

## Understanding the Contract

When reviewing a contract, it may initially appear disorganized, but this is often an illusion. Upon closer inspection, you should recognize that a contract typically contains both administrative and financial terms and conditions. Administrative terms usually present minimal risk and exposure to financial liability, while financial terms involve more significant risk. However, it's crucial not to become complacent with administrative clauses, as they can still lead to disputes. For example, the term "Cooperation with Others" may seem benign, but failing to attend meetings or respond to information requests can cause delays and claims, leading to damages asserted by your customer.

Also, while reviewing a contract, some terms and conditions may appear trivial or like fillers. However, every term and condition plays a specific role and presents potential risks to your organization. The contract language might sometimes be consolidated under unrelated headings. Ideally, terms should be outlined from the most to least important, but this approach is not always followed.

Contracts are often recycled across projects, focusing on risks identified in previous iterations. Despite a potentially poor layout, it's essential to read the entire contract without making assumptions. Later in this guidebook, we will discuss headings in greater detail.

# Terms and Conditions: Understanding the Difference

As we delve into the intricacies of contracts, it's crucial to establish a clear understanding of two fundamental concepts: terms and conditions. While often used interchangeably, these terms have distinct meanings in the legal context.

- **Term**: A term is a provision within a contract that outlines a specific obligation for one or both parties. Think of them as the building blocks of the agreement, defining the rights and responsibilities of each party. Terms can cover various aspects, such as payment schedules ("Contractor shall be paid monthly in arrears"), delivery dates ("Goods shall be delivered on or before July 1st"), confidentiality obligations ("The parties agree to keep all confidential information disclosed during the project confidential"), or performance standards ("The software shall be delivered with a 99.9% uptime guarantee"). While most terms are explicitly stated in writing, some, like implied warranties (the assumption that a product is fit for its intended purpose), may not be explicitly written but are still legally enforceable.

- **Condition**: A condition is a contractual provision that acts as a "trigger." It determines when or if a specific term within the contract becomes active or inactive. In other words, conditions control the timing and circumstances under which obligations arise or are discharged.

There are two main types of conditions:

1. **Condition Precedent**: This type of condition creates an obligation. For example, a contract might state that a buyer's obligation to pay for goods arises only after the seller delivers them. The delivery is the condition precedent that triggers the payment obligation. Another example could be a bonus clause in an employment contract that states that an employee will receive a bonus only if they meet a certain sales target.

2. **Condition Subsequent:** This type of condition terminates an existing obligation. For instance, a contract might stipulate that a lease agreement

will end if the tenant fails to pay rent on time. The non-payment of rent is the condition subsequent that terminates the lease. Another example could be a construction contract stating that it will terminate if the project is not completed by a specific date.

## Legality of Purpose

For a contract to be enforceable, the work or services performed must be legal. For example, a contract to design and construct a laboratory for the sale or distribution of illicit substances (e.g., drugs or paraphernalia) would be considered unenforceable by the courts. In other words, an illegal contract is no contract at all and cannot be enforced. Such contracts are deemed void, as if they never existed. Consequently, if either party breaches the contract, they will not be entitled to any remedy or relief from the courts.

## The Parties

Typically, a contract involves at least two parties. Any persons or organizations that have not signed the contract are considered third parties and do not have a direct contractual relationship, known as privity of contract. Privity of contract is a common law doctrine that prevents a third party (not a party to the contract) from enforcing a term, even if the contract confers a benefit on that third party.

## Competent Parties

For a contract to be enforceable, all parties involved must be competent and possess the legal and mental capacity to form one. This means they must understand the nature and consequences of entering into an agreement. Contracts with minors, mentally incapacitated individuals, intoxicated persons, convicted felons (in most states), and undocumented immigrants are generally not legally binding. Additionally, the individuals signing the contract must have the authority to bind their organization to the agreement. This last point will be discussed later.

## Conditional Acceptance and Counteroffers

As we discussed, if your subcontractor gives you an offer with added strings attached, the response is considered a counteroffer, not an acceptance. A counteroffer isn't considered acceptance because it materially changes the terms of the proposed contract. Think of it this way: a counteroffer rejects the original offer and substitutes it with a new one. For instance, if you ask a mechanic to repair a piece of heavy equipment for $3,000, and the mechanic says, "I'll agree to that price if you pay for my travel expenses to the site," the mechanic has made a counteroffer. You would have to accept the counteroffer for an agreement to be formed.

It's important to note that under the Uniform Commercial Code (UCC), which governs the sale of goods and has been adopted in some form by every state, a qualified acceptance may create a binding contract despite adding new conditions, unless these conditions cause surprise or hardship. However, to avoid ambiguity, it's crucial to clearly state that any counteroffer to your terms and conditions will be rejected.

Consider this common scenario: Your subcontractor returns your purchase order, signed on the first page (with your standard terms and conditions). However, they've crossed out your terms and added a statement that their own terms and conditions apply. In this case, acceptance has not occurred, and your subcontractor has made a counteroffer. It's essential to respond promptly in writing, either accepting or rejecting their counteroffer. Silence could be construed as acceptance.

In such scenarios, it's advisable to reject the counteroffer and negotiate using your own terms and conditions. Your terms should be well-crafted to favor your company, ensuring your interests and legal obligations are fully protected. They should include provisions for confidentiality, intellectual property, delivery, warranty, and liability.

Using your own terms and conditions offers several advantages:

- Protection: Ensures your interests are safeguarded and legal obligations are clearly defined.
- Consistency: Standardizes your business relationships, reducing the risk of misunderstandings and disputes.
- Negotiation Power: Allows you to negotiate more favorable terms and make changes as needed.

By prioritizing your own terms and conditions, you take control of the contract and pave the way for a more successful business relationship. To illustrate the importance of this, let's explore an issue John had on one of his projects.

## Time and Delivery

Finally, the offer may include specific requirements, such as time and delivery method, that you must meet for acceptance. For instance, the other party might require you to respond with a formal written letter or make a phone call at a specific time and day. The critical point to keep in mind is that a contract is not formed if you respond in any way other than as specified by the other party. While these requirements may seem very formal, it is common for contracts to have specific acceptance criteria. Today, most contracts clearly define how acceptance is achieved.

Consider the following example:

> **Acceptance**. Contractor supplying the goods, parts, and products ("Goods") or supplying services, including any resulting products, starting performance, or taking any payment, will be considered as Contractor's clear acceptance of this Agreement.

This clause outlines several actions for acceptance of the contract: (i) agreeing by signing the contract, purchase order, order acknowledgment, or other documents; (ii) commencement of performance; or (iii) acceptance of payment. Acceptance clauses may include more details than our example, but the principle remains the same.

## Enforceability

I've mentioned the word "enforceable" several times throughout this chapter. So, what does that mean exactly? For a contract to be enforceable, one party must make a clear and straightforward offer to perform work or services. The offer must be definite, seriously intended, and communicated to the other person. Sometimes, one party disputes whether the other party accepted an offer. Acceptance hasn't occurred if one party's response to an offer doesn't show a willingness to be bound by the terms of the agreement or if the response includes added conditions or strings attached.

When additional terms or strings are attached, it becomes a counteroffer. The party receiving the counteroffer may accept, reject, or continue to negotiate. We'll discuss this crucial point further later in this chapter. Finally, acceptance hasn't occurred if the proposed offer is based on false information or lies, or if the offer was made in jest. For example, I often joke with my younger son about mowing the entire yard. I might say, "I'll pay you a million dollars to mow my grass," but he knows I'm joking about spending that much money for a 20-minute task.

## Importance of Thoroughly Reviewing Contract Terms and Conditions

For your convenience, I have listed the headings for terms and conditions in alphabetical order in the next chapter. As mentioned, it is rare to find contract terms and conditions presented in a logical sequence. The terms and conditions included here represent only a few of the standard clauses you may encounter in construction and supply contracts.

It is impossible to provide a comprehensive list of all potential terms and conditions you may come across in your career. Always be prepared to review each contract thoroughly, as each will present unique clauses and requirements tailored to the specific project and parties involved.

Careful review and understanding of each clause are critical to identifying potential risks and obligations that could impact the project's success. Contract terms can vary widely based on the nature of the work, the parties involved, and the industry standards. Therefore, it is essential to approach each contract with a meticulous eye, ensuring that every term and condition aligns with your project goals and risk management strategies.

## Common Mistakes

We have emphasized the importance of ensuring that your contract documents are unambiguous, consistent, clear, and concise. These lofty goals are difficult to achieve in the best circumstances. But we should remember that people create these documents. People are imperfect and often prone to fatigue, slips, lapses, and mistakes. If mistakes are found, most of the time, it's after the concrete has been delivered and poured and the first section of steel is erected. Correcting these mistakes is costly and often ends in disputes or litigation.

Most contractors will attempt to interpret the requirements when faced with ambiguous language, and the outcome may or may not produce the intended result. Most bidding documents will ask contractors to ask for clarifications, but after the contract award, most contracts compel the contractor to submit requests for clarifications.

> **Errors and Omissions**. Contractor is responsible for thoroughly reviewing and comparing the Contract Documents with each other and with the information provided by Owner, and reporting any errors, inconsistencies, or omissions found immediately. If Contractor carries out any construction activ-

ities while aware or should have been aware that it involves an error, inconsistency, or omission in the Contract Documents without notifying Owner, Contractor will be fully responsible for such actions and will bear the full cost of corrections.

Do you recall the discussion about requests for information? This is a perfect time to use this form.

## Determining When a Contract is Complete

Determining when a contract is truly complete isn't always straightforward. The answer often lies in the details—specifically, within the contract itself. While it may seem like a simple question, contract completion is a nuanced process that depends entirely on fulfilling the specific obligations outlined in the agreement.

Think of a contract as a checklist. Each item on the list represents a contractual obligation that must be satisfied in order for the contract to be considered complete. These obligations can vary widely, depending on the nature of the contract. They might include (but not limited to):

1. Delivery of Goods or Services: Has the agreed-upon product or service been fully delivered to the customer's satisfaction?
2. Payment Terms: Have all payments been made according to the schedule outlined in the contract?
3. Documentation: Have all required documents, such as certificates of completion or acceptance forms, been executed?
4. Inspections and Approvals: Has the work been inspected and approved by the relevant parties or agencies?
5. Warranty Obligations: Have any warranty periods commenced or expired?
6. Subcontractor Payments: Have all subcontractors been paid for their work?

To determine whether a contract is complete, you must meticulously review the contract's terms and conditions. Look for any clauses that define completion, termination, or final acceptance. Pay close attention to any specific requirements or milestones that must be met before the contract can be considered fulfilled.

## Conclusion

In this chapter, we've explored the anatomy of a contract, dissecting its key components and understanding their functions. We've examined the preamble, recitals, definitions, and the main body of the contract, highlighting how each element contributes to a comprehensive and enforceable agreement. We've also discussed common drafting pitfalls and emphasized the importance of clear, concise language and thorough review to avoid ambiguities and potential disputes. By now, you should have a solid grasp of the structure and language of contracts, empowering you to confidently review, negotiate, and manage your agreements.

In the next chapter, we'll shift our focus to the specific terms and conditions commonly found in contracts. We'll delve into the nuances of these provisions, exploring their potential risks and offering strategies for mitigating them. We'll also discuss the importance of understanding the interplay between different clauses and how they can impact your rights and obligations. By the end of this chapter, you'll be equipped with the knowledge to identify potential pitfalls, negotiate more favorable terms, and protect your interests in any contractual agreement.

# 4

# DRAFTING CLEAR AND UNAMBIGUOUS CONTRACT DOCUMENTS

It may seem daunting if you have never created a scope of work. But unbelievably, this is the most exciting part of the overall process, and this document will be used throughout the life of your project. It would be best if you had a clear idea of your specific objectives before hiring a subcontractor or putting a shovel in the ground. Your role is to orchestrate this symphony and ensure your team members (and subcontractors) can deliver a result that meets the project's specifications. If you aren't into opera, then think about it in the context of sports. It's the same analogy but applied a little differently. You are the master of developing this plan!

Before we start, we need to reiterate the importance of definitions. You may think, "Are we going to cover this topic again?" Yes! It is critical that you get it right. If you have been in the construction or manufacturing business long enough, you will see that contracts contain a long list of definitions. They may have a section dedicated for the reader to explore, or the definitions may be sprinkled throughout the contract, making the reader flip through the pages, searching for their meaning. When people ask me if all these definitions are needed, my answer is this: There are over 600,00 words in the English language, and some are spelled the same, but they have different meanings. You will also see words that mean one thing in one industry but take on a different meaning in another. The words you choose may take on a different life depending on your perspective. The words you choose should be unambiguous or have their meaning clearly defined.

Think of it this way. It's common to define your contract in the introduction section, like this example:

> This Consulting Agreement ("<u>A</u>greement") is made and entered into this 15th day of June 2025 (the "<u>Effective Date</u>") by and between Jones Limited Consulting, Inc., a Delaware corporation having its principal office located at 1234 Six Forks Road, Raleigh, NC 28616 ("<u>Consultant</u>"), and XYZ Communications, Inc., a New York corporation having its principal office located at 155 Capital Blvd, Raleigh, NC 28616 ("<u>XYZ</u>").

You have identified the contract and defined it as the **<u>A</u>**greement (the first letter is bolded here and underlined for emphasis). Throughout your contract, if you are referring to your contract, you will say this "Agreement." If you refer to it elsewhere as a contract or agreement, you are creating an ambiguous situation. What contract or agreement are you referring to here? This may seem trivial, but it may have significant implications in a dispute or litigation. Okay, let's pretend you are the manufacturer of a unique, one-of-a-kind ice machine for outside grilling enthusiasts, and its name brand is the "Super Tumbler." Instead of calling it an "ice maker machine" (throughout your contract), you state it is an ice maker (make, model, or other descriptive information) and then define it as (the "<u>Super Tumbler</u>"). Once you define it, you will use this defined term throughout your contract. Again, the best way to ensure your contract is clear is to define the terms and ensure their consistency throughout all contract documents.

## Where it all Begins

One of the biggest mistakes project managers make, both new and experienced, is failing to identify their needs and what they hope to achieve. The more time you spend clarifying your needs, the better the result. Let's pretend you need to build a widget, and you want to reuse the exact requirements that were previously used. Are you sure it will meet your needs? What if you want the latest and greatest bells and whistles? Have you considered the changes in manufacturing technologies that may reduce the cost of the widget? If you insist on reusing the requirements, the manufacturer may have to retool, driving up manufacturing costs.

It all starts with creating your requirements, but if your project is still in the conception phase, these requirements may be abstract, and they need to be molded into something you can use to breathe life into your specifications. To develop and refine your requirements into something tangible, you must work with internal (and sometimes external) stakeholders to help you identify your requirements and create a concrete set of specifications. It's sometimes a case of, "I don't know what I don't know."

It's common to see organizations conduct market research by taking their requirements and soliciting requests for information from companies to help them develop and refine a description of the result that will meet their needs. Think of it this way. Requirements are your road map, and they contain information that helps to describe the required results rather than how to accomplish them. They also help you define your objectives, needs, goals, and tasks, as well as how the result will be created and implemented. After you collect this information, it's used to develop a set of project documents (e.g., specifications).

## *Insight Story: I Need the Equipment Now!*

John arrived at the site trailer early to meet with his assistant project manager and review the project's equipment list. He was tall and seemed to have a commanding presence. He was in his early thirties, with black hair and brown eyes. He had his professional engineering license and recently completed his master's degree, but he rarely spoke about any of his accomplishments. I was driving to work when I received a call from John.

"Hey, sorry to call you this early, but I need your help," John's voice came through the speaker.

"No problem, John. What's up?" I responded, always ready to assist.

"I just realized I forgot to order a critical piece of equipment with a long lead time. It needs to be ordered today, or my project schedule will be in shambles," John explained, a hint of stress in his voice.

"Okay, what are your options?" I asked, trying to get a handle on the situation.

"I know you prefer not to use our suppliers' terms, but can you take a look and see if we can make an exception this time?" John asked hesitantly.

"Of course. Send them over, and I'll review them," I assured him.

Upon reaching my desk, I checked my email. The supplier's terms, as expected, were one-sided and heavily favored them. I picked up the phone to discuss the risks with John.

"John, I've reviewed the terms. They're not ideal, but given the urgency, we can accept them for this order. However, I need to warn you about the potential downsides," I cautioned.

"I understand. I'm between a rock and a hard place. If I don't get this equipment ordered now, I'll be facing liquidated damages," John replied, sounding frustrated.

"Alright, I'll send you an email authorizing the order based on our conversation," I confirmed.

Months passed, and one morning, I received a forwarded email from John. In the email, the supplier notified us of a three-month delay in the equipment delivery. John called a few minutes later, clearly agitated.

"Did you see the email?" he asked urgently.

"Yes, just now," I replied.

"This delay is unacceptable. What are our options? Can we go after them for delay damages?" John inquired, hoping for a solution.

"Let me pull up the terms and take a look," I said, trying to remain calm.

A quick search for "delays" and "damages" in the supplier's terms revealed the harsh reality.

"John, their terms state that the proposed schedule was for convenience only and they aren't liable for any delay damages. They also have the right to adjust the schedule at any time before delivery," I explained, hating to be the bearer of bad news.

"So we have no recourse?" John asked, defeated.

"Not according to their terms. Your best bet is to appeal to their goodwill or offer to pay for expedited delivery," I suggested, wishing there was a better solution.

This incident underscored the importance of using our own company's terms and conditions. Without clear terms protecting us as the customer, we were at the mercy of the supplier. To safeguard your company, ensure your terms cover key aspects like goods/services, payment, delivery, warranties, termination rights, and any flow-down terms from your customers. By doing so, you minimize liability, protect your interests, establish trust, and streamline contract reviews. Always make your company's terms the starting point for negotiations—it's the best way to level the playing field and ensure a fair and successful outcome.

> **BEST PRACTICES**
>
> Using a requirements document or previously used specifications is easy, but you shouldn't assume they will meet your needs. For instance, technology is constantly evolving, and your needs may be met by taking a different approach. Additionally, it may prevent other companies from responding to your requests and proposing the latest approaches or technologies.

It sounds simple enough, but recognize that we live in an imperfect world, and Murphy's Law creeps into everything. You may think, "Why are these documents so important?" Consider this point. These documents are the cornerstone of your project's foundation and outline your customer's vision, scope, cost, schedule, quality, and performance (among other things). You may also think, "Why is it so difficult to jot these things down and get them right?" Your customer may have failed to involve the right stakeholders, effectively communicate those requirements, or need help understanding their requirements.

It's common to find ambiguous or boilerplate information from previous projects included in the requirements. Your customer's requirements evolve and change throughout the project. These scenarios create ambiguities in the requirements, which always surface later. For contract and project managers, ambiguity is an absolute nightmare, eroding clarity and trust. Clear and concise requirements are essential to the project's overall success. Your project may only succeed if you understand your customer's requirements, and you may spend more time and money fixing these ambiguities.

Since we understand the importance of unambiguous requirements, we can move on to the next step. Once the customer has developed its requirements and is certain they are clear and concise, it will use them to develop a set of specifications. Specifications are the documents that provide you with the definition of the project's scope and objectives. They explain what will be delivered to your customer once the project is completed and typically include the materials, products, installation procedures and constraints, inspection, testing requirements, and quality aspects. It should also include details of all your customer's required or desired items. They may also include the technical data needed to plan and implement the project. The specifications may list functional attributes or consist of diagrams or schematics. They can also be in the form of prototypes, mockups, and models.

During the bidding phase, you should see a flurry of people huddled in a small room pouring over the customer's specifications, inspecting it for clarity by reading and re-reading it. This is the time to ask questions to ensure no details are missed. Once the project is awarded, dedicate the same amount of time to performing the same task. It's essential to review the requirements and specifications together to ensure they are clear, complete, and accurate.

Please think back to the last time you asked someone to do something; the result wasn't what you saw in your mind. I always go into my sons' bedrooms and ask them to clean up the clothes from the middle of the floor. I walk down to the first floor and hear them frantically cleaning. It sounds like a couple of elephants jumping up and down, ready to fall through the ceiling. When I return a few hours later and open the door, I find that the middle of the floor has been cleaned, but the clothes have been relocated to a corner of the room or thrown unceremoniously in the closet. Did they do what I asked them to do? Sure, they did! It's my fault—I needed to be more specific about what and how I wanted it. While I have oversimplified this by using the scenario, it does ring true.

## *Insight Story: I Want My Grass to be Green!*

Let's reframe this in another story. You started a new job that requires you to travel, and you only have the time to do some of the yard and house maintenance you were able to do last spring. You and your partner hire a yard maintenance company to do everything that needs to be done outside. You create a list of your high-level requirements to give to the companies interested in working for you.

- The cost of lawn services must be under $2,500 for the season.
- The grass should be green and healthy.
- Provide an additional quote for spraying the yard with insecticide.

You have a mental image of your ideal yard and know what services should achieve your goals and objectives. You eventually find a contractor that assures you they can meet your requirements. You like their company's logos on their vehicles and their professional demeanor. You shook hands, signed the contract, and later found you were not getting the services you believed you were paying for when you gave them your check. The services only resemble what you originally had in mind.

You may have envisioned mulch placed around your trees and shrubs, no weeds in the cracks of your sidewalk and driveway, and especially in the flower beds! The green grass you envisioned is richer, healthier green than the pale green you see. In this scenario (and I have learned this lesson the hard way), the more precise your wording is, the better! Consider this. What does "green" mean? What do the words "as required" and "all weeds removed" mean? That is precisely my interpretation. All weeds around my house, including the flower beds and the weeds growing up between the cracks in my concrete, should be removed, and the grass should be fertilized enough to get that dark green color. Let's assume you spent more time researching lawn care companies and found that some offer unique services that others do not. According to this research, you use your requirements document to create your specifications.

- No services before 7:00 am or after 6:00 pm on weekdays. No work on Sundays unless approved.
- Proof of insurance for all employees must be provided before starting services.

- Grass should be cut and maintained at 2 ½ inches.
- Grass should be fertilized as the manufacturer requires (monthly, quarterly, yearly) for Bermuda grass.
- Spray insecticide (specifically for mosquitoes) on a monthly basis.
- Remove all weeds from the flower beds, sidewalks, and driveway.
- All debris (tree limbs and trash) will be removed from the yard.

While not perfect, this is a terrific way to refine your list. Let's explore a scenario that John needs help resolving.

## Recycling Contracts is Bad!

Recycling old contracts and scopes of work is a recipe for disaster. These outdated documents are often riddled with gaps, ambiguities, and outdated terms, virtually guaranteeing disputes down the line. Every project deserves unique, carefully tailored contracts and scope of work.

In my workshops, the pushback is predictable: "I'm swamped! Drafting new documents for every project is unrealistic." Others mistakenly claim that reusing old documents saves time and money. This is a dangerous illusion.

Let's be clear: I'm not advocating against templates. Templates are valuable tools that provide a framework and structure for your thinking. I use them constantly, along with a checklist to ensure thoroughness. But let me ask you this: What's the true cost of incomplete or ambiguous project scopes? It's a ticking time bomb. The unknowns are vast, and your potential liability is staggering.

Here's the bottom line: The more time invested upfront in crafting meticulous contracts and scopes of work, the less likely a dispute will erupt, saving everyone involved significant time and money. Remember, lawyers bill by the minute—those perceived savings from cutting corners will vanish faster than sandcastles in a hurricane.

## BEST PRACTICES

Investing the time to create comprehensive, project-specific contracts and scopes of work is an investment in the smooth execution of your projects and the protection of your bottom line.

### Getting it Together: Project Requirements and Scopes of Work

It's common for your customers to establish their requirements and use that document to create their specifications and your scope of work. If the customer lacks the expertise or personnel to develop these documents, they may hire a consultant to create them. When created internally by the customer, there is a certain level of investment or "skin in the game." However, there are instances where you, as the contractor, must take the customer's specifications and develop your scope of work.

Sometimes, you may need to develop the scope of work and include it in your proposal. You may also need to create a scope of work for your subcontractors. As a contractor, failing to invest the necessary time and effort to produce a clear, concise, and unambiguous document can lead to changes, delays, cost overruns, and disputes[3]. Unless you have significant experience in project management and feel comfortable with the risks, it's advisable to have at least one other project manager review the documents you produce.

When you receive a call from your boss assigning you a project, you might think, "Where do I start?" It's easy to feel overwhelmed, especially when faced with a pile of complex documents. You must turn that information into clear

---

3  Isaac Sakyi Damoah, Anthony Ayakwah, and Paul Twum, "Assessing Public Sector Road Construction Projects' Critical Success Factors in a Developing Economy: Definitive Stakeholders' Perspective," *Journal of Project Management* 7, no. 1 (2022), https://doi.org/10.5267/j.jpm.2021.7.003.

documents for subcontractors and suppliers. Feeling overwhelmed is normal, and congratulations—you are now part of the club.

When I started working in the contract's profession, I was thrilled to have a job with a large defense contractor, but I also felt anxiety and doubted my ability to do the work. If you are new to contracts and project management, you can probably relate to these feelings. If you are experienced, you can sympathize with those experiencing it for the first time. How do you get over the anxiety? I have learned over the years to approach tasks in small steps until I reach my objective.

Breaking down the process into manageable parts helps mitigate the initial overwhelm. Start by thoroughly reviewing all relevant documents. Outline the key requirements and specifications. Consult with experienced colleagues or mentors. Take time to draft your scope of work meticulously, ensuring clarity and precision. Each small step brings you closer to creating effective documents that can guide your project to success without unnecessary complications.

Last year, I took my two sons to Moab to hike Arches and Canyonlands. The Southwest is a fantastic place to visit; looking across the canyons, it feels surreal, and the views are truly breathtaking. Before we left on our trip, I taught my sons the importance of making lists. I love creating lists—long lists, detailed lists, and even lists about other lists. We made one for each of our suitcases, backpacks, tent gear, supplies, and, of course, a grocery list. Since we were flying, I wanted to ensure we had everything we could possibly need neatly packed away in our suitcases.

Moab is surrounded by desert, and when you see a sign that says, "No Gas for 90 Miles," you better go gas up! We created our lists and followed them to the letter. Was it a perfect trip? Yes, but did we have everything we thought we needed? Absolutely not! Murphy's Law always comes knocking when you least expect it. But remember, a list is a starting point. It helps to guide you. Things can and will go wrong, but this is a great time to anticipate problems and prepare for them before you are stranded.

Creating an outline gives you an idea of what needs to be done rather than how you plan to do it. A quick web search may reveal a long list of things you should consider, or you can explore the Internet for useful materials. Don't be afraid to use the tools you have available to accomplish your goals. Consider asking your colleagues if they have any materials that may be useful to you.

Whatever approach you decide to take, start by creating a list of the requirements and specifications. These documents will provide different aspects of the project, including performance, delivery, schedule, acceptance, and quality. This structured approach ensures that you cover all bases and helps mitigate the risks of unexpected issues. Remember, the value of a list is not just in its creation but also in how it guides you through the process, helping you to anticipate and prepare for potential challenges.

## Specifications

A specification is a description of your needs. It's meant to provide potential subcontractors with a detailed, accurate, and complete statement of your needs so that they can offer solutions[4]. Think of it this way. Your project's specifications should cover every item you may need on your project, along with where they are to be used and how much should be used, and the specific materials to be used and fabricated. The specification should be clear and concise, allowing you to evaluate potential offers. It should also provide the basis for performance measurement and may serve as evidence in a dispute.

Like most documents that make up your contract, it's common to find huge gaps in an important topic area, contradictions, or ambitious language. The first version is never perfect, and it takes multiple revisions to get it close to being right. You should consider these documents to be "living documents." They will change faster than the water current flowing through an inlet. The constant clarifications or additions to the specification may result in change orders, so be

---

4  Damoah, Ayakwah, and Twum, "Assessing Public Sector."

prepared for that eventuality. It's essential to capture the revisions and modifications to the specifications in a revision log, but remember to modify your plans, drawings, bill of materials, and other contract documents that the changes may impact.

> **BEST PRACTICES**
>
> Let's suppose you are happy with the scope of work your subcontractor included in their proposal. In that case, you should be cautious about incorporating their entire proposal into your contract by reference. It may contain terms and conditions, assumptions, or exclusions that aren't acceptable or create loopholes or ambiguities.

## General Drafting Guidelines

Now that we have that out of the way, let's focus on the fun stuff. Here are some aspects you should consider when drafting a scope of work, and let's work through these as a checklist framed as questions:

1. What is the problem you are attempting to solve?
2. Who owns the problem?
3. What are you attempting to accomplish?
4. How will you know when it is accomplished or resolved?

Writing well is difficult to master. But it's an incredibly important skill, and it takes a lot of experience and practice to put things down on paper that are easily understood. At least, that's been my experience. Its immense power allows us to inform, convince, entertain, and evoke strong emotions. As necessary are the words you choose to write down; the presentation of your work is equally important. The documents you produce are a direct reflection of your skills and abilities. Let's explore ways to create documents that naturally flow and are professionally labeled and formatted.

**Formatting**

1. The first piece of advice I have to offer is to consider the layout and appearance of the document when you print it. Are the margins appropriate, or are they so wide that they seem to fall off the page? There should be lots of white space. Why? It is easier to read and digest if the text is not jumbled and close together.

2. Is your font type and size appealing? Most of my contracts are written in Times Roman, size 10 font with a line spacing of 15. If you are unfamiliar with this terminology, use the search engine box at the top of the Microsoft Word program.

3. In contracts or scopes of work, do not use bullet points. This is a huge pet peeve of mine, and it isn't easy to describe it in letters. Adopt the appropriate number system that works for you.

4. Do not overuse boldface, italics, and underlining. Their overuse often distracts and desensitizes the reader.

5. Do not be afraid to use graphics, tables, charts, or other diagrams to convey your message. You should ensure they are appropriately labeled.

**Your Choice of Words**

In general, you should use straightforward words and not attempt to impress anyone with your vocabulary knowledge. The words you choose may express certainty or vagueness. For instance, words such as "similar, like, type, average," and "about" often create uncertainty. When drafting a scope of work, remember it is a legal document with potential risks. As I mentioned, if you are using words unique to a particular profession, then use those words, but be consistent and define them if appropriate.

I mentioned the term "consistent." Let me emphasize this point. If you refer to a steel beam as a "support member" in one section of your scope of work and then refer to it as a "brace" in another, you have created an ambiguity. Be careful and consistent in how you use your words.

Avoid using buzzwords or jargon specific to your profession, as they can be overused, unclear, or awkward. For example, "bandwidth" in IT refers to the capacity to transmit information, but it's often misused to mean someone doesn't have enough time or resources. If you must use such terms, define them clearly the first time, or in a dedicated definitions section. This ensures everyone understands your meaning. For instance, providing a clear definition of "scope of work" helps avoid ambiguity. Let's consider the following example in the definitions section:

> **Scope of Work**" means the description of Work to be performed by Contractor as outlined in this Agreement, including as more specifically outlined in Exhibit A.

You may find it defined in the contract similar to this example:

> **Scope of Work**. Subcontractor shall furnish all services, supervision, labor, materials, tools, rental equipment, supplies, products, goods, parts, and equipment (collectively, the "Scope of Work") as described in the Contract Documents.

Every profession has their own unique jargon and an extensive list of acronyms that often confuses uninitiated people. To hear them speak, you may wonder, "Am I on the right planet?" Either by design or by accident, using abbreviations, jargon and acronyms often creates ambiguity. If you use them, keep in mind that some people may not understand them. If you are in the federal contracting arena, you may be able to relate to my feelings. I genuinely believe there is a division of people whose sole purpose is to do nothing but create acronyms. I guess they serve their purpose in some way. If you find yourself using acronyms that are uncommon in your industry, define them the first time you use them and be consistent throughout the document. Did you check the other contract documents to ensure consistency?

A professor told me to use an active voice rather than a passive one, and I had to research these terms to understand what he was trying to tell me. Here it is in simple terms. In the active voice, the subject of the sentence acts; in the passive voice, the subject receives the action. This topic is difficult to explain, and it takes writing, rewriting, and learning to get this right. I recommend using a word editing software program to catch spelling, missing words, typos, punctuation, and other errors to ease your pain.

## Shall, Will, May, and Should

It's common to see scopes of work with words that do not hold the subcontractor accountable. For instance, the words "should" and "may" do not create a compelling reason for your subcontractor to perform. If you want to hold them accountable, use the word "shall." When referring to an obligation under the contract, refer to it as "will." The term "shall" create a higher duty than "will." Let's consider the following examples [***Bolded here and italicized for emphasis***]:

> <u>Work Description</u>. Subcontractor ***shall*** exercise reasonable skill and judgment in the performance of the work and shall provide all necessary equipment, material, tools, labor, and supervision ("<u>Work</u>") that are required to replace the existing water meters with new water meters.
>
> <u>Termination for Convenience</u>. Contractor ***may*** terminate the Purchase Order at any time without cause before its completion by sending Subcontractor written notice of such termination. Upon such termination, Contractor ***shall*** pay to Subcontractor, in full satisfaction and discharge all liabilities

and obligations owed to Subcontractor, an equitable amount for all Work satisfactorily performed by Subcontractor as of the date of termination.

**Access to Site**. Contractor *will* give Subcontractor access to Contractor Equipment during Business Days.

Here's a point I have had to make a few times in my workshops. Do not let your ego become unchecked. When you write things down, they become part of your project's written record. This record may become available to other people, litigants, and the court. Unnecessary or unprofessional comments may haunt you later in your project and career. Always consider your tone and message when drafting contract documents.

## Summary

In summary, Chapter 4 underscores the necessity of clear and precise contract drafting to prevent misunderstandings and disputes. It offers a step-by-step guide to the contract drafting process, beginning with the identification of project needs and the development of comprehensive requirements and specifications. The chapter emphasizes the importance of clear communication and precise language and the avoidance of ambiguity in contract documents. Additionally, it provides valuable insights into best practices for contract drafting, including incorporating proposals into final agreements, addressing errors or inconsistencies, and understanding the implications of the "four corners" rule in contract interpretation.

In the following chapter, we'll journey into the core of contracts: the terms and conditions. We'll dissect the various provisions typically found in contracts, each with its own potential benefits and drawbacks. Understanding these clauses and how they interact is vital, as they delineate the rights, duties, and liabilities of all parties involved. We'll equip you with practical strategies for spotting potential pitfalls, negotiating advantageous terms, and mitigating risks associated with specific contract provisions. By the chapter's conclusion, you'll possess the knowledge and confidence to navigate the intricacies of contract terms and conditions, safeguarding your interests and ensuring the smooth execution of your projects.

# 5

# TERMS AND CONDITIONS

Before we delve into the terms and conditions commonly found in most contracts, it's important to clarify a few key points. The example terms and conditions provided in this guidebook have been rewritten and simplified for better understanding. Throughout this guidebook, we will use the terms "word" and "term" synonymously. When you see a capitalized word in a contract, it is usually intended to have a specific meaning within that context, such as "Delivery." However, this is not always the case. It is common to encounter capitalized terms that are not clearly defined in the definitions section or the contract body, or that are inconsistently capitalized.

Important keywords should be clearly defined to avoid ambiguity. This can be done in two ways: either by defining the term in the dedicated definitions section of the contract or by defining the term the first time it appears in the contract by capitalizing it, placing it in parentheses, and using quotation marks (e.g., "Project Site"). As a personal preference, I underline defined terms when using them within the body of the contract. This helps me quickly locate the defined terms when scanning the document.

For instance, in our example above, the definition of "Project Site" may be found within a sentence or included in the definitions section. The definition in the definitions section might read as follows:

**Project Site**: The location where the work specified in this contract will be performed. By maintaining consistency in defining and capitalizing key terms, we ensure clarity and avoid misunderstandings in contract interpretation.

Or you may define it in the body of the contract similar to this:

PROJECT SITE. The project is located at 777 Division Street, Raleigh, NC ("Project Site").

Before delving into specific terms and conditions, a few housekeeping notes are necessary. The terms in this guidebook are arranged alphabetically, not by importance. It's crucial to remember that most contract terms are interconnected and should be considered in relation to one another. For example, if a subcontractor supplies faulty equipment, understanding your recourse involves reviewing multiple clauses like warranty, termination for default, indemnification, insurance, and limitation of liability (if present). Okay, now that we have the house cleaning done, let's jump right into our first term.

## Acceptance of Products and Services

Clarification: The term "Acceptance" in this context refers to the customer's acknowledgment that the delivered goods or services meet the contract's requirements. This is distinct from the earlier discussion about contract formation.

Acceptance plays a crucial role in determining contract completion. It occurs when the customer, after having had a reasonable chance to inspect, confirms that the goods or services conform to the contract or chooses to accept them despite any non-conformity. Your contract should include an acceptance clause outlining the inspection criteria and procedures for accepting your products or services.

To ascertain if Acceptance has taken place, carefully review your contract's terms and associated documents. Often, contracts stipulate that the customer must either reject non-conforming items or explicitly accept them within a defined timeframe.

Let's examine the interplay of relevant clauses:

> **Project Site**. The project is located at 123 Main Street, New York, NY 12345.
>
> **Acceptance.** Contractor will promptly, but no later than 25 calendar days after the Delivery ("Inspection Period"), examine and inspect all Work performed by Subcontractor. Contractor will notify Subcontractor of any defects or nonconformity to the agreement. If Contractor does not notify Subcontractor in writing of any nonconforming work and provide Subcontractor with written evidence or other documentation required by Subcontractor, the Work will be considered accepted at the end of the Inspection Period.
>
> **Warranty**. Subcontractor warrants that the Work will be in compliance of all laws and regulations and free from defects in material and workmanship ("Warranties") for a period of 12 months after the date of Delivery to the Project Site (the "Warranty Period"). This warranty is conditional upon: (i) Contractor fully paying the purchase price, (ii) Contractor providing written notice of the defect, described reasonably, to Subcontractor within 10 days of the time when Contractor discovers or ought to have discovered the defect, and (iii) the proper storage, installation, operation, use and maintenance of the Work in compliance with Subcontractor's operation and maintenance manuals.

**Delivery**. All deliveries under this agreement will be FOB Project Site and all transportation and handling charges will be paid for by Subcontractor.

**Payment Terms**. Unless otherwise specified in the purchase order, Contractor will pay all invoiced amounts within 30 calendar days after the date of Delivery and receipt of Subcontractor's invoice.

As you can see in our example above, acceptance is often linked to other contract terms like delivery, inspection, payment, and warranty. Determining the exact moment of Acceptance can be challenging, so it's essential to carefully read through your contract to understand if you've met all your obligations and to identify when Acceptance officially occurs.

## *Insight Story: Defective Equipment*

Let's imagine a scenario where you've delivered equipment to a project site. This equipment is sensitive to weather, and its packaging isn't meant for long-term outdoor storage. You included an operation manual detailing warranty exclusions and steps the customer needs to take to protect the equipment. The contract requires your customer to inspect the equipment within 25 days of delivery and report any issues.

Months later, when the equipment is about to be installed, the customer notices what they believe are defects—internal and external rust. They submit a warranty claim. Upon checking your records, you find no inspection report and no indication that the required inspection took place upon delivery. Before the equipment is moved or damaged, you visit the site to investigate. You ask the customer to protect and cover the equipment from further damage.

Your investigation reveals the customer failed to inspect on time and didn't protect the equipment as required in the operation manual. In this best-case scenario, you can reject the claim based on the contract's terms. However, this highlights the importance of thorough documentation. Consider these questions and potential risks:

- What could happen if you didn't include an inspection and acceptance requirement in your contract?
- What if your contract required you to add more waterproof packaging?
- What if your customer argued your packaging failed to protect the equipment adequately?

These scenarios emphasize the need for comprehensive contract clauses and meticulous record-keeping to protect your interests.

### BEST PRACTICES

Make it a habit to take pictures of equipment and its packaging before loading it onto the truck and unloading it at the project site. This small effort could save you major headaches if issues arise later. Remember, even if a customer initially accepts products or services, most contracts allow them to later raise concerns about defects within the warranty period.

Now, imagine you're the customer. If you don't inspect your subcontractor's work and reject any non-conforming items in writing within the inspection period, you might lose your ability to make claims later on. Ideally, acceptance should be documented through a written notice or a signed acceptance form, but this doesn't always happen. As a contractor, it's your responsibility to track and record when acceptance occurs.

No matter which side of the deal you're on, inspection and acceptance are powerful risk-mitigation tools when used correctly. You want your customers to inspect and accept your work so you can get paid. Customers want to use payment terms to motivate you to deliver your best work. It's a bit of a strategic game, with each side using terms and conditions to their advantage. Sadly, without clear terms and documentation, disputes often arise, and subcontractors often lose.

If your contract lacks a formal inspection and acceptance process or forms, try to negotiate their inclusion during negotiations. If it's too late and the contract is signed, don't hesitate to ask your customer for confirmation of acceptance (even an e-mail works) after your work is complete. If you need a reason, just blame it on your contracts manager or finance department.

## Audit

This clause outlines your customer's right to require you to open your books for an audit periodically. The purpose of the audit is to ensure the project is being completed according to the terms and conditions of your agreement. Suppose you are completing the project on a time and materials basis. In that case, your customer may want the right to audit your books and records to ensure it reimburses only those costs allowable under the terms of your contract. Let's consider the following clause:

> **Auditing**. Contractor shall keep accurate records, documents, and papers of all amounts billable to and payments made by Owner under this agreement, related to the Work as per recognized accounting practices, as required by laws and regulations, in a format that will allow for auditing, for a period of 3 years after payment of the last invoice related to this agreement or resolution of any claim, whichever is later.

Let's consider the following questions and their associated risks:

- How will this clause affect you if you complete the work on a firm-fixed-price basis? If your work is priced on a firm-fixed-price basis, this clause could potentially expose you to audits and requests for cost data, even though your price is already set.

- Will you have to disclose how you arrived at your pricing, potentially revealing proprietary and sensitive pricing information? You might be required to reveal how you determined your pricing, potentially divulging proprietary and sensitive information about your business practices.

- Do the auditing rights include the records of your subcontractors? It's important to clarify whether the auditing rights extend to the records of your subcontractors, as this could have further implications for confidentiality and data sharing.

The risks associated with audit clauses are potentially significant. Let's consider this scenario: Your customer requests additional work through a change order based on your firm's fixed price proposal. Later, they claim your pricing is now open for scrutiny and demand to see your detailed cost breakdown. Are you obligated to provide this information under the example clause?

While the clause doesn't explicitly exclude fixed-price proposals from audits, it doesn't explicitly include them either. This ambiguity creates a potential risk. Unless your legal counsel can find a compelling argument to the contrary, you might be forced to disclose your pricing details.

This highlights the importance of carefully scrutinizing audit clauses in contracts and negotiating clearer language to protect your proprietary information. Don't assume that fixed-price proposals are automatically shielded from audits; clarify this point in the contract to avoid potential disputes and unwanted disclosures down the line.

### BEST PRACTICES

During contract negotiations, explicitly exclude your customer's right to audit firm-fixed-price agreements. In your proposals and change order forms,

> clearly state that FFP pricing is not subject to audit. Consider attaching a labor rate and equipment rental rate sheet as an exhibit to both the contract and your proposals. This allows both parties to agree on pricing upfront, preventing future disagreements regarding change orders.

Another crucial aspect is the auditing and record retention period. Familiarize yourself with relevant laws and regulations governing contract document retention. While accepting these terms is common, they can be burdensome and expensive. Ensure that a reasonable standard is applied and that your agreements with subcontractors have corresponding terms. This consistency helps mitigate risks and ensures all parties are held to the same expectations regarding audits and record retention.

## Assignment

This clause might seem like a lot of legal jargon, but it's actually pretty important and common in contracts. In plain terms, "assigning" a contract means transferring its benefits and obligations from one party to another. It's like passing a baton in a relay race.

Unless your contract says otherwise, you can usually assign most of your contractual rights to someone else. But if there's an anti-assignment clause, it might restrict your ability to do so or require the other party's permission. This clause can work both ways, either allowing or disallowing assignments for both parties.

Let's take a look at some examples of these clauses:

> **Assignment.** Contractor shall not assign this agreement, or any part of it, or delegate its responsibilities under this agreement without Owner's prior written consent. Unless otherwise agreed upon in writing by Owner, any assignment will

not release or discharge Contractor from any obligations under this agreement.

Or

**Right to Assign**. Without the written consent of the other party, neither party can assign or transfer any part of this agreement, except to an affiliate, provided that (i) the assignee agrees in writing to be bound by the terms of this agreement and (ii) the assigning party remains liable for obligations under the agreement. Any other attempt to transfer or assign is void.

If you anticipate needing to assign your contract due to an acquisition or merger, it's wise to revise or find a clause that aligns with your needs. Consulting an attorney might be beneficial if you want the flexibility to assign your rights and obligations to another party.

Consider this point: Under the current example clauses, could your customer potentially assign your contract to a competitor? While the second example offers some protection, it doesn't explicitly exclude competitors. To address this, you could add a limitation such as: "No such assignment shall be made to a competitor of Contractor." This would safeguard your intellectual property from falling into the hands of rivals (a topic we'll delve into later).

## Changes

Change is a natural part of any project. It's so common that most contracts anticipate and adapt to it[5]. Let's take a closer look at a typical changes clause and understand how it works to protect both parties.

---

5  Lana Lovrenčić Butković, "A New Framework for Ranking Critical Success Factors for International Construction Projects," *Organization, Technology and Management in Construction: an International Journal* 13, no. 2 (2021), https://doi.org/10.2478/otmcj-2021-0030.

**Owner Changes**. Owner reserves the right to make ***reasonable*** changes to the Agreement through a written Change Order at any time. These changes can include, but are not limited to, modifications to the drawings or specifications, changes in the quantity ordered, adjustments to the delivery schedule, changes to the method of shipment or packing, and adjustments to the place of delivery. No changes will be recognized unless they are confirmed in writing by Owner. If a change results in an increase or decrease in the cost or time needed for performance of any part of the Work, an appropriate adjustment will be made to the price or delivery schedule, and the Agreement will be modified by written amendments or revisions signed by authorized representatives of both parties. [bolded here and *italicized* for affect]

The changes clause provides a safety net for both you and your customer. It gives your customer the flexibility to make reasonable adjustments to the project scope—whether that means adding, removing, or modifying work—while ensuring that these changes are managed within the general scope of the contract. Crucially, the change clause also outlines a clear process for determining how the value of these changes will be handled, protecting both parties from financial surprises.

To illustrate, let's examine a typical example of a mutual changes clause that you might find in a contract:

**Changes**. If either party wishes to alter the scope of the work outlined in this agreement, they must submit a written request for the change to the other party. The parties will then promptly negotiate and agree on the terms of the change. Owner will not be responsible for any additional costs or changes to the work unless explicitly outlined in a Change Order or written Directive. Any changes to the schedule for completion of the work must also be agreed upon in writing in a Change Order. Contractor must not begin any additional work or changes to the scope of work until they have received written authorization from Owner.

A well-crafted changes clause does more than just allow for changes; it provides a clear framework for managing them. It outlines a mechanism for you, the contractor, to promptly notify your customer when you believe a change to the project scope has occurred, triggering the need for a change order. This clause typically specifies a timeframe for this notification, ensuring that both parties are aware of the change and can begin discussions to address it promptly.

For example, consider this alternative changes clause that incorporates these notification and timeframe elements:

**Change Order Request**. Contractor shall not make any changes to the Work without the written consent of Owner. Any request for changes in the scope of work, cost or completion time ("Change Order Request") must be submitted to Owner in writing within ten (10) calendar days of the event requiring the change. Contractor must provide a written certification of the reason for the request and, if applicable, the time involved. The submission of a written Change Order Request is a condition precedent for Owner to consider any such request.

This example goes beyond simply permitting changes. It sets a clear expectation that you, as the contractor, will proactively communicate any perceived changes to the project scope within a specified timeframe. This early notification allows both parties to address the change before it becomes a major issue, minimizing the risk of disputes and delays. It also reinforces the collaborative nature of the contract, ensuring that both you and your customer are working together to achieve a successful project outcome.

Suppose you need to provide the required information within the time limits outlined in the changes clause. What actions should you take? At a minimum, consider sending a formal notice to your customer stating there is a cost and/or schedule impact and that it's being evaluated. This language may work for you with minor adjustments:

> As of [Date], project conditions have necessitated additional coordination, accelerated efforts, and increased labor hours. This is an ongoing situation, and the full impact on project costs and schedule is currently under evaluation.
>
> We anticipate providing you with a detailed accounting of these impacts, including supporting documentation, by [Date]. Please note that these figures may be subject to revision as we continue to assess the evolving situation.
>
> We appreciate your understanding and cooperation as we work together to address these changes.

### BEST PRACTICES

- Document Everything: Keep meticulous records of all the additional work, costs, and schedule impacts. This will be crucial when you submit your formal change order.

- Communicate Early and Often: Don't wait until the end to inform your customer. Keep them informed about the developing situation and your ongoing assessment of the impacts.
- Collaborate: Work with your customers to find solutions that address both their needs and your concerns about the extra work.
- Review the Changes Clause: Refer back to the specific language in your contract's changes clause. It may provide guidance on the notification process, required documentation, or dispute resolution mechanisms.
- Consider Mediation or Negotiation: If you and your customer can't agree on the change order, consider alternative dispute resolution methods like mediation or negotiation before escalating to legal action.

Why This Approach Works:

- Proactive: It demonstrates your commitment to addressing the changes promptly and professionally.
- Transparency: It keeps the customer informed about the situation and your ongoing assessment.
- Collaboration: It opens the door for a collaborative discussion to find solutions that work for both parties.
- Protective: It establishes a paper trail documenting your notification of the changes and your efforts to address them.

Before you even think about taking on additional work, meticulously review your contract's change order requirements. This point should be non-negotiable. Never proceed with extra work without either a signed change order or a clear, written directive from your customer's authorized representative. It may seem inconvenient, but it's your first line of defense against misunderstandings and disputes down the road.

Ensure your contracts include a robust system for identifying and addressing changes as they happen. This system should allow for swift estimation and negotiation of the change's cost and schedule impact. The faster you can get those change orders in place, the smoother your project will run.

## Compliance with Laws and Regulations

Compliance requirements are woven throughout most contracts. These requirements are more than just formalities—they carry serious risks. Ignoring or mishandling them can expose your company to penalties, fines, reputation damage, and even significant financial loss. These risks stem from failing to adhere to laws, industry regulations, or established best practices.

Notice how compliance clauses often interconnect with other contract provisions. They may be linked to auditing clauses that give the other party the right to inspect your records, termination for default clauses that allow for contract termination if you fail to meet compliance standards, indemnification clauses that require you to compensate the other party for damages resulting from your non-compliance, and warranty and representation clauses that affirm your commitment to complying with relevant regulations.

To illustrate how these clauses work together, let's consider the following examples:

> **Compliance with Laws and Regulations**. Contractor shall adhere to all relevant federal, state, and local laws and regulations, including court orders and decrees, related to the performance of this Agreement. This includes compliance with worker's compensation laws, wage and salary regulations, non-discrimination laws, and licensing requirements. When necessary, Contractor will provide Owner with evidence of compliance. Contractor shall also indemnify and protect Owner from any loss, liability, or expense, including legal fees,

resulting from Contractor's failure to meet the obligations outlined in this Section 12.

**Compliance Audit**. Contractor shall comply with all applicable laws and regulations and provide Owner with proof of compliance upon request. Owner has the right to conduct audits to ensure compliance with NERC Standards related to the Facilities. Contractor agrees to assist in these audits and provide Owner access to and copies of any records related to compliance activities.

**Termination for Cause**. Owner has the right to terminate this contract if Contractor breaches any material term, condition or provision of this contract, if such breach is not cured within the period specified in Owner's notice of breach or any subsequent notice or correspondence delivered by Owner to Contractor, provided that cure is feasible. Owner may also terminate this contract immediately without penalty and without advance notice or opportunity to cure if Contractor fails to comply with any applicable international, federal, state, or local laws, rules, ordinances, regulations, or orders when performing within the scope of this contract.

**Indemnification**. To the fullest extent permitted by law, Contractor shall fully indemnify and hold harmless the Owner and its directors, officers, agents, employees, shareholders, and affiliates (hereinafter the "<u>Indemnified Parties</u>") from any third-party claims, legal actions, and expenses, including attorney fees, related to or arising from Contractor's violation of any laws or regulations.

> **Representations**. Contractor shall ensure compliance with all relevant laws, regulations, codes, ordinances, and requirements of federal, state, local, and foreign government agencies in relation to the conduct of its business operations.

Did you notice that our example clauses included indemnification language? Indemnification clauses are often intertwined with compliance requirements, as they outline who is responsible for covering costs or damages in the event of non-compliance.

While our example clauses list several laws and regulations, it's important to remember that your specific contract may cover a much broader range of compliance areas. This could include adherence to environmental and safety regulations, obtaining and maintaining necessary permits, complying with labor laws, and providing appropriate employee benefits.

Thoroughly reviewing this clause is essential to ensuring that you fully understand the scope of your compliance obligations. If you have any doubts or questions, it's always wise to consult with legal counsel to ensure you can meet all requirements and avoid potential liabilities. Remember, non-compliance can lead to costly penalties, fines, or even legal action.

### BEST PRACTICES

Your company's risk mitigation plan should be seamlessly integrated with its overall business plan. Effective risk management isn't just about identifying and understanding potential risks—it's about proactively mitigating them and adapting your strategies as needed. This necessitates ongoing monitoring and the creation of robust controls to address evolving challenges.

To effectively mitigate compliance-related risks, consider incorporating these critical factors into your ongoing risk management plan:

- Project Kickoff Meetings (Preconstruction): Gather your project team before work begins to discuss potential compliance risks specific to the project. This could include permitting requirements, stormwater mitigation plans, security protocols, and safety regulations. Clearly define roles and responsibilities for each team member regarding compliance efforts, ensuring everyone understands their part in maintaining compliance[6].
- Regulatory Monitoring: Keep an eye out for regulatory updates and changes in your industry. Anticipate any new risks that may arise from these updates, and proactively adjust your strategies accordingly.
- Regular Internal Audits: Conduct periodic internal audits to assess your compliance status. These audits help identify any weaknesses or gaps in your current practices, allowing you to address them before they escalate into major issues.
- Compliance and Change Management: Whenever you implement changes to your project or process, integrate compliance evaluations into your change management activities. Assess how these changes may affect your compliance status, and adjust your strategies as needed.

By weaving these practices into your business operations, you create a proactive and adaptable risk management approach. This not only minimizes the likelihood of compliance violations but also fosters a culture of responsibility and awareness within your organization. Remember, effective risk management is an ongoing process that requires constant vigilance and a willingness to adapt to new challenges.

---

6   Shadi Shayan, Ki Pyung Kim, and Vivian W. Y. Tam, "Critical Success Factor Analysis for Effective Risk Management at the Execution Stage of a Construction Project," *International Journal of Construction Management* 22, no. 3 (2019), https://doi.org/10.1080/15623599.2019.1624678.

## Confidentiality

Before diving into discussions involving sensitive or proprietary information with your customer, it's crucial to consider establishing a legal framework to protect both parties' interests. This often involves negotiating and signing a mutual confidentiality agreement (NDA). Several types of NDAs are available, including one-way (unilateral) and two-way (mutual) agreements, as well as agreements designed for multiple parties.

While a deep dive into these agreements is beyond the scope of this guidebook, it's important to be aware of them and their potential benefits. They can protect your "secret sauce"—your unique processes, technologies, or other valuable information—from being disclosed or misused by the other party. These agreements typically outline what information is considered confidential, how it can be used, and the duration of the confidentiality obligations.

If you haven't signed an NDA during preliminary discussions, you can still address confidentiality within your main contract. In fact, it's quite common to see contracts that incorporate confidentiality clauses. Let's explore the purpose of these clauses and some potential pitfalls to watch out for.

One common pitfall is the one-way confidentiality clause. This type of clause only protects the confidential information of one party, usually the one who drafted the contract. However, a well-crafted confidentiality clause should be mutual, safeguarding the sensitive information of both parties. It should clearly define what information is considered confidential and establish clear guidelines for its use and protection.

Let's examine the following example clause to illustrate how a mutual confidentiality clause might be structured:

> **Confidential or Proprietary Information.** Confidential or Proprietary Information refers to any information or data disclosed by either Owner or Contractor, (each a "<u>Disclosing Party</u>") to the other party (each a "<u>Recipient</u>"), including

but not limited to technology, ideas, concepts, drawings, designs, inventions, discoveries, improvements, patents, patent applications, specifications, trade secrets, prototypes, processes, notes, memoranda, reports, visual representations of the Disclosing Party's past, present or future research, technology, know-how, and concepts, computer programs, software code, written documentation, products, information about vendors, members, customers, prospective customers, employees, and prospective employees, market research, sales and marketing plans, distribution arrangements, financial statements, financial information, financing strategies, and opportunities, and business plans, all of which relate directly or indirectly to the Disclosing Party's products, services, or business. If any Confidential or Proprietary Information is disclosed orally or by observation or viewing, it must be identified as proprietary before disclosure, and after disclosure, it must be reduced to writing within thirty (30) calendar days and delivered to the Recipient.

This example demonstrates how a confidentiality clause can be drafted to protect the interests of both parties involved. It specifies what constitutes confidential information, outlines permitted uses, and establishes a duration for the confidentiality obligations.

Why the fuss about confidentiality clauses? Imagine you just landed a massive contract, a dream project with a hefty budget to build a revolutionary piece of equipment using your patented technology and hard-earned expertise. It's a one-of-a-kind creation. You deliver this masterpiece to the project site, ready for integration into a larger system.

Then, the phone rings. It's your customer, and they've hit a snag. They need some of your secret sauce—your proprietary knowledge—to complete the integration. Do you hand it over? If you do, where do you draw the line? What are the limits on how they can use that information? What if their integration partner is your fiercest competitor?

This scenario isn't far-fetched. It happens every day in the real world. That's why having a confidentiality clause in place is absolutely crucial. It's your insurance policy against unwanted information leaks and potential exploitation. Think of it as protecting your precious recipe in the cookie jar.

Now, let's get back to the specifics. A well-crafted, mutual confidentiality clause shields both you and your customer from unauthorized disclosure. Unless explicitly stated otherwise in the contract, you're obligated to keep their confidential information under lock and key. Sharing it outside your organization could land you in hot water, potentially leading to legal action and costly damages.

## BEST PRACTICES

When scrutinizing a confidentiality clause, keep these crucial points in mind:

- Safeguard Your Secrets: If your company is sharing confidential information, ensure it's clearly marked and protected under the clause. Don't leave any room for ambiguity about what's considered confidential.
- Demand Mutuality: Insist on a mutual confidentiality clause that shields both parties' sensitive information. If the clause only protects the other side, your secrets are vulnerable.
- Define Permitted Use Carefully: The clause should explicitly outline the allowed uses of confidential information. Strike a balance between narrow enough to safeguard your interests and broad enough to accommodate potential collaborations.

- Document Retention for Auditing: Specify how long each party must retain confidential information and any related records. This is critical for demonstrating compliance during audits or disputes.
- Separate Clauses for Specific Protections: Don't lump confidentiality, non-solicitation, and anti-lobbying provisions into one clause. Create separate clauses to address each of these issues individually. This allows for greater clarity and flexibility in enforcing each provision.

Additional Considerations:

- Exceptions: Review any exceptions to confidentiality, such as disclosures required by law or to authorized third parties. Make sure these exceptions align with your company's policies and legal obligations.
- Remedies: Understand what remedies are available in case of a confidentiality breach. Are there financial penalties? Injunctive relief? Ensure the clause provides adequate protection for your interests.
- Survival: Determine how long the confidentiality obligations last after the contract ends. Some information may need ongoing protection even after the business relationship concludes.

By paying close attention to these factors, you can ensure that your confidentiality clauses are robust, comprehensive, and tailored to your company's specific needs. This will help protect your valuable information and minimize the risk of costly disputes or leaks.

## Contract Documents

To simplify contract drafting and interpretation, I often define the term "Contract Documents" early on. This is because contracts frequently involve a multitude of documents that, together, form the foundation of the agreement. While this seems straightforward, the list of these documents can be extensive: the agreement itself, schedules, solicitation documents, requests for proposals, general and special conditions, plans, drawings, specifications, addenda, modifications, pricing schedules, various forms (like change orders and lien waivers), and sometimes even the prime contract if applicable. Your own proposal could even become part of this collection!

Listing all of these documents multiple times throughout the contract would be tedious. Therefore, a common practice is to create a comprehensive list and include it under the umbrella term "Contract Documents." However, it's crucial to get this list right. If a document isn't included in this catch-all term, it could lead to confusion, disagreements, or even legal disputes about what actually constitutes the agreement.

When reviewing contracts from customers, you'll often find they employ a similar approach. The definition of "Contract Documents" might be located in the body of the contract, within the Entire Agreement clause, or even within the Order of Precedence clause. We'll delve deeper into the Entire Agreement and Order of Precedence clauses later in this chapter.

To get a better understanding, let's examine some examples of Contract Documents clauses:

> **Contract Documents**. Owner and Contractor have entered into, or are considering entering into, one or more purchase orders ("Applicable Purchase Orders") and related documents, such as scopes of work, drawings, and specifications (collectively referred to as the "Contract Documents"), that will be in addition to this Agreement and outline the specific responsibilities and obligations related to the deliverables, services, and work being provided by Contractor.

Or

**Contract Documents.** The terms and conditions outlined in this agreement ("Agreement"), along with any attachments, exhibits, supplemental terms and conditions, the scope of work, specifications, blueprints, designs, drawings, notes, instructions, renderings, and other information (collectively the "Contract Documents"), whether physically attached or incorporated by reference, comprise the complete and exclusive agreement between Contractor and Subcontractor.

### BEST PRACTICES

It's important to note that if your own quote or proposal is meant to be included as part of the Contract Documents, it should be explicitly referenced in this list. For example, you might see it listed as "Contractor's Proposal, dated March 4, 2026." This ensures there's no ambiguity about whether your proposal is considered a binding part of the agreement.

## Contractor Responsibilities

This clause details your comprehensive responsibilities throughout the project. These responsibilities encompass the planning, execution, and timely completion of all project tasks as outlined in the project schedule. The specific scope and extent of your responsibilities will vary depending on the nature and complexity of the project.

In general, your responsibilities include[7], but are not limited to:

---

7  Rami J.A Hamad, Bassam A. Tayeh, and Hamdan A. Al Aisri, "Critical Factors Affecting the Success of Construction Projects in Oman," *Journal of Sustainable Architecture and Civil Engineering* 29, no. 2 (2021), https://doi.org/10.5755/j01.sace.29.2.29269.

- Project Planning: Developing a detailed project plan that outlines the scope of work, resource allocation, timelines, and risk mitigation strategies.
- Execution: Carrying out all project tasks in accordance with the project plan, industry standards, and any applicable regulations.
- Time Management: Ensuring the project progresses on schedule and is completed within the agreed-upon timeframe.
- Communication: Maintaining open and transparent communication with the client throughout the project, providing regular progress updates, and addressing any concerns promptly.
- Quality Control: Implementing quality control measures to ensure the project meets or exceeds the agreed-upon standards.
- Safety: Adhering to all safety regulations and ensuring a safe working environment for all personnel involved in the project.
- Financial Management: Effectively managing project costs and providing the client with accurate and transparent financial reports.
- Problem-Solving: Proactively identifying and resolving any issues or challenges that arise during the project.

This clause serves as a general framework for your responsibilities. A more detailed and project-specific list of responsibilities will be provided in the project scope of work document.

> **Contractor Responsibilities**. Contractor shall be held fully accountable for all aspects of engineering, procurement, and construction, including coordination of all work and fulfillment of any obligations outlined in this Agreement. This includes work performed by Contractor, its subcontractors, lower-tier subcontractors, or any other individuals or entities

employed or utilized by Contractor or its subcontractors, either directly or indirectly.

> **BEST PRACTICES**
>
> During contract negotiations, conduct a meticulous review of the responsibilities and obligations outlined in this clause to ensure they align precisely with your organization's initial proposal and capabilities.

## Coordination with Others

The "Coordination with Others" clause can be a potential minefield for contractors and subcontractors. It typically assigns responsibility for coordinating work with other parties on the project, even those with whom you have no direct contractual relationship (i.e., no privity of contract). This lack of privity means you have limited power to enforce timelines or hold third parties accountable for delays or disruptions.

### *Key Challenges:*

- Lack of Control: You are held responsible for coordinating with entities you cannot directly control or influence.
- Potential Delays: Third-party delays can have an impact on your schedule and budget, potentially leading to cost overruns and disputes.
- Limited Recourse: Without a contract, you have limited legal recourse against third parties for delays or non-performance.

### *Strategies for Protection:*

1. Thorough Review and Negotiation:
   - Scrutinize the Clause: Carefully analyze the "Coordination with Others" clause during contract negotiations. Look for broad or ambiguous language that could expose you to excessive risk.

- Negotiate Limitations: Seek to limit your responsibility to coordinating with parties you have a direct contractual relationship with. If coordination with third parties is required, push for clear definitions of responsibilities, timelines, and communication channels.
- Request Indemnity: If possible, negotiate an indemnity clause where the client agrees to hold you harmless for delays or damages caused by third parties outside your control.

2. Proactive Communication and Documentation:
   - Establish Clear Communication: Set up clear communication channels with all parties involved in the project, including third-party subcontractors, vendors, and suppliers.
   - Regular Meetings: Schedule regular coordination meetings to discuss progress, identify potential issues, and proactively resolve conflicts.
   - Detailed Documentation: Maintain meticulous records of all communications, agreements, and potential delays or disruptions caused by third parties. This documentation can be crucial in cases of disputes.

3. Risk Mitigation:
   - Contingency Planning: Develop contingency plans to address potential delays or disruptions caused by third parties. Identify alternative solutions or resources that can be mobilized quickly.
   - Insurance: Consider obtaining insurance coverage that protects you from financial losses due to third-party delays.

4. Legal Remedies (if necessary):
   - Dispute Resolution: If a dispute arises with a third party, explore alternative dispute resolution methods like mediation or arbitration.

- Last resort: If all else fails, consider legal action against the client for breach of contract if they fail to fulfill their obligations to facilitate coordination or provide necessary information.

    **Coordination with Others**. Contractor shall work in harmony with other suppliers, contractors, and consultants by coordinating their schedules and activities to prevent delays or disruptions to their work or the timely completion of the project.

It would be reasonable for you to negotiate a change to this clause during contract negotiations and require your customer to coordinate the activities of its forces and each third party with your work. You would then agree to "participate" in project review meetings with your customer and third parties. Here are several approaches you may take to achieve this during negotiations:

    **Coordination with Others**. Contractor shall participate with other separate contractors, suppliers, consultants, and Owner in reviewing and revising the Project Schedule as needed. Contractor shall make any revisions to the Project Schedule deemed necessary after a joint review and mutual agreement. The Project Schedule shall then constitute the schedules to be used by Contractor, separate contractors, and Owner until further revisions are made.

Or

    **Coordination with Others**. The Client shall be solely responsible for coordinating the activities of its own forces and each third party (including, but not limited to, other contractors, subcontractors, vendors, and suppliers) with the Contractor's work. The Client shall ensure that all parties involved in the project are aware of the Contractor's schedule, requirements, and any potential conflicts or dependencies. The Contractor agrees to participate in reasonable project review meetings with the Client and third parties as requested by the Client.

Unless you can devote substantial time to perform the required coordination and are willing to incur the additional cost, you should limit your obligations to coordinate with third parties.

### BEST PRACTICES

Effectively managing project delays requires a combination of proactive documentation, preparedness for unforeseen circumstances, and adherence to contractual agreements.

1. Comprehensive Documentation Plan:
   - Site Diary: Maintain a detailed site diary that records all project-related events, including:
     o Material deliveries and delays
     o Weather conditions and their impact on work
     o Unforeseen problems or obstacles
     o Critical decisions made and their rationale
     o Any other factors affecting project progress
2. Photographic and Video Evidence: Consider incorporating photographs and videos into your documentation plan. These can provide valuable visual evidence of site conditions, work progress, and any delays or issues encountered.

3. Contractual Review: Before implementing any documentation practices, carefully review your contract to ensure they are permissible and do not violate any confidentiality or intellectual property clauses.

4. Preparedness for Unforeseen Circumstances:
   - Contingency Planning: Develop comprehensive contingency plans that outline how you will respond to various types of delays, such as weather events, material shortages, or labor issues.
   - Communication Protocols: Establish clear communication protocols with all project stakeholders, including the client, subcontractors, and suppliers[8]. Ensure everyone knows who to contact and how to report delays or issues promptly.
   - Flexibility: Be prepared to adapt your schedule and resources as needed to accommodate unforeseen circumstances.

4. Regular Review and Analysis:
   - Schedule Monitoring: Regularly review the project schedule and compare it to actual progress. Identify any potential delays early on and take proactive measures to mitigate them.
   - Data Analysis: Examine the data collected in your site diary and other documentation to identify patterns or trends that may contribute to delays. Use this information to improve your planning and risk management strategies for future projects.

By implementing these best practices, you can better anticipate and respond to project delays, minimizing their impact on your schedule, budget, and overall project success. Remember, thorough documentation not only serves as a valuable record of events but can also be crucial evidence in case of disputes or claims.

---

8   Shayan, Pyung Kim, and Tam, "Critical Success Factor."

# Default

The terms "breach" and "default" are often used interchangeably, but they have distinct meanings in contract law. Understanding this distinction is crucial for effectively managing contractual relationships.

*Breach vs. Default:*

- Breach: A breach occurs when one party fails to fulfill its obligations under the contract. This can range from minor deviations to major non-performance.
- Default: A default is a specific type of breach that triggers certain consequences, as outlined in the contract's default clause. These consequences may include a notice-and-cure period, termination of the contract, or the right to seek damages.

*Types of Contract Breaches:*

- Actual Breach: This occurs when a party fails to perform its obligations as required by the contract. Examples include missed deadlines, non-payment, or delivering substandard work.
- Anticipatory Breach: This occurs when a party indicates, either explicitly or implicitly, that it will not fulfill its future obligations under the contract. This can trigger the non-breaching party's right to take action before the actual breach occurs.
- Minor Breach: This involves a relatively insignificant deviation from the contract terms that does not substantially affect the contract's overall performance.
- Material Breach: This is a significant breach that undermines the purpose of the contract or deprives the non-breaching party of the essential benefits it expected to receive.

*The Default Clause:*

A contract's default clause defines the consequences of a breach, particularly a default. It typically includes a notice-and-cure provision, which gives the breaching party an opportunity to rectify the default within a specified timeframe. If the default is not cured, the non-breaching party may have the right to terminate the contract and/or seek damages.

*Key Considerations:*

- Clarity: The default clause should be clear and unambiguous, specifying the events that constitute a default and the consequences that will follow.
- Fairness: The notice-and-cure period should be reasonable, giving the breaching party a genuine opportunity to remedy the default.
- Remedies: The non-breaching party's available remedies should be proportionate to the severity of the breach.

By understanding the nuances of breaches and defaults and carefully reviewing the default clause in your contract, you can better protect your interests and effectively manage contractual relationships.

> **Default**. If at any time during the term of this Agreement, Subcontractor fails to commence the Work under the provisions of this Agreement or fails to diligently provide Work in an efficient, timely, and careful manner and in strict accordance with the provisions of this Agreement or fail to use an adequate number or quality of personnel or equipment to complete the Work or fail to perform any of its obligations under this Agreement, then Contractor shall have the right, if Subcontractor does not cure any such default after five (5) calendar days written notice thereof, to terminate this Agreement and complete the Work in any manner it deems desirable, including engaging the services of other parties therefore.

Any such act by Contractor shall not be deemed a waiver of any other right or remedy of Contractor. If after exercising any such remedy, the cost to Contractor of the performance of the balance of the Work is in excess of that part of the contract sum which has not been paid to Subcontractor hereunder, Subcontractor shall be liable for and shall reimburse Contractor for such excess.

## Default: Handling Subcontractor Disputes and Termination

It's not uncommon for projects to encounter challenges due to subcontractor performance issues. These issues can range from defective or incomplete work to significant delays, often leading to strained relationships and the potential for back-charges and termination.

### *Insight Story: The Project From Hell*

As part of my role, I travel the country, leading workshops and educating project teams and executives on the complexities of contract terms and dispute resolution. These workshops are a highlight of my job, often providing insights that no textbook could offer.

After transitioning from a contracts manager to a construction claims manager, I noticed an unsettling quiet at my desk—the phone calls I was accustomed to receiving suddenly ceased. Initially, I reveled in the peace, but it soon dawned on me that this silence could be a harbinger of trouble.

At the end of a recent workshop, I spotted John, a seasoned project manager known for tackling the most challenging assignments. As we headed towards the breakroom, he approached me with a playful jab.

"Well, well, look who decided to take a break from their jet-setting lifestyle to grace us with their expertise," John quipped, a playful glint in his eye.

"Business travel, my friend, is a far cry from a vacation," I replied with a smile, shaking his hand warmly. "It's good to see you, John."

"You too," he sighed, the amusement fading from his face as he slumped into a nearby chair. "But I'm knee-deep in a real mess. Delays, budget overruns—it's a complete disaster."

He began to recount his ordeal with a subcontractor, the deteriorating relationship, and the cascading impact on his main client. His furrowed brow and troubled expression spoke volumes. "Any ideas on how to salvage this situation?" he asked, his voice laced with desperation.

"Let's discuss this further after the workshop," I suggested, recognizing the complexity of his predicament.

Later, in my office, John and his assistant project manager, Sarah, appeared, their faces etched with worry.

"Got a minute to spare?" John inquired, peering anxiously through the doorway.

"As long as it's not dinnertime, I'm at your disposal," I joked, trying to lighten the mood. John's usual jovial demeanor was nowhere to be found.

"We're working on a water meter installation project, and it's been an absolute nightmare," he explained. The subcontractor, who claimed to be an expert recommended by their client, was significantly behind schedule. "I'm honestly considering terminating their contract."

As John outlined the issues, I listened carefully, absorbing every detail. "I'll need to review the subcontract and any formal correspondence you've had with them," I stated, knowing that the devil was in the details.

John promptly returned with the subcontract and a disorganized stack of e-mails. "Here's everything. No formal notices, just a series of email exchanges."

"Have you explicitly communicated that they're behind schedule?" I questioned, sifting through the haphazard collection of e-mails.

"I've mentioned it numerous times, both over the phone and in multiple e-mails," John replied, his voice laced with frustration.

"And have we contributed to any delays on our end? Missing drawings, access issues, anything like that?" I probed, determined to leave no stone unturned.

"Absolutely not," he insisted, shaking his head emphatically.

"I'll need a few hours to thoroughly review all of this," I said, acknowledging the gravity of the situation. "Do you happen to have call logs or meeting minutes documenting these conversations?"

"Just the e-mails," John admitted, his shoulders slumping.

"Okay, I'll get back to you as soon as I've had a chance to analyze everything," I assured them as they left my office, a glimmer of hope returning to their eyes.

Alone once more, I immersed myself in the contract documents, recalling a mentor's wisdom: contract review is like solving a complex puzzle, each clause interlocking with another to form an intricate web of obligations and rights. The key was not to jump to hasty conclusions but to meticulously examine each piece of the puzzle to understand the bigger picture. Only then could I guide John out of this predicament. I reviewed the following terms in John's subcontract:

> **Scope of Work.** Subcontractor shall ensure that the products they provide and any installation services they offer are delivered and completed in accordance with the project schedule outlined in the contract.
>
> **Delivery.** Time is of the essence. The timely completion of the Installation Services and delivery of the Products is of significant importance and a fundamental aspect of this Agreement.

**Termination for Cause**. Under this Agreement, Subcontractor shall be considered in default if any of the following occur: (i) Subcontractor breaches any of its obligations in the Agreement and does not remedy the breach within ten (10) calendar days of receiving written notice from Contractor, unless the breach cannot be remedied within that time frame, in which case Subcontractor must provide evidence that the issue will be corrected or that they are making progress towards a solution. (ii) Subcontractor refuses or neglects to provide the necessary workforce, materials, or equipment of the appropriate quality or quantity to properly perform the work outlined in the Agreement. (iii) Subcontractor fails to complete the work promptly and diligently in accordance with this Agreement's provisions.

**Notices**. Any written communication required or allowed under this Agreement must be signed by the sender and delivered by hand, sent via registered mail, or sent via email (with a subsequent confirmation sent via registered mail) to the intended recipient at the address specified in this Agreement.

**Delay Damages**. Subcontractor shall be held liable for any delay damages, including liquidated damages, that are imposed on Contractor as a result of Subcontractor's actions or failures to act.

**Assurances**. If at any point during the course of the agreement, Contractor finds that Subcontractor is not fulfilling their obligations under this agreement, Contractor may require Subcontractor to submit a corrective action plan outlining the steps they will take to correct the issue within three (3) business days. Contractor may request modifications to the corrective action plan if they determine it does not sufficiently address the deficiency. Subcontractor must promptly and diligently carry out the corrective action plan and show Contractor that the problem has been resolved. If Subcontractor fails to implement the corrective action plan, Contractor may terminate this agreement.

After reviewing the subcontract, I headed down to John's office, a sense of urgency propelling me forward. I knocked lightly and poked my head around the corner. "John, got a minute?"

He looked up from a pile of papers, a weary expression on his face. "Sure, come in," he said, gesturing towards a chair.

I settled in as he reached for the coffee pot. "Coffee?" he offered, a forced smile playing on his lips. "It's hot and strong—just the way I like it." He poured a steaming cup and slid it across the desk towards me.

I picked up the mug, peering inside with a raised eyebrow. "When was the last time you washed this thing?" I couldn't help but ask, noticing a suspicious ring of grime around the rim.

John chuckled, unfazed by my observation. "Yours, maybe sometime last week, but mine? Never seen the inside of a dishwasher. Adds character, don't you think?" He winked, taking a hearty gulp from his own mug.

I decided to decline the coffee, placing the mug back on the desk. "Thanks, but I'll pass." I spread the subcontract out before us, then turned to the first highlighted section. "John, I know this subcontractor is causing major headaches, and it's putting you behind the eight ball. But as much as you want this resolved quickly, we need to be strategic here."

John leaned back in his chair; his frustration was palpable. "Just tell me what needs to be done."

I pointed to the highlighted section. "The subcontract is pretty clear about our obligations. First, we need to send them a formal notice letter detailing the issues and our expectations. Then, we have to give them a chance to rectify the situation."

John's eyes widened in disbelief. "But that's not fair! I've already talked to them multiple times. They know they're screwing up. Why should we waste time with a letter? I have another subcontractor ready to jump in right now!"

I could sense his impatience, but I held firm. "I understand your frustration, John, but we have to follow the procedures outlined in the contract." I pointed to another highlighted section. "We're obligated to give them formal notice and a reasonable opportunity to cure the problem. If they fail to do so within ten days, then we can take further action."

I slid a pre-drafted notice letter across the desk. "Here's what I propose we send them."

John sat silently for a long moment, carefully reading through the letter. His expression was unreadable, but I could almost hear the gears turning in his head as he weighed his options.

## Notice Letter

SENT BY E-MAIL AND CERTIFIED MAIL
March 16, 2025
My Company, Inc.
157 Evens Street
Beautiful City, NC, 28567

My Best Friend Subcontracting, Inc.
Attention: Joey Best, Owner
1125 Atlantic Circle
Sand Piper, NC 28589
SUBJECT: DELAYS AND RESERVATION OF RIGHTS

Dear Mr. Best:

This letter is a follow-up to our telephone conversation and a notice of schedule delays. As you are aware, My Company, Inc. ("My Company") and My Best Friend Subcontracting, Inc. ("My Best Friend") entered enter an agreement dated February 16, 2025 (the "Subcontract") for the installation of 12,000 water meters for Beautiful City (the "Project"). Capitalized terms used herein without definition shall have the meanings assigned to them in the Subcontract.

As of the date of this letter, the installation of the water meters is sixty (60) calendar days late. For your company to regain the project schedule, it needs to install an additional 50 water meters each day or add additional crews to work during the week and on the weekends at your company's sole expense.

Please provide me with a corrective action plan and updated project schedule within three (3) business days. If you fail to adequately staff the project or take other sufficient measures to regain the project schedule within ten (10) business days, we will take necessary actions to bring the installation of the water meters back on schedule.

Please be informed that we will back-charge your company for any damages we incur due to its delays. We reserve all our rights and remedies in this matter.

If you have any questions or want to discuss this further, don't hesitate to contact me at (919) 555-1212.

Regards,

John Hardy, PMP
My Company, Inc.

John glanced at his watch; his voice tight. "They're further behind than the time frame you've outlined in that letter."

I could sense his mounting frustration. The temptation to lecture him about foresight and early intervention was strong, but I knew that wouldn't be productive. Instead, I offered a solution.

"I'll email you the letter as a Word doc," I said. "Adjust the deadlines as needed. The main objective here is to officially put them on notice, get their corrective action plan, and give them a chance to catch up. That's the first step." I leaned back, hoping a softer approach might ease the tension. "Before we can declare them in breach of contract, we have to give them an opportunity to perform and meet the revised deadlines. It's about creating a paper trail to protect us if things go sideways."

I took a deep breath, then continued, "Realistically, I see two possible outcomes here. We either bring in another subcontractor to help them catch up, or we terminate their contract and find someone else to finish the job. Neither option is ideal, and both come with their own set of challenges that you'll need to navigate."

"So, which path should I take?" John asked, his frustration giving way to a hint of confusion.

"My role is to lay out your options, explain the risks, and offer recommendations," I clarified. "Ultimately, the decision rests with you. You're the one responsible for the success and profitability of this project."

I paused, letting the weight of that responsibility sink in. "Ask yourself this, John: which option is the lesser of two evils?"

I gave him a moment to think before elaborating. "Bringing in another subcontractor to help them finish the work could lead to cost overruns. It might be the only way to get back on schedule, but it will likely cost more than you anticipate, and it will take time for the new subcontractor to ramp up. Plus, there's the risk that the original subcontractor might claim they lost out on profits and should be compensated."

I could see the worry lines deepening on John's forehead. "The second option, termination, isn't much better. It's a drastic step, and you should only consider it if you've thoroughly vetted a replacement and have a solid contract in place with firm deadlines. Be prepared to pay a premium for a new subcontractor on short notice."

John sighed, running a hand through his hair. "You're not painting a very rosy picture here."

"I'm not sugarcoating it, John. These situations are never easy. I encourage you to discuss the options with your executive team. They might prioritize the client relationship above all else and direct you to take a specific course of action. But whatever you decide, the starting point is that notice letter." I tapped the document on his desk. "Let me know how I can help."

I stood up to leave, casting one last glance at the grimy coffee mug. There was no magic bullet for this situation, and experience told me that termination would likely be more costly and time-consuming than trying to work with the existing subcontractor. But ultimately, the decision was John's to make.

## John's Subcontractor Dilemma

Let's delve into John's specific situation to illustrate how to navigate such scenarios:

- The Problem: John's subcontractor is consistently behind schedule, causing delays in the overall project timeline. The quality of their work is also subpar, requiring rework and additional resources.
- Initial Steps: John first attempted to resolve the issue amicably through open communication and discussions with the subcontractor. He clearly outlined the performance deficiencies and provided a reasonable timeframe for improvement.

- Escalation: Unfortunately, the subcontractor's performance did not improve despite John's efforts. This led to further delays and additional costs for the project.
- Consulting Legal Counsel: Recognizing the potential for a serious dispute, John consulted with an attorney to understand his legal options and obligations under the contract.
- Reviewing Contractual Provisions: John and his attorney carefully reviewed the contract, particularly the default clause and any notice-and-cure provisions. This helped them determine the appropriate course of action.
- Notice and Cure Period: John provided the subcontractor with a formal written notice of default, detailing the specific breaches and giving them a reasonable opportunity to cure the defaults within a specified timeframe.
- Termination: When the subcontractor failed to cure the defaults within the notice-and-cure period, John exercised his right to terminate the subcontract. He then hired a replacement subcontractor to complete the work and backcharged the original subcontractor for the additional costs incurred.

*Key Lessons and Recommendations:*

- Early Intervention: Address performance issues with subcontractors as soon as they arise. Open communication and a collaborative approach can often resolve problems before they escalate.
- Documentation: Meticulously document all communications, performance issues, and attempts to resolve problems. This documentation can be crucial in cases of disputes or legal action.

- Legal Counsel: Consult with an attorney to understand your contractual rights and obligations. They can advise you on the best course of action and represent your interests in negotiations or litigation.
- Contractual Compliance: Follow the procedures outlined in your contract, including notice-and-cure provisions, to ensure that you are acting within your legal rights.
- Mitigation: Take proactive measures to mitigate the impact of subcontractor issues, such as hiring additional resources or adjusting the project schedule.

Remember, terminating a subcontractor is a serious step with potential legal and financial consequences. It's essential to approach such situations with careful consideration, thorough documentation, and professional legal advice. By doing so, you can protect your interests and ensure the successful completion of your project.

### BEST PRACTICES

- Contractual Compliance: Please comply with the notice and cure provisions outlined in your contract. Skipping these steps can jeopardize your position and weaken your legal standing.
- Foresight: Anticipate the potential consequences of each course of action before making a decision. Weigh the risks and benefits of termination versus working with the subcontractor to find a solution.
- Strategic Thinking: Remain calm and collected, even in the face of frustration. Avoid impulsive decisions, especially when it comes to terminating a subcontractor. Take the time to thoroughly review your contract and understand your options.

- Collaboration: Engage with your executive leadership team before taking any action. Their insights and guidance can be invaluable in navigating complex situations and mitigating potential risks.

## Additional Thoughts

Here's a crucial point to consider: What if your contract didn't include any notice and cure clauses? In many jurisdictions, the law implies a right for the breaching party to remedy their default. This means that even without explicit contractual language, you could be held liable for breaching the contract yourself if you didn't give your subcontractor a fair chance to correct their performance issues.

This underscores the importance of proceeding cautiously and strategically, even when dealing with a frustrating situation. Always consult with legal counsel or a contract expert to ensure you understand your rights and obligations, especially in the absence of explicit contractual provisions.

## Differing Site Conditions

It's common to find a Differing Site Conditions (DSC) clause in most construction contracts. But before we dive into a real-world scenario, let's clarify what a DSC actually means:

> A Differing Site Condition is an unexpected physical condition encountered at the project site that differs significantly from what was anticipated or indicated in the contract documents, such as plans, specifications, and geotechnical reports. These conditions are tangible—think buried debris, unexpected soil types, or hidden utilities—not intangible issues like labor shortages or material price increases.

Let's consider a hypothetical situation: You've been awarded a subcontract to construct foundation piers for an existing electrical substation. As you begin excavation, you unearth a massive amount of buried debris that prevents you from driving the piles as planned. This unforeseen obstacle forces you to devise costly workarounds, significantly altering your construction methods and driving up expenses. You realize that this situation wasn't accounted for in your original bid, and the cost to complete the job has skyrocketed.

The question is: who is responsible for absorbing these additional costs? You consult your subcontract and discover the following clause:

> **Changed Conditions**. If during the course of the project, Contractor discovers subsurface or concealed conditions that are materially different from those outlined in the Contract Documents, or conditions of an unusual nature that are not typically found in construction of this type, Contractor must promptly notify Owner in writing before disturbing the conditions, no later than seven (7) days after the first observation of the conditions. Owner will then investigate and, if the conditions cause an increase or decrease in the cost or time required for the project, Owner will agree to an adjustment to the contract price or project schedule. If Owner determines that the conditions are not materially different from those outlined in the Contract Documents and no adjustment is needed, Owner will notify Contractor in writing with reasoning. Any disputes about the adjustment must be made within seven (7) days of Contractor receiving notice of Owner's de-

termination and if the parties cannot agree, the dispute resolution procedure outlined in the Contract Documents will be followed.

Your investigation reveals a significant issue: the project site was once used as a county landfill. Thankfully, the Changed Conditions clause in your subcontract provides a clear path forward. If you encounter subsurface or concealed conditions that differ materially from the contract documents, you must notify the owner in writing within seven calendar days. The owner is then obligated to investigate, and if they determine the conditions are materially different and impact the project's cost or schedule, they must agree to an equitable adjustment. This clause effectively shifts the risk of unforeseen conditions from you to the owner.

However, the situation isn't always so straightforward. Consider these scenarios:

- Owner Disagreement: What if the owner disputes your claim, arguing that the conditions aren't materially different, are not unusual, or should have been discovered during your initial site investigation?
- Refusal to Adjust: What if the owner refuses to acknowledge the impact on time and cost or insists that you share in the additional expenses?

These situations can quickly escalate, straining relationships and potentially leading to costly disputes. It's crucial to be prepared for these challenges and have a strategy for addressing them. This might involve negotiation, mediation, or, in the worst-case scenario, litigation.

### BEST PRACTICES

If you discover conditions on the project site that are materially different from what's shown or indicated in the contract documents, or significantly different from what's typically expected for this type of work, read your contract and consider taking these immediate actions:

1. Cease Work: Stop all work in the affected area, except in emergencies involving life or property. Avoid further disturbing the subsurface or physical conditions.

2. Notify Immediately: Contact your customer by phone to alert them to the issue. Your contract may require this, but even if not, it's best practice. In your records, note the date and time of your call. If you can't reach them by phone, send an email outlining the situation.

3. Document Thoroughly: In your site diary, record the event in detail. Take photos and videos if allowed by your contract. Mark up relevant drawings, geotechnical reports, and other contract documents. Ideally, attach these documents to your formal notice letter, but don't delay sending the notice if they aren't immediately available. You can state in the letter that supporting documents will follow.

4. Await Written Authorization: Do not resume work in the affected area until you receive written permission from your customer. If they verbally authorize you to proceed while they investigate, please request that this authorization be confirmed in writing.

5. Prepare a Claim (if applicable): If the situation requires it, prepare a change order or claim, supported by all relevant documentation.

6. Seek Legal Counsel: If your customer denies your change order or claim, consult an attorney. They can help you assess your options and protect your interests.

Remember, early and thorough documentation is crucial in these situations. By taking swift and decisive action, you increase your chances of a successful resolution, whether through negotiation or, if necessary, legal recourse.

# Delays

Project delays are an unfortunate but unavoidable reality in the construction industry. Seasoned project managers understand it's not a matter of if but when these costly and disruptive events will occur. A multitude of factors can trigger delays, ranging from severe weather and unforeseen site conditions to equipment malfunctions, construction errors, and external interference. These delays invariably lead to increased costs and extended project timelines.

To mitigate these risks, contracting parties often include clauses in their agreements to address potential delays. The force majeure clause, for instance, deals with unforeseeable and excusable events that delay one or both parties, typically without incurring additional costs. However, the No Damages for Delay clause is a different beast altogether and can be a minefield for the unwary.

## The No Damages for Delay Clause: A Double-Edged Sword

This clause essentially absolves the owner from compensating the contractor for additional costs incurred due to delays, regardless of the cause. The contractor's sole remedy is an extension of the project timeline, with no other claims permitted.

Let's examine a typical example:

> **<u>No Damages for Delay</u>**. Contractor shall not be able to seek any compensation for losses resulting from any delay or disruption, regardless of the cause, and the only remedy available to Contractor in the event of a delay or disruption will be an extension of the project timeline. Contractor will not be able to make any other claims.

This clause is a clear illustration of the owner shifting the risk of delays onto the contractor. While courts generally uphold such clauses, there are exceptions. Every contract carries an implied obligation of good faith and fair dealing, and some states have enacted laws limiting or creating exceptions to these clauses. For example, the clause may not be enforceable if:

- The owner engaged in interference, fraud, misrepresentation, or gross negligence.
- The delay extended the project for an unreasonable duration.
- The delay was not contemplated by either party.
- The delay resulted in a breach of a fundamental obligation of the contract.

## Damages for Delay Clause: The Flip Side

In the absence of a liquidated damages clause, which specifies a predetermined amount of damages for delays, contracts may include language allowing the owner to withhold payment for delays. This provision can be found under a heading like "Damages for Delay" or embedded within other terms and conditions. Here's an example:

> **Damages for Delay**. If Contractor fails to complete the work on time, they shall be held responsible for any damages directly incurred by the Owner.

It's important to note that this language doesn't require a specific heading and can appear anywhere in the contract.

### BEST PRACTICES

If your contract contains clauses like "No Damages for Delay," it's vital to proactively document and promptly notify your customer of any delays. Your notices should clearly outline the nature and cause of the delay, particularly if it stems from active interference, fraud, misrepresentation, gross negligence, or bad faith on the part of the owner. This meticulous documentation can often make or break your case in a dispute or litigation, as it establishes a clear record of the events and their impact on your ability to perform.

## Delivery Milestones

In the ancient Roman road system, milestones marked distances, reassuring travelers of their progress. In the modern construction world, milestones serve a similar purpose—they're the checkpoints along the complex journey of design and construction.

Each milestone represents a significant stage in the project, and it's essential to fully complete one before moving on to the next. Understanding your contractual obligations and ensuring your ability to meet these milestones is crucial. Why? Because your customers, subcontractors, and suppliers may rely on your successful completion of each milestone to begin their own work.

Let's take a look at a couple of typical milestone clauses:

> **Milestones**. The Parties acknowledge that time is of the essence in meeting the deadlines outlined in this Agreement and that any delays may cause harm to Owner. Therefore, Contractor must meet certain Milestones promptly or be held liable for any resulting damages. Additionally, Contractor must provide any necessary documentation to prove the completion of Milestones within ten (10) business days of receiving such a request from Owner.

Or

> **Construction Milestones**. The Parties agree time is of the essence. The Parties acknowledge that timely completion of the construction of the Project as outlined in Exhibit B ("Mile-

stones") is of paramount importance in this Agreement. If Contractor fails to meet these Milestones in a timely manner, Owner may suffer damages. Within seven (7) days after completing each Milestone, Contractor must provide Owner with written notice and supporting documentation to demonstrate that the Milestone has been achieved. If Contractor misses the deadline for three (3) or more Milestones or misses the deadline for any one Milestone by more than ninety (90) days, Contractor must submit a plan ("Remedial Action Plan") to Owner within ten (10) business days, outlining a plan (including accelerating the work, for example, by using additional shifts, overtime, additional crews or resequencing of the work, as applicable) to achieve the missed Milestones and all subsequent Milestones no later than the Final Acceptance Date. The submission of a Remedial Action Plan will not absolve Contractor of their responsibility to meet all subsequent Milestones and the Final Acceptance Date.

## Milestone Clauses: Essential Strategies

Milestone clauses are integral to construction contracts and are often intertwined with pivotal provisions like "Time is of the Essence," Liquidated Damages, and Delay for Damages clauses. When outlining your scope of work or project plan, consider the following strategic approaches:

- Define Milestones: Establish a transparent, objective process for achieving each milestone. Include precise definitions and the corresponding payment terms to avoid ambiguity and ensure clear expectations.
- Build in flexibility: Recognize that changes are part of the construction landscape. To allow adjustments in the payment schedule, incorporate

adaptability into your milestone plan. This flexibility should allow for additional work and potential value enhancements.

- Address Partial Payments: Consider the implications of incomplete milestones, especially if the contract is terminated prematurely. Ensure that your plan includes provisions for reasonable compensation for work already performed, detailing how partial achievements will be valued.
- Establish Certification Protocols: Clearly designate who will certify milestone completion. This role could be assigned to a contract administrator, a third-party expert, or another defined authority within the contract.

By proactively integrating these key considerations, you can forge a more resilient and fairer milestone plan. This approach not only safeguards your interests but also promotes a smoother, more predictable project completion.

## BEST PRACTICES

Since milestone achievement is often tied to payment terms, it's crucial to define clearly:

- Milestone Criteria: What specific, measurable tasks or deliverables constitute successful completion of each milestone? This should be clearly stated in the contract.
- Payment Schedule: How much will be paid upon achieving each milestone? This should also be clearly defined to avoid disputes later.

Additionally, consider including language that addresses:

- Diligent Effort: Requiring the contractor to demonstrate that they've made reasonable and diligent efforts to meet each milestone, even if unforeseen circumstances cause delays.
- Partial Payment: Establishing a framework for partial payment if a milestone is partially completed before contract termination or other unforeseen events.

- Dispute Resolution: Outlining a process for resolving disputes regarding milestone completion or payment, such as mediation or arbitration.

By addressing these aspects in your contract, you can create a more transparent and equitable milestone framework that benefits both parties and reduces the risk of disagreements or costly delays.

## Dispute Resolution

While often overlooked in the excitement of a new project, the dispute resolution clause is crucial when things go awry. During the initial "honeymoon phase," disagreements seem distant, and you might be confident in your ability to resolve any issues amicably. However, complex projects often involve changes, disputes, and claims. When cost overruns, schedule delays, and other unexpected problems arise, emotions can run high, and relationships can sour. It's essential to have a plan in place to address these issues before they escalate and damage your hard-earned relationships.

## The Importance of Dispute Resolution Clauses

Dispute resolution clauses, often considered standard "boilerplate" provisions, are frequently overlooked. Yet, these clauses provide a valuable mechanism for avoiding the time, expense, and publicity of litigation. They offer the peace of mind that comes from knowing that disputes will be handled efficiently and privately. If there is no clause, you and your customer are left to navigate the complexities of governing law and local regulations, which can be a daunting and costly endeavor.

There are various approaches to dispute resolution, including arbitration, mediation, and litigation. Many contracts include a stepped resolution process, starting with negotiation and escalating to more formal methods if needed. Consider this example clause:

**Dispute Resolution**. The Parties shall make a good faith effort to resolve any disputes arising from the contract ("Dispute") through negotiation. If a Dispute cannot be resolved through normal business operations, either party may provide written notice to the other. Executives with the appropriate decision-making authority from both parties shall meet within ten (10) calendar days of the written notice and as often as deemed necessary to exchange information and attempt to resolve the Dispute. If the Dispute is not resolved within forty-five (45) calendar days after the initial notice, the Parties agree to resolve the Dispute through arbitration.

This clause outlines a negotiation-arbitration process, but other methods like mediation can also be included.

- Mediation is a structured negotiation facilitated by a neutral third party. The mediator's role is to guide the parties towards a mutually agreeable solution.
- Arbitration is a more formal and legalistic process, often involving hearings, evidence presentation, and a binding decision by an arbitrator.
- Litigation is the most costly and time-consuming option, involving a public court process.

### *Key Points to Remember*

- Act Quickly: The sooner you resolve a dispute, the less expensive it will be.
- Cost Considerations: Be aware that your contract may not allow you to recover dispute resolution costs.

- Prioritize Negotiation: Start by attempting to resolve disputes through direct, face-to-face negotiation at the project management level. If unsuccessful, escalate to senior leadership.
- Involve Key Players: The more involved the actual project participants are in the resolution process, the more likely it is that the outcome will be based on facts rather than legal arguments.
- Retain Knowledge: Losing key personnel can mean losing valuable historical knowledge about the project and the dispute.

### BEST PRACTICES

It's not uncommon for customers to postpone resolving open issues, change orders, disputes, and claims until the end of a project. While your contract might allow this, it's crucial to understand that waiting until the end can significantly weaken your negotiating position. You might find yourself forced to accept settlements far below the true value of your claims.

Therefore, it's strongly recommended to proactively address these issues as they arise, rather than letting them fester until the project's conclusion.

Here's how you can safeguard your interests:

- Timely Communication: If you can't resolve an issue through informal discussions, don't hesitate to invoke the dispute resolution clause in your contract.
- Meticulous Documentation: Keep detailed records of all communications, meetings, and decisions related to the dispute. This includes e-mails, letters, meeting minutes, photos, and any other relevant documentation.

- Formal Notices: If your contract requires formal notices for specific issues (e.g., delays, change orders), ensure you send them promptly and in accordance with the contract's terms.

By taking a proactive and well-documented approach, you'll be in a stronger position to negotiate fair resolutions and protect your financial interests.

## Entire Agreement

The Entire Agreement clause may seem like standard legal boilerplate, but its implications can be significant and have been the subject of numerous legal battles. Essentially, this clause ensures that the written contract and any documents referenced within it represent the complete understanding between the parties. It aims to prevent either party from relying on prior discussions, negotiations, or promises that aren't explicitly included in the final agreement.

Let's take a look at a common example:

> **Entire Agreement**. The Parties agree that this Agreement, along with all documents referred to within it, is the sole and complete agreement between them and supersedes any and all prior discussions, correspondence, negotiations, drafts, agreements, promises, assurances, warranties, representations, and understandings, whether in writing or spoken, regarding the subject matter of this Agreement.

While this clause might seem innocuous, it can have a profound impact on how a contract is interpreted and enforced. To illustrate, let's follow John as he navigates a real-world scenario that highlights the importance of this clause.

### *Insight Story: Updated Equipment List*

Yesterday morning, John and his assistant project manager, Sarah, were huddled in the site trailer conference room. John had just placed an order for some essential equipment and sent an update to Jane, the customer's project manager, who worked downtown and whom he'd only briefly met during the project kickoff.

As he finished the email, John's mind drifted to the other reports looming on his to-do list. "That equipment list was pretty detailed," he mused aloud.

Turning to Sarah, he said, "Let's make a list of the reports we need to tackle tomorrow."

Later that morning, John's phone rang. It was Jane, but her voice sounded tense. "John, it's Jane. Got a minute? We might have a problem."

"Sure, I've got a few minutes before my next call," John replied, his curiosity piqued. "Did you get the equipment list I sent this morning?"

"I did," Jane said, her voice clipped. "That's why I'm calling. I think there's a discrepancy."

"Okay, let me pull up the list," John said, shuffling through papers on his desk. "Alright, I've got it. What are you looking at?"

"Column 4," Jane replied. "It lists equipment that you've indicated I need to provide."

"Yes, that's correct," John confirmed. "We didn't include those items in our proposal."

"John," Jane's voice grew sterner, "your contract requires you to provide all necessary equipment. Do you have the contract handy?"

John could hear the rustle of pages as he frantically searched for the contract. "Take a look at Section 3," Jane directed.

He found the section, which stated:

> **Acceptance.** Subcontractor shall provide all necessary elements, including but not limited to services, supervision, labor, materials, tools, equipment, rentals, supplies, products,

goods, and parts (referred to as "Work" in this Agreement) to construct a fully functional facility as outlined in the Contract Documents. Subcontractor shall take full responsibility for ensuring that all aspects of the Work are completed properly, efficiently, on schedule, and safely.

"John, it clearly states you're responsible for all equipment," Jane reiterated.

"But Jane, we specifically excluded that equipment in our proposal," John countered, flipping to the last page of his proposal, titled "Exclusions."

"I'm not sure that's relevant," Jane said. "Your proposal isn't part of the contract. We awarded you the contract based on your pricing and ability to complete the work, and we agreed that you would supply all equipment."

A wave of frustration washed over John. "Jane, let me review the contract, and I'll call you back first thing tomorrow," he said, barely able to mask his irritation.

As he hung up, the phone slipped from his grasp and clattered to the floor. He retrieved it and slumped back in his chair, his eyes scanning the contract until they landed on the "Contract Documents" clause:

> **Contract Documents**. The Contract Documents include this Agreement, the related drawings and specifications, any additions or changes made to them, and any modifications made after the Agreement has been signed. These documents aim to provide Subcontractor with all the necessary information and instructions for properly executing and completing the Work. All the documents are closely interrelated and are to be considered as one document. Any instruction or requirement specified in one document is considered binding and applies to all the documents. Subcontractor is expected to perform the Work in accordance with the Contract Documents and to

use their own judgment to carry out any additional tasks that are necessary to achieve the intended results.

John sighed heavily, clinging to a sliver of hope that he could resolve this before it escalated into a full-blown dispute. He knew his leadership team would expect a clear explanation of how this misunderstanding occurred.

With a racing mind, he began to draft a summary:

- We were asked to submit a proposal for equipment supply and installation.
- During pre-negotiations, we assumed our proposal (and potentially e-mails and verbal discussions) would be part of the contract, and we outlined specific exclusions.
- We received the final contract and reviewed the terms, conditions, and related documents, still assuming our proposal (with exclusions) was incorporated.
- The customer now asserts that we are responsible for the excluded equipment.
- The contract doesn't reference our proposal, so as it stands, we are liable for supplying the equipment.
- Unless this is resolved quickly, we're likely headed for a dispute.

Shortly after, I received an email from John with the synopsis, asking for my feedback. Recognizing the gravity of the situation, I decided to call him directly.

"John, your summary looks accurate," I said. "I'm sure our leadership team will have more questions, but it provides a good overview."

I could hear the tension in John's voice. "I don't understand. Our pricing was based on those exclusions," he lamented.

"I know this is frustrating," I said, trying to offer reassurance. "But if this ends up in court, the courts typically look at the "four corners" of the contract to determine the parties' intent. They'll interpret the contract as a whole, considering each clause and ensuring consistency with the primary purpose. This means that the final agreement usually overrides any prior discussions, negotiations, or documents unless they are specifically incorporated into the contract."

There was a pause on the other end of the line. "That's what I was afraid of," John muttered.

"We need to talk to our proposal and contract teams," I said, my voice firm. "We have to ensure they're incorporating our proposals into the contracts and, ideally, referencing them in the Entire Agreement clause or the order of precedence. That would give us a much stronger position."

I assured John that I was available if he had further questions, though I knew this was far from resolved. The pressure was on for John to find a solution that met the leadership team's expectations. While he could have taken steps to avoid this situation, such as a more thorough pre-kickoff meeting with Jane, the root of the problem lay in the proposal and contract drafting process. This was a lesson learned the hard way, and one that could be prevented in the future with more rigorous contract management.

## BEST PRACTICES

During contract negotiations, be vigilant about incorporating the key elements of your proposal into the final agreement. Remember, a purchase order is considered to be a contract. If you've invested time and effort in outlining clarifications, exclusions, assumptions, scopes of work, and responsibility matrices in your proposal, these details are crucial enough to merit inclusion in the formal contract.

However, be prepared for pushback. Some customers might resist including your entire proposal due to its boilerplate terms and conditions. In such cases, if you've successfully negotiated specific terms, consider removing the boilerplate language and insisting on incorporating your clarifications, exclusions, and other essential details. Alternatively, you may attach these documents as exhibits to the contract.

Protecting your margins is paramount. Don't let essential details slip through the cracks during contract negotiations. By ensuring your proposal's key components are integrated into the final agreement, you can safeguard your interests, minimize misunderstandings, and avoid costly disputes down the road.

## Error or Inconsistency in Contract Documents

Even the most meticulous contract drafters can make mistakes, especially when dealing with the voluminous documents commonly associated with large, complex projects. I once worked on a contract that spanned over 2,000 pages—the potential for errors in such a massive document is immense.

That's why it's crucial to include an "Error or Inconsistency in Contract Documents" clause in your agreements. This clause mandates that both parties promptly notify each other in writing if they discover any errors, omissions, inconsistencies, ambiguities, or discrepancies in the contract documents.

Let's look at a typical example of such a clause:

> **Error or Inconsistency in Contract Documents**. If either party discovers any errors, omissions, inconsistencies, ambiguities, or other discrepancies in the Contract Documents, they must notify the other party in writing within three (3) business days. Owner will not be held responsible for any verbal explanations, directions, or interpretations, and Contractor is not required to follow any verbal explanations, directions, or interpretations.

This clause serves several important purposes:

- Clarity: It ensures that both parties are working from the same understanding of the contract's terms.
- Timely Resolution: It encourages prompt identification and resolution of errors before they escalate into costly disputes.
- Documentation: It creates a written record of the issue and any agreed-upon solutions, which can be invaluable in the future

## *Insight Story: Is Anyone up for a Quick Swim?*

John gazed out the window of his office trailer, the white sandy beach, and the tantalizing aroma of hotdogs and hamburgers from nearby food trucks tempting his grumbling stomach. Suddenly, a new truck caught his eye.

"Huh, haven't seen that one before," he mumbled to himself.

Turning to his assistant project manager, Sarah, he asked, "What's that new food truck out there?"

"Looks like a taco truck," she replied, glancing out the window.

"Well, there goes my lunch plans," John chuckled, his stomach rumbling in agreement.

He turned back to the stack of dusty paperwork on his desk. "Can't put this off any longer," he sighed, pulling out a file for a small project installing water pumps in a resort's jacuzzi and pool. It was a welcome respite from his larger, more demanding projects, allowing him some downtime with his family.

As he flipped through the specifications, a familiar pump model caught his eye. He'd used it on a previous project, and it had a glaring flaw: it remained open during power outages. John doubted that Jake, the customer's project manager, was aware of this issue.

"This has to be a design error," he thought, a sense of unease settling in.

He quickly drafted a Request for Information (RFI) form, attaching it to an email for Jake. He outlined the potential problem with the pump and asked for guidance.

Jake's response came swiftly in the form of a phone call. "John, I just read your email," he said, his tone puzzled. "I'm not quite following your concern."

John explained the pump's malfunction during a power outage on his previous project and the potential for significant water damage. "I'd appreciate it if your engineers could review the design and suggest an alternative," he concluded.

Jake remained unconvinced. "John, I don't see the issue. Please proceed with the pump specified in the contract."

John was taken aback by Jake's dismissive response. "Jake, could you confirm that in writing, please?" he asked, sensing trouble brewing.

"No, just proceed as contracted," Jake replied curtly.

Knowing he needed a written record in case this issue resurfaced, John fired off an email:

> Jake,
>
> Thanks for your call today. Following up to make sure we're on the same page. During our call, I described a potential design error with the pool pump and the problems it could cause. I requested a design review, but you instructed me to use the pump specified in the contract. I'll order it today and follow up after installation.

John ordered and installed the pump without incident. But the day after final acceptance, a power outage struck. The hotel's first floor was flooded, and the second floor sustained significant water damage. A week later, a formal notice from Jake arrived, blaming the damage on faulty pump installation and promising a detailed claim within two weeks.

John reached out to me; his voice strained with worry. "Can you swing by the beach today?" he asked.

"Always up for a beach trip," I replied, envisioning a change of scenery.

"Great, come around lunchtime," John said. "Some of the best food trucks are right in front of our old site trailer. We can grab a bite and chat."

When I arrived, we took a quick walk around the hotel, but the damage was obscured by ongoing repairs. We crossed the street to a food truck serving mouthwatering shrimp plates, and John filled me in on the situation.

"It's hard to say who's at fault," I mused. "Was it a faulty installation, like Jake claims? We need a root cause analysis to know for sure."

John nodded. "I've found a third-party engineering firm we can use."

"Have we worked with them before?" I inquired.

"No, but they come highly recommended," John replied.

"That's good," I said, "but credibility is key. We need an unbiased assessment, regardless of whether the findings favor us or not."

John nodded in understanding.

"I'd also recommend notifying the pump manufacturer and allowing them to participate in or conduct their own tests," I added.

John agreed. "I'll get on that today."

As we finished our lunch, I reminded him, "Don't overshare with the manufacturer. Just inform them of the failure. We don't want to jump to conclusions or admit any fault. Let the lawyers handle it if it turns out to be our problem."

Later, John emailed me to confirm he'd taken the necessary steps and forwarded his email to Jake. Jake, however, denied any knowledge of the pump's potential issues and even the conversation where he allegedly instructed John to use it. He cited the following clause from their contract:

**Owner Instructions**. Under no circumstances shall Owner be liable for any verbal explanations, directions, or interpretations, and Contractor is not required to follow any verbal explanations, directions, or interpretations.

A month later, John called with an update. "The engineering firm determined that the pump did indeed remain open during the power outage, causing the flood," he reported, relief evident in his voice.

"That's great news!" I replied. "Did we recover the cost of the analysis?"

"Partially," John sighed. "We spent a lot of time, resources, and legal fees fighting their claim, but in the end, we reached a settlement."

"I'm glad you documented everything," I said. "If you hadn't sent that RFI and follow-up email, things might have turned out very differently."

### BEST PRACTICES

If you uncover any errors or inconsistencies in contract documents that could impact either party or the project, notify your customer in writing immediately. Whether it's a formal notice or an RFI, provide supporting documentation like photos, plans, specifications, and detailed descriptions. Remember, thorough documentation is your best defense.

## Expediting

Expediting clauses are often included in contracts to address potential delays in equipment delivery, material supply, or work performance. These clauses typically grant the owner the right to demand that the contractor accelerate their efforts to meet the project schedule, often by adding shifts, resources, or even subcontracting portions of the work.

Consider this common example:

> **Expediting**. If at any point, Owner realizes that the Equipment will not be delivered to the Project Site by the date(s) specified in the Delivery Schedule or the Work is not meeting the Project Schedule, Owner has the right to require Contractor to speed up the deliveries and/or Work by adding extra shifts, equipment or by subcontracting. Contractor will be responsible for any additional costs incurred in expediting the deliveries and/or Work.

Delays can stem from various sources, including supplier issues, manufacturing problems, labor shortages, and unforeseen events. Any delay can have a domino effect, impacting the overall project schedule and potentially leading to significant consequences.

If the owner notices you're falling behind, they might issue a notice or directive to expedite and recover the lost time. They may also request written assurance that you'll meet the schedule. Effective expediting can help you get back on track, but be aware that delays can trigger additional costs, such as liquidated damages or other delay-related penalties. Failure to meet the schedule could even put you in default of the contract.

## The Risk of Expediting

Expediting can be a double-edged sword for contractors. While it's reasonable to bear the cost of expediting delays caused by your own actions, it's unfair to absorb the costs of delays caused by the owner or factors outside your control.

To protect yourself, consider adding language like this to the expediting clause during contract negotiations:

> **Expediting**. If at any time, the Owner determines that the Equipment will not be delivered to the Project Site on the date(s) outlined in the Delivery Schedule, or the Work is not

in compliance with the Project Schedule, the Owner has the authority to instruct the Contractor to accelerate the deliveries and/or Work, including by adding extra shifts and equipment or subcontracting. The Contractor will be accountable for any extra costs incurred while expediting the deliveries and/or Work unless the delay is caused by factors beyond the Contractor's control, in which case the Owner shall be responsible for the additional costs.

By incorporating this or similar language, you ensure that you're not unfairly penalized for delays that aren't your fault, while still allowing the owner to take necessary action to keep the project on track.

## Flow-down (or Flow-through) and Incorporated by Reference

A flow-down clause is designed to align the interests of the owner, contractor, and subcontractor by requiring the contractor to incorporate similar terms and conditions from their contract with the owner into their subcontracts.

Incorporation by reference clauses is even more expansive than flow-down clauses. They aim to extend all rights and obligations between the owner and contractor to the subcontractor. This means you could be held accountable for terms and conditions you never negotiated or even considered during your proposal process, potentially leading to unforeseen and negative consequences. Let's examine two typical examples:

> **Prime Contract**. As well as the obligations and responsibilities outlined in this Subcontract, the terms of the Prime Contract also apply to Subcontractor, and Subcontractor is bound to Contractor by the same terms and conditions by which Contractor is bound to Owner under the Prime Contract.

Or

> **Incorporation of the Prime Contract**. This Subcontract incorporates, by reference, all the terms of the Prime Contract, and Subcontractor is bound to Contractor in the same way that Contractor is bound to Owner for all obligations.

If you encounter such language in your subcontract, it's crucial to recognize that it essentially binds you to the same arrangement the contractor has with the owner. This can impose obligations that you never negotiated or even contemplated when preparing your proposal, sometimes with unpleasant surprises. These clauses can bury significant legal obligations deep within the prime contract documents, which you may not have received or reviewed yet.

## Mitigating the Risks

If your subcontract includes either of these clauses, it's vital to take proactive steps to mitigate the associated risks:

1. Obtain the Prime Contract: Request a complete copy, including all exhibits and conditions. Even if it's partially redacted, having access to the prime contract is essential to understanding the full extent of your obligations.
2. Conduct a Comparative Review: Carefully compare the prime contract and your subcontract side-by-side. Highlight any inconsistencies, conflicts, or provisions that could impose additional burdens or risks on you.
3. Seek Clarification: Don't hesitate to ask your customer or legal counsel for clarification on any points of confusion or concern.
4. Negotiate the Order of Precedence: Aim to include a clause in your subcontract that prioritizes its terms over those of the prime contract in case of conflict. Here's an example:

> **Order of Precedence**. In case of any discrepancy between the terms of this Subcontract and the terms outlined in the Prime Contract, the precedence will be given in the following order: (i) this Subcontract, (ii) the Prime Contract, and (iii) all attachments to the Prime Contract.

By proactively addressing these issues during contract negotiations, you can protect yourself from unexpected obligations and ensure that your subcontract accurately reflects your negotiated terms and risk tolerance.

## Force Majeure

Force majeure clauses are standard inclusions in most contracts, offering protection against unforeseen events that can disrupt project performance. While there are many variations, tailoring this clause to your specific needs is crucial. Legal nuances vary by state, so it's important to understand the applicable laws.

> **Force Majeure**. In the event that a party is unable to fulfill their obligations under this Agreement due to an act, event, or condition beyond their reasonable control, such as natural disasters, changes in laws, strikes, or delays caused by third parties, they must immediately notify the other party in writing within two (2) working days and provide proof of the delay. The party claiming the event must also take steps to mitigate the delay. Deadlines will be extended for the duration of the delay caused by the Force Majeure event. If a party is excused from performing their obligations for 180 calendar days, the other party has the right to terminate the Agreement without liability.

When crafting or reviewing a force majeure clause, consider the following questions:

1. Is the clause mutual? Does it protect both parties equally, or is it one-sided?
2. Notice Requirements: Are there clear notice requirements, and are the time limits reasonable?
3. Force Majeure Events: Are these events well-defined, and do they encompass the potential disruptions relevant to your project and location? Think about natural disasters, pandemics, governmental actions, etc.
4. External Factors: Do the events covered fall outside the control of the contract and the parties involved?
5. Impact on Performance: Would these events render performance substantially different from what was initially contemplated by the parties?
6. Foreseeability: Are the events unforeseeable at the time of contracting?
7. Control: Are the events genuinely beyond the control of the party claiming force majeure?
8. Extensions: Does the clause allow for reasonable extensions to the delivery or project schedule in the event of a force majeure event?
9. Termination: Does the clause allow for termination of the contract by either party if the event is prolonged?

Financial Obligations: Does the contract explicitly state that the inability to pay is not a valid force majeure event?

## Termination Rights: A Critical Consideration

Force majeure clauses typically allow either party to terminate the contract if the disruptive event persists for a specified period. However, this termination should be "for convenience," meaning without assigning fault, unless the party experiencing the force majeure event has breached the contract in some other way.

Be wary of language like this:

> Notwithstanding the foregoing, in the event that the delay resulting from the Force Majeure event continues for more than thirty (30) days, Owner shall have the right to terminate the Agreement, and any such termination shall be deemed to be a termination for default by Contractor.

This type of language is unacceptable because it undermines the purpose of the force majeure clause, which is to excuse performance in the face of uncontrollable events. It exposes the contractor to potential damages for default, negating the clause's protective intent.

### *Key Takeaway*

A well-drafted force majeure clause can provide crucial protection against unforeseen events. By carefully considering the specific risks relevant to your project and tailoring the clause accordingly, you can mitigate the potential for costly disputes and ensure a fair outcome for all parties involved.

### BEST PRACTICES

In the event of a force majeure, it is critical to promptly review all contracts that may be impacted to determine your notification obligations and legal rights. Despite the possibility that your customer is aware of the event, it is still imperative to issue a formal notice. If the contract lacks specific time constraints for notification, aim to inform your customer as soon as feasible, ideally within 48 hours. Additionally, you should explore alternative methods to fulfill your contractual obligations. Ensure that all efforts and measures taken during this period are thoroughly documented to maintain a clear record of your attempts to comply.

# Governing Law (or Choice of Law) and Venue

The governing law clause is a crucial boilerplate provision that can significantly impact on the contract and its potential legal implications. While often overlooked, its importance becomes evident when disputes arise, potentially requiring litigation in a distant jurisdiction.

This clause enables parties to agree on a specific state's laws to interpret their agreement. This serves two key purposes:

1. Providing certainty: It clarifies the agreed-upon terms and expectations for both parties.
2. Identifying the governing law: It specifies the legal framework for resolving any disputes arising from the contractual relationship.

Many large corporations favor Delaware law due to its well-established body of case law upholding contract provisions, offering predictability in dispute resolution.

Example Clause:

> **Governing Law**. This Agreement and any claims or legal actions related to it, including those arising from contract, tort, or statute, and any representations or warranties made in connection with it, will be governed and enforced by the laws of the State of Delaware, including its statutes of limitation.

It's important to note that the governing law clause determines the applicable state law but not necessarily the location for litigation. This is often addressed by a separate venue or jurisdiction clause, which specifies the state with jurisdiction over disputes.

Combined Clause Example:

> **Governing Law; Venue.** This Agreement shall be governed by and interpreted in accordance with the laws of the State of

Delaware, without regard to conflict of laws principles. Both parties agree to submit to the jurisdiction of the federal and state courts located in the State of Delaware for any disputes arising out of or related to this Agreement and will not challenge the jurisdiction of such courts or bring any action in any other court.

While Delaware is a popular choice for both governing law and venue due to its extensive case law, other factors warrant consideration when selecting a venue:

- Litigation Expenses: Attorney fees can vary significantly depending on location.
- Travel Costs: Litigation in a distant state can incur substantial travel expenses.
- Time Commitment: Litigation requires a significant time investment from all parties involved.

By carefully considering these factors, parties can make informed decisions about both the governing law and venue, ensuring a comprehensive and effective contract.

## BEST PRACTICES

It's not uncommon for clients to initially state that governing law and venue clauses are non-negotiable. However, it's worth noting that these terms can often be revisited and adjusted, even after a dispute has arisen.

Should you encounter resistance in securing your preferred governing law and venue, consider proposing a modification from mandatory to permissive language within the clause. This allows for the possibility of selecting an alternative forum at a later stage, should the need arise, offering a compromise that may be mutually agreeable. Consider incorporating the following option into your agreements [bolded here for emphasis]:

> **Governing Law; Venue**. This Agreement shall be governed by and interpreted in accordance with the laws of the State of Delaware, without regard to conflict of laws principles. The parties agree that any disputes arising out of or related to this Agreement shall be subject to the exclusive jurisdiction of the federal and state courts located in the State of Delaware. **Notwithstanding the foregoing, the parties may mutually agree in writing to modify this provision to select an alternative governing law or venue for any specific dispute.**

## Headings

Contract drafters meticulously detail agreements to define roles and responsibilities for each party. Often, this process begins with boilerplate templates or term sheets, customized to address specific needs and risks. Headings play a crucial organizational role, guiding the reader through the contract's structure.

However, it's important to understand that headings are not meant to be all-encompassing or definitive summaries of the content beneath them. To reinforce this, contract drafters often include a "headings clause."

Example Headings Clause:

> **Headings.** The headings in this Agreement are for convenience and reference only and shall not affect the interpretation or construction of any provision of this Agreement.

Purpose of the Headings Clause:

- Clarification: This clause explicitly states that headings are not intended to limit, define, or expand the meaning of any contractual provision.
- Interpretation: It prevents headings from being used to resolve ambiguities or conflicts within the contract's body.
- Risk Mitigation: While not foolproof, the headings clause can serve as a safeguard against potential misinterpretations based solely on headings.

**Key Takeaway:**

Headings are a helpful tool for navigating contracts, but they should not be relied upon as a definitive source of meaning or interpretation. The headings clause ensures that the substance of the contract takes precedence over any potential inferences drawn from headings alone.

## BEST PRACTICES

While headings in contracts offer a convenient way to navigate the document, they can be misleading if relied upon exclusively. Here's why:

- Inconsistent Content: It's not uncommon for clauses to contain information that doesn't perfectly align with the heading. A clause might include provisions related to both delays and termination, even though the heading only mentions one, as in the force majeure example.
- Ambiguity: Headings are often brief and may not fully capture the nuances of the underlying provision. This can lead to misinterpretations if you don't carefully read the entire clause.
- Legal Interpretation: Courts generally treat headings as organizational tools, not as definitive statements of content. This means that if there's a conflict between the heading and the actual text of a provision, the text will usually prevail.

> **BEST PRACTICES**
>
> When reviewing a contract:
>
> - Read every clause in its entirety: Don't rely solely on headings to understand the terms.
> - Be mindful of inconsistencies: Look for language that doesn't seem to fit the heading and clarify any ambiguities.
>
> By taking these steps, you can ensure that you have a complete and accurate understanding of the contract's terms, regardless of what the headings might suggest.

## Indemnification

Indemnification clauses are powerful tools for managing risk in contracts, but their complexity can pose significant financial consequences, potentially even leading to bankruptcy. Together with additional insured provisions, they are primarily used to transfer risk associated with third-party claims for personal injury, property damage, and intellectual property disputes. Understanding these clauses is vital, as they often interact with other contract provisions, including insurance, warranties, and limitations of liability.

## Understanding Damages

Before delving into indemnification, let's clarify the common types of damages you might encounter in contracts:

- Actual Damages: Tangible losses like lost profits, supervisory expenses, or overhead.
- General Damages: Non-monetary losses resulting from an action or inaction.
- Direct Damages: Losses flowing directly from an act, such as project labor costs.

- Indirect Damages: Costs supporting the project indirectly, like administrative expenses.
- Compensatory Damages: Money awarded to compensate for proven harm, such as lost time or opportunities.
- Special/Consequential Damages: Additional costs directly caused by a breach or wrongful act, which require explicit proof.
- Punitive/Exemplary Damages: Damages exceeding actual losses, meant to punish malicious or reckless conduct.
- Liquidated Damages: Pre-agreed amounts payable for specific breaches.
- Unliquidated Damages: Not pre-determined, established by a judge or jury.

## Indemnification: Taking on the Responsibility of Others

Indemnification occurs when one party (the Indemnitor) contractually accepts legal and financial responsibility for another party (the Indemnitee). This can extend to claims arising before, during, or after a project. Agreeing to indemnify beyond your own negligence can expose you to liabilities you wouldn't typically face under the law.

## Beware of Ambiguous Language

Phrases like "relating to," "arising out of," or "in connection with" are often used in indemnification clauses. These terms are intentionally broad and open to interpretation, creating potential for unintended liabilities. Always aim for clear, specific language that defines the exact scope of your responsibility.

## Three Key Obligations: Indemnifying, Defending, and Holding Harmless

- Indemnify: Promise to pay for the other party's losses.
- Hold harmless: Protect the other party from lawsuits by third parties.

- Defend: Pay the other party's legal fees when they are sued by a third party.

## Types of Indemnification and Example Clauses

**Broad Form**: The most comprehensive and risky type, covering all claims regardless of fault.

Example Clause:

> **Indemnification**. Contractor agrees to indemnify and hold harmless Owner, its subsidiaries and affiliates and all of their respective directors, officers and employees (collectively "Indemnified Parties") for any damages, losses, costs, expenses, demands, claims, suits, and actions resulting from or related to the Contract, regardless of the cause of such damages, losses, costs, expenses, demands, claims, suits, and actions, and whether or not the Indemnified Parties are negligent or intentionally cause such damages, losses, costs, expenses, demands, claims, suits, and actions.

**Intermediate Form**: Less risky than broad form, but still potentially problematic. Covers damages where the indemnitor is partially or fully at fault.

Example Clause:

> **Indemnity**. Contractor shall indemnify and hold harmless the Owner for all damages, losses, or claims that arise as a result, in whole or in part, from the negligence, errors and omissions, or failure to perform by Contractor, his employees, his agents, or his subcontractor.

**Narrow Form**: The most limited and reasonable form, covering only damages directly caused by the Indemnitor's negligence.

Example Clause:

> **Indemnification**. Contractor shall indemnify Owner for any damages resulting from the provision of materials and services, but only if such damages are caused by the Contractor's negligence, mistakes, or failures to fulfill their duties.

### Word Placement is Critical

The placement of words like "negligent" significantly impacts the scope of the clause. Ensure the adjective "negligent" directly modifies the relevant actions to avoid unintended liability.

### Seek Mutual Indemnification

Whenever possible, negotiate for mutual indemnification, where both parties agree to protect each other. This promotes fairness and shared responsibility.

### Limit Your Liability

Negotiate to cap your indemnification obligations, ideally to the extent of your negligence or a specific dollar amount. If unlimited liability is unavoidable, ensure you have sufficient insurance coverage to protect your business.

### Key Takeaway

Indemnification clauses are complex and carry significant financial risk. Careful review with legal counsel and adequate insurance coverage are essential to protect your company from unexpected liabilities.

## Inspection

The inspection clause is a standard provision in supply and construction contracts. It grants the customer or their representatives the right to inspect and test products and services and work to ensure compliance with contract specifications and quality requirements. This right extends to the contractor's facilities, supplier facilities, and the project site.

**Owner's Right to Inspect.** The Owner, with five business days' notice, has the right to inspect the work at the project site during regular business hours. This inspection right does not interfere with the Contractor's safety precautions or release them from their contractual obligations. The Owner may reject work due to latent defects, but this does not relieve the Contractor of their obligations or impose any on the Owner.

Or

**Owner's Right to Inspect During Manufacture.** The Owner has the right to inspect facilities where machinery or equipment is being manufactured at reasonable times with prior notice. Similar to the clause above, this does not absolve the Contractor of obligations or impose any on the Owner.

It's crucial that inspections and tests occur at reasonable times, typically during regular business hours, without causing undue disruption to the Contractor's operations. Inspections do not imply acceptance of work or manufacturing methods, nor do they relieve the contractor of responsibilities. Contractors should include similar inspection terms in their subcontracts as a best practice to maintain consistent rights throughout the project hierarchy.

## BEST PRACTICES

To streamline the inspection process, consider requiring subcontractors to submit progress reports. These reports help assess the project's phase, identify potential issues, and focus inspections on areas of interest. By proactively managing inspections and fostering communication, both parties can ensure the project's successful completion.

## Limitation of Liability

The limitation of liability clause is a heavily negotiated and critical provision in any contract. Far from boilerplate, it's a carefully constructed tool designed to limit your company's risk exposure. Its consequences for all parties can be enormous, making it one of the most important terms in your agreement. Investing time in reviewing, negotiating, and understanding this clause is essential.

### Why is a Limitation of Liability Clause Important?

A well-planned limitation of liability clause acts as a safety net. It allows you to predict and control the extent of your potential liability in the event of a contract breach, capping it at a specific, agreed-upon dollar amount.

### Types of Damages and the Need for Limitation

Before diving into the clause itself, let's explore the types of damages you might be liable for without a limitation clause. If your customer omits this clause, you could be held responsible for all reasonably foreseeable damages they incur, including both direct and indirect damages.

### What a Limitation of Liability Clause Does

This clause allows the parties to reduce or eliminate certain types of damages. Commonly excluded damages include:

- Consequential Damages (or special damages): These are unpredictable and potentially unlimited. Limiting them reduces risk, but it may leave a party without recourse for indirect losses.
- Indirect Damages: These are losses not directly caused by the breach. Think of data loss during a computer repair—the cost to restore the data is indirect.

- Incidental Damages: These are extra costs incurred to fix or mitigate a breach, such as towing and repair fees for a faulty used boat.
- Punitive Damages: These are court-imposed penalties for egregious behavior, like fraud or gross negligence.

Example Clause

Consider this example of a limitation of liability clause:

> **LIMITATION OF LIABILITY**. NEITHER CONTRACTOR NOR OWNER SHALL BE LIABLE, WHETHER IN CONTRACT, WARRANTY, FAILURE OF A REMEDY TO ACHIEVE ITS INTENDED OR ESSENTIAL PURPOSES, TORT (INCLUDING NEGLIGENCE), STRICT LIABILITY, INDEMNITY OR ANY OTHER LEGAL THEORY, FOR LOSS OF USE, REVENUE OR PROFIT, OR FOR COSTS OF CAPITAL OR OF SUBSTITUTE USE OR PERFORMANCE, OR FOR INDIRECT, SPECIAL, LIQUIDATED, INCIDENTAL OR CONSEQUENTIAL DAMAGES, OR FOR ANY OTHER LOSS OR COST OF A SIMILAR TYPE; AND CONTRACTOR'S MAXIMUM LIABILITY UNDER THIS CONTRACT SHALL BE THE CONTRACT PRICE.

The capitalized and bolded text emphasizes the importance of this clause. In some jurisdictions, this "conspicuousness" is required for enforceability.

## Enforceability and Carveouts

While often debated, limitation of liability clauses are generally enforceable unless they are ambiguous, unconscionable, or contradict public policy.

Parties can also negotiate "carveouts" or exceptions to the limitations. These might include claims for:

- Death or bodily injury
- Breach of security or confidentiality
- Infringement of intellectual property
- Attorney's fees and litigation costs

**Example Carveout Language**

> ... however, these limitations shall not apply to claims arising from a breach of warranty, any infringement of third-party intellectual property, negligence, or any attorney's fees and other litigation costs that either party becomes entitled to recover.

## *Insight Story: The Project that We Could Not Complete*

Throughout my career, I've witnessed both the triumphs and pitfalls of successful companies. While many excel in their industries, a single misstep can lead to devastating financial losses, brand damage, and irreparable client relationships. This story illustrates how one company's risky decision, despite a limitation of liability clause, resulted in costly consequences.

The company I worked for was a leader in manufacturing and installing HVAC systems. When a city manager, a satisfied customer, inquired about recommendations for a wastewater treatment plant, our sales team saw dollar signs. A proposal was quickly drawn up, even though we had no experience in wastewater treatment.

Relying on our reputation, the city eagerly requested a formal proposal. We partnered with an outside contractor and drafted a design using our in-house engineers—experts in HVAC, not wastewater. Upon completion, we struggled to commission the facility due to unforeseen sludge management issues. Despite hiring consultants, no viable solution was found.

Two years passed and the plant sat dormant. Communication with the city ceased. When a $10 million demand letter arrived (double the project cost), panic ensued. As I reviewed the contract, our limited liability clause stood out. It capped our liability at the $5 million contract price and excluded consequential damages.

Our failure's root causes were clear. Eager to expand, we ventured into an unfamiliar market without the necessary expertise. Our partnership didn't fill this gap, and by the time we recognized our shortcomings, it was too late.

In the end, we settled with the city, paying the full contract price and covering demolition costs. We never worked for them again. The damage to our reputation and customer relationship? Immeasurable!

This experience highlights the importance of understanding your core competencies and the risks of venturing into uncharted territory. While a limitation of liability clause can mitigate financial losses, it cannot repair the intangible costs of a damaged reputation and lost trust.

## BEST PRACTICES

To enhance the enforceability of your limitation of liability clause, make it conspicuous by using capitalized and bolded text. Ensure the language is clear, concise, and unambiguous. Consider specifically excluding consequential, incidental, indirect, and punitive damages, and clearly define a cap on your overall liability. This will help protect your business from unexpected and potentially excessive financial burdens.

## Liquidated Damages

Should you consider liquidated damages in your contract? The answer isn't always black and white. They can be a valuable tool in certain situations, providing predictability and avoiding disputes. However, they're not a one-size-fits-all solution and require careful consideration based on the specific contract and potential risks involved.

## What Are Liquidated Damages?

Liquidated damages clauses serve two key functions:

- Reduce or eliminate: They cap the customer's potential actual damages (direct losses due to delay).
- Predetermined amount: They specify a fixed sum payable to the customer if you breach the contract's terms.

For example, if the clause states "$2,000 per day for unexcused delays," the customer can only recover that amount for each day of delay, even if their actual damages are higher.

## Example Clauses

Common in construction and supply contracts, liquidated damages clauses are often tied to project milestones. Here are a few examples:

> **Delay Liquidated Damages**. The Parties understand that it is difficult to determine the exact dollar amount of damages that would result from Contractor's failure to complete the project on time. The Parties agree that in such an event, Owner would be damaged, and it would be impractical to calculate the exact damages. Therefore, the Parties agree that any damages payable in such a situation will be considered as liquidated damages, and not a penalty, which are a fair and reasonable estimate of the damages that may occur. These liquidated damages,

referred to as "Delay Liquidated Damages," will be payable on demand and will be the sole remedy for Owner's delay-related damages. This provision will remain in effect even after the completion or termination of the Agreement. The Delay Liquidated Damages do not cover the cost of completing the work or any damages resulting from defective work.

Or

**Liquidated Damages**. The Parties acknowledge that it is difficult or impossible to determine with precision the dollar amount of damages that would be incurred by the Owner as a result of the Contractor's failure to achieve Substantial Completion within the Contract Time provided by the Contract Documents. Therefore, the Contractor agrees that liquidated damages in the amount of Two Thousand Dollars ($2,000.00) per calendar day of delay beyond the Contract Time, as adjusted for time extensions, shall be assessed and recovered by the Owner as compensation for such delay, without the Owner being required to present any evidence of the amount or character of actual damages sustained. These liquidated damages are intended to represent an estimate of actual damages and not a penalty, and the Contractor shall pay them to the Owner without limiting the Owner's right to terminate the agreement for default as provided elsewhere in the contract.

Or

**Late Deliveries And Liquidated Damages**. Supplier must follow the delivery schedule outlined in the Purchase Order. If there is a delay, Supplier must notify the Contractor in writing of the reason for the delay and provide a recovery schedule. If the delay is not caused by force majeure or the Contractor, Supplier must pay liquidated damages of 1% of the unit price for each week of delay, up to a maximum of 5% of the unit price.

## Advantages for You (the Contractor)

Accepting liquidated damages offers several benefits:

- Predictability: You know your maximum liability upfront.
- Dispute avoidance: The agreed-upon amount prevents costly litigation over damages.
- Potential cap: You can negotiate a maximum total for liquidated damages.

## Example Cap Language

Contractor will be held responsible for any delay damages incurred by Owner as a result of the Contractor's actions, but Contractor's total liability for all types of delay damages will not exceed $50,000.

## Advantages for Your Customer

Customers also benefit from liquidated damages clauses:

- Guaranteed Compensation: They receive a predetermined amount without needing to prove actual losses in court.
- Enforcement: They can deduct liquidated damages directly from your payment.
- Deterrent: Knowing the consequences may encourage timely performance.

## Weighing the Pros and Cons

The downside? If you're facing a liquidated damages claim, it likely means you've missed a deadline, potentially impacting your project's profitability. However, this is often preferable to facing a lawsuit for much larger, unpredictable damages.

## Enforceability and Additional Considerations

For a liquidated damages clause to be enforceable, it must meet specific criteria:

- Difficult to Calculate: The damages resulting from the breach must be uncertain or difficult to quantify at the time of contracting.
- Reasonable Estimate: The liquidated damages amount must be a reasonable pre-estimate of the actual damages that may result from the breach. It cannot be a penalty.
- Exclusivity (with potential exceptions): Liquidated damages should generally be the customer's exclusive remedy for delay, unless the contract specifies exceptions (e.g., for gross negligence, willful misconduct, or other egregious breaches).

Be wary of "carveouts" that allow additional damages beyond the liquidated amount. As a contractor, such provisions could significantly increase your risk.

No Liquidated Damages Clause?

If the contract lacks this clause, your customer could seek both actual damages and, potentially, consequential damages for unexcused delays.

## Key Takeaways for Subcontracts

Avoid copying the prime contract's clause directly into subcontracts. Instead, negotiate indemnity provisions that specifically address liquidated damages to protect yourself from losses caused by your subcontractor's delays.

## BEST PRACTICES

To ensure effective and fair liquidated damages provisions in your contracts, consider these essential points:

- Include a Liquidated Damages Clause: Make it clear that this clause is the customer's sole remedy for delays, precluding claims for actual and consequential damages.

- Review for Carveouts: Scrutinize any language that allows for additional damages beyond the liquidated amount, especially for unexcused delays. Seek to remove or modify such provisions.

- Ensure Alignment: If your contract includes liquidated damages, ensure that the limitation of liability clause and a mutual waiver of consequential damages are consistent. As a contractor, negotiate a carveout in the limitation clause to preserve your right to recover the agreed-upon liquidated amount.

- Focus on Substantial or Final Completion: Avoid tying liquidated damages to interim milestones. Instead, link them to the project's substantial or final completion.

- Negotiate a Grace Period: Establish a reasonable grace period (e.g., 30 days) after substantial completion to address minor punch-list items without triggering liquidated damages.

- Ensure the Clause's Survival: For contractors, explicitly state that the liquidated damages provision survives contract termination.

- Address Subcontractor Delays: Include indemnity provisions in subcontracts to protect yourself from liquidated damages or other costs arising from your subcontractor's unexcused delays.

- Tailor Subcontract **Clauses**: Avoid blindly copying the prime contract's liquidated damages clause into subcontracts. Instead, analyze the potential impact of subcontractor delays and negotiate clauses accordingly.

By implementing these best practices, you can create liquidated damages provisions that are fair, enforceable, and protect your interests.

## No Damages by Contractor

Changes, disputes, and disagreements are all part of projects. It is reasonable for your customer to want your assurance that when these things happen, you (and your lower-tier subcontractors) will continue working with no delays. The same can be said about you and your subcontractors.

Consider the following scenario: Your company signed a significant contract for a construction project. As the prime contractor, you selected a handful of subcontractors to complete portions of the project. Until today, the project has not experienced significant delays and appeared to be on schedule, but that harmony only lasted a little while.

Last week, you received a claim from one of your subcontractors for work that was considered extra. You reviewed the claim and their scope of work and determined the work they claimed was extra work is outlined in the contract documents. Yesterday, you sent them a written response to their claim outlining your conclusions, and you gave your subcontractor's project manager a call to review it. Your subcontractor gets frustrated by your decision and tells their workers to pick up their tools and leave the project site. Today, you receive a call from the subcontractor's owner telling you they will return once you agree to pay them for the extra work.

Do the subcontractor's actions sound reasonable? It depends! To answer this question, we need to understand what you and the subcontractor agreed to in the contract.

1. Are there clauses that outline how changes are to be addressed?
2. Can the subcontractor unilaterally decide to stop work and leave the project site?

3. Does the dispute resolution clause outline how you and the subcontractor will manage disputes?

Before we dig into this scenario much further, I would like to caution you about some risks. It is not unusual for contractors and subcontractors (depending on which side of the table you are on) to unintentionally (or intentionally—you be the judge) leave out specific equipment that is a necessary part of their scope of supply or work that's needed to complete the project. It may be because they don't have stringent estimating controls, or they give you low pricing to win the contract, and they intend on making up the difference through change orders. Subcontractors may accomplish this by leaving out certain aspects in their proposal (i.e., assumptions and/or exclusions) or in the scope of work you are responsible for preparing.

How do you ensure continued performance when there is a dispute? Again, your change order process should outline how to manage changes. If you and your subcontractor disagree, the clause should clearly state that your subcontractor must continue their performance and that the dispute will be addressed under the dispute resolution clause.

Let's consider the following example:

> **No Delay by Subcontractor.** To the fullest extent allowed by law, even if a dispute, controversy, or question arises regarding the interpretation of any provision of this Agreement, the performance of any work, the delivery of any material, the payment of any sums of money to Subcontractor, or otherwise, Subcontractor agrees that they will not directly or indirectly halt or delay any work or delivery of materials required under this Agreement. Any disputes or controversies will be resolved through the Dispute Resolution Clause.

If a dispute arises, this example clause requires your subcontractor to continue their supply or work.

What if your subcontractor leaves the project site and continues to demand payment before returning to the project site? Great question! Let's explore this further. In addition to ensuring that your change process is straightforward (and agreed upon), you will need to review your termination for default clause. Let's take a look at the following clause:

> **Termination for Default**. Subcontractor will be considered in default if they: (a) fail to carry out the work promptly and efficiently, (b) fail to perform the work in a professional, skilled, cooperative, safe and careful manner, (c) fail to provide adequate and competent supervision, (d) fail to provide enough properly skilled workers, (e) fail to provide the necessary materials and equipment of the appropriate quality and quantity, (f) fail to promptly fix any defective or inadequate work, (g) fail to promptly pay their sub-subcontractors or suppliers or fail to fulfill their financial obligations on the project, (h) fail to maintain the project schedule or significantly delay the work of the contractor or other subcontractors, (i) fail to provide adequate assurance of their ability to fulfill their obligations under the Agreement within two business days of a written request, or (j) fail to submit any required progress, procurement, and man-hour completion schedules.

Subsection (h) states that if your subcontractor fails to maintain the project schedule or materially delays the work, it is in default.

Is this enough to terminate your subcontractor for default? No, it is not enough based solely on this clause. First, you have more homework to do. According to the UCC, if your subcontractor makes a statement or engages in an action that indicates it will not fulfill its contractual obligations or will not be able to perform within the time required under the agreement, then it is an anticipatory breach of contract. Since we have their statement, is that enough? Again, it depends, but I would not terminate the subcontractor based solely on a verbal statement. Has the date for their performance come and gone?

Besides the changes and termination for default clauses, I suggest adding more requirements to ensure you have your bases covered and documenting the event in as much detail as possible. Let's consider the following clause:

> **Adequate Assurances**. If the Parties have agreed to a Project Schedule and Subcontractor fails to provide enough evidence of their ability to fulfill their responsibilities under the Agreement within two (2) business days of a written request from Contractor, and Contractor has a valid reason to be concerned, it will be considered a default under the Agreement.

We need to mention a few more things. Even if you have the no delay clause, termination for default clause, and adequate assurance clause, is it a good idea to terminate your subcontractor? It depends, but I would make it my last option. I suggest you consult a litigation attorney to ensure your bases are covered. Covering your bases means documentation, documentation, and more documentation. You must demonstrate that you did everything in your power to collaborate with and encourage your subcontractor to fulfill its obligations. Why? You do not want the termination for default deemed by the court to be a termination for convenience. We will go into greater detail about this Insight Story "I've had it. Let's Terminate Them Today."

## No Damages for Delay

I hope you see how a contract can transfer the risk to other parties. The clause we will discuss now is no exception. We all know that changes are a fact of life, especially on large and complex projects, and delays often follow changes. Delays, like changes, come with a cost. Here's a question for you to consider: If you are delayed by other individuals or companies that are not within your control, who will pay for those delays?

Let's consider the following example:

> **No Damages for Delay**. Contractor acknowledges that it will not seek compensation from Owner for any expenses, including but not limited to damages, charges, interest, additional costs or fees, which may arise as a result of delays or interruption to work caused by Owner, parties under Owner's control, or any other external factors during the performance of the work under this Agreement. The only remedy available to Contractor in the event of delays, stoppage or suspension of work is an extension of the timeframe given to complete the work under this Agreement, equal to the duration of the delay, stoppage or suspension.

This clause asserts that delays are part of construction projects, and you will be responsible for your additional costs. Does that sound like a good deal?

Several states have adopted statutes prohibiting no damage for delay clauses in public works contracts. Some states have banned or at least restricted their use, watering them down. The courts have outlined a few exceptions to these clauses, but no matter how carefully crafted, they will be subject to court interpretation. Let's cover this and discuss the options you may have to carve out these exceptions.

The exceptions include delays that weren't mentioned in the contract or were not foreseeable or contemplated (i.e., Force Majeure) by the parties at the time of the contract signing. Additional exceptions include delays resulting from active interference, bad faith, fraud, misrepresentation, a fundamental breach of contract, or if the delays continue for an unreasonable time and constitute an intentional abandonment of the contract by your customer. This list is not exhaustive, and some states may recognize other exceptions to no-damage for delay clauses. Understanding how this clause is applied under the law governing your contract would be a great start.

If I were reviewing a contract and discovered our example clause or similar language, I would redline it. If that approach is not an option, consider inserting language that allows for the above exceptions. For instance, insert the following exception into the clause: "except for delays caused solely by acts of Owner that constitute intentional interference with Contractor's performance of the Work."

It is understandable for you, as a contractor, to limit your unknown risk by using this or a similar clause. I know, this is absolutely a double standard! We don't want the risks being pushed down by our customers, but we will require our subcontractors to live with it. Even if you include the clause, it doesn't guarantee (nothing in life is absolutely for sure) that your company will not be liable for delay damages. You may add language to the no damages for delay clause that provides additional protection for your company. Consider adding language that makes any payment from your customer a condition precedent to paying them for delay damages.

## Notices

In my workshops, the notices clause receives a lot of attention from me, but it's one of the most intentionally overlooked contract clauses by project managers. Why is that? Maybe they don't understand its importance and the potential consequences of ignoring it, or since it seems benign, they don't understand its relevance. I don't want to jump to conclusions, but I have my suspicions. Let's explore this concept and see if we can understand why.

But before we get in too deep, presenting a notice clause is a great place to start. Let's consider the following clause:

> **Notices**. Any communication required or allowed under this Agreement must be in writing, signed by the sender, and delivered either in person, via mail with proof of receipt, or by email (with a follow-up hard copy sent via mail) to the recipient.

So let's consider the elements of the Standard Notice Clause. Notices must be:

- Sent when there is a need to notify your customer (or subcontractor) of an important event.
- In writing
- Signed by the party giving such notice.
- Sent by registered letter or e-mail (followed by registered letter).

I have to be open and honest with you. I do understand why some project managers are hesitant or do not follow the requirements outlined in this clause. I imagine they do not want to seem confrontational, or their customer has clarified that they do not want to receive anything that may be construed as a legal document. We will learn how to manage situations like this later in this guidebook!

It's common to find notice requirements generously sprinkled throughout contracts for specific events that may or may not occur on your project. It's understandable. Your customer wants to be aware of events that may affect their projects, so you must notify them. It is that simple! The other language in the notice clause outlines the notice's procedural aspects. Don't gloss over them and assume they are optional. If you do, you may find real and unintended consequences for failing to follow the notice requirements outlined in your contract.

A scenario is the best way to illustrate the importance of the notice clause. Imagine this: you are a newly minted project manager working on a project. You are the prime contractor. The project consists of building a new elementary school to replace an existing high school. Once you get onboard, you select several subcontractors to complete portions of your scope of work. You select an electrician, plumber, and drywall installer. You have your project kickoff meeting with your subcontractors and suppliers and cover each company's scope of work.

Once the project is ready, you verbally ask all three companies to work together and coordinate their schedules. The project is going well, and you have heard no complaints from your customers or suppliers. You have completed the project on time and within budget.

You are now closing out your subcontracts and requesting payment applications and final lien waivers. A few days after your request, you receive a formal claim from your electrician for delay damages. In their claim, they assert that the sheetrock crew had installed the drywall in most of the building before the electrical wiring could be installed. They asserted that they had to remove the drywall, which resulted in additional labor costs, schedule delays, and acceleration costs to meet the project's substantial completion date.

By the way, while you were reviewing the electrician's claim for damages, you just received a similar claim from your plumber and a call from the sheet rock company telling you they will be submitting a claim for damages/rework to the drywall. Does this story sound too far-fetched? No! This scenario is relatively common and will quickly end in dispute resolution or litigation.

To prevent this scenario from occurring, let's break this down and discuss everyone's obligations. Before we take laps in that pool, we should start by answering a few questions. For the sake of this scenario, let's assume your contract had our example notice clause. These questions are touchy-feely but relevant to our discussion, so please answer them truthfully.

1. If this scenario happened to you, how would it make you feel?
2. Did it catch you off guard and surprise you? Or better yet, did it make you mad?
3. Is there anything you could have done to prevent this event?
4. What will your customer say when you send your subcontractor's claim up the flagpole?

I won't spoon-feed you my thoughts, but this scenario is unacceptable. There are many issues with it. Honestly, my first impulse would be to call them and deny their claims, but that approach is unrealistic and will not solve the problems. It would be best to start by reviewing the notice requirements in your subcontracts. Remember that they may be scattered throughout, so you must thoroughly review your contract. You should also review any clauses relating to changes and delays while your contract is open.

Here is what you should consider. This clause works both ways. Not only is your subcontractor obligated to notify you when events occur on the project, but you are also under the same obligation to notify your customer. Let's explore why giving and receiving written notices is essential. It allows the party receiving the notice to:

- Exercise control over the cost and effort expended in resolving the problems.
- Make its determination as to the character and scope of the problem.
- Determine the course of action for coping with the problems encountered.
- Document the facts and circumstances while they are fresh in everyone's mind.
- Ensure that both parties have a record of the dates and facts that initiated the event.

Under your contract, you must notify your customer when events occur on your project, and the same goes for your subcontractor's obligation to notify you. It's not just a contractual duty. The courts have expressed that you have a good-faith obligation to notify the other party.

The clause we used in our example could be better. It fails to provide you with adequate protection and should be rewritten. However, one clause will probably not protect you. This scenario's potential risk should be addressed in other clauses too. I typically include language that addresses notices, claims, and changes, as well as requirements to notify us when events occur. Let's consider the following language:

> **Claims**. If a dispute or disagreement arises in relation to the Work, Subcontractor must immediately provide written notification within five (5) business days of becoming aware of the event. If Subcontractor fails to do so and Contractor is not given the opportunity to inspect the Work, keep accurate records of the cost incurred, or review Subcontractor's project records, Subcontractor waives any right to pursue the claim under the Agreement.

Does the language seem familiar? If not, please review the things you should consider in the notice clauses (above). Let's break this clause down into its elements. When events occur on your project, your subcontractor must give you written notice. Suppose your subcontractor fails to provide you with written notice within five (5) working days and does not allow you to: (i) examine the work; (ii) keep a strict accounting of the time and costs; or (iii) review their project records. In that case, they waive their rights to assert a claim. This clause would have made the project manager in our story much happier.

## BEST PRACTICES

You should pay close attention to all notice clauses within your customer's contract, especially those individuals that must be notified, how they will be notified, and when they will be notified. The terms and conditions in your customer's contract should resemble or mirror the terms in your subcontracts.

When I cover this section in my workshops, one question I am asked is, "Will an e-mail or text message serve as notice?" This question is challenging, and I almost always respond with,—it depends. With the advent of technology, the courts are looking at this question differently. The various state courts are divided on this question, and there is no definite answer.

Let's consider the elements of a notice clause again. I've included them here again for easy reference.

- When you want to notify your customer (or subcontractor) of an important event, you must send a notification.
- It has to be in writing.
- It has to be signed by the party giving such notice.
- It has to be sent by registered letter or e-mail (followed by registered letter).

The first two elements include an obligation to notify your customer in writing when an event occurs. An e-mail seems to fulfill these requirements since you notified your customer of the event in writing. However, the meaning of the words "notify" and "in writing" are up for debate. Okay, element three requires that the notice be signed by the party giving notice. Again, there is some ambiguity here. Do electronic signatures count? Does your contract allow you to add electronic signatures? We are now at the last element. Notices must be sent by registered letter or e-mail, followed by a registered letter. Our analysis of this clause shows that an e-mail does not serve as an official notice because it was not sent by registered letter.

But don't discount e-mail! Some state courts do not take the strict interpretation we used in our analysis and look at the entire set of circumstances. However, you should ensure that you follow the requirements outlined in your contract. If you are able, modify the terms during contract negotiations. Consider adding the clauses below:

> **Electronic Signatures**. Both parties agree that this Agreement and any associated documents may be signed electronically and that electronic signatures will be considered valid and legally binding.

As I mentioned, other notice requirements may contain waiver language. One reason is that your customer may have notice requirements in their contracts with the end customer or other contractors performing work on the project.

> **Notice by E-mail**. If a notice is sent via e-mail, the sender's receipt of a delivery confirmation report that verifies the e-mail was received shall serve as presumptive evidence of receipt unless the sender receives a notification indicating that the e-mail was not delivered to the recipient.

These two examples may answer some of our questions and assure you that the process you follow will be correct. Later in this guidebook, we will cover notices and correspondence in greater detail. Before we move on, I want to emphasize that you should give the other party a call before you send official notice letters. Naturally, some people will get more upset about being blindsided by the letter than its content. Take the time to call them.

# Order of Precedence

We briefly mentioned this clause in our earlier discussion about flowdowns and incorporated it by reference contract clauses. The order of precedence clause is usually found among the boilerplate terms and conditions of the contract, but you may find that some standard-form contracts do not include it.

What is an order of precedence? Great question. It ranks the specific contract document's importance in the chain of documents when resolving a conflict or ambiguity. How does this affect me and my project? I am so happy you asked this question! Let's examine this question further.

A contract may contain (or reference) other documents that are part of your project. For instance, you may have a construction agreement, but multiple exhibits are attached to the end of the contract. The exhibits may include the project's specifications, schedules, safety requirements, and code of conduct, and this list of potential documents goes on.

Let's take a look at an example order of precedence clause:

> **Order of Precedence**. Any ambiguity, conflict or inconsistency between the documents comprising this Contract shall be resolved according to the following order of precedence:
>
> i. The Contract
> ii. Attachment D
> iii. Attachment A
> iv. Attachment C
> v. Attachment B

When you have a large amount of attached or referenced documents, there are almost always ambiguous or conflicting terms, instructions, guidelines, roles, and obligations. Once all the contract documents are attached to the contract, they typically run into hundreds of pages. It's challenging to spot every inconsistency.

Now that we have a picture of how the order of precedence clause works, let's talk briefly about your proposal and revisit our earlier discussion on the entire agreement clause. It's common for companies to spend considerable time and resources preparing their proposals. Much time is often spent understanding the customer's requirements and developing the proposal's deliverables, schedule, and pricing (to mention a few) to meet those requirements.

If there are many unknowns, it's common for companies to address these unknowns by including a list of excluded deliverables (or work), along with their assumptions, and their pricing is directly tied to those exclusions and assumptions. You must review your subcontractor's proposals in detail or be prepared for change orders!

What if your proposal isn't referenced or included in your contract? Will the crucial aspects of your proposal (e.g., assumptions and exclusions) apply? If your proposal is not referenced or physically included as an exhibit, you may be unable to successfully argue that it is part of your agreement. As I mentioned, if you can't negotiate with your customer to include it (without your terms and conditions), then push to have the essential portions included as exhibits.

The last point I want to make is this: If your proposal is not referenced, attached, or included, it is *not* part of your contract. You should consider not taking any verbal assurances from your customer that it is or that you'll work through any discrepancies.

## BEST PRACTICES

Check each of the contract documents included in the contract's order of precedence for order of precedence language. For instance, it's typical for special or supplemental terms and conditions to contain a separate order of precedence clause that can conflict with the contract's order of precedence.

This might seem counterintuitive, but this is exactly the issue that the order of precedence clause is designed to address. If you find an inconsistent order of precedence clause in other contract documents, consider deleting it or revising it to reference the contract's order of precedence clause. This will ensure clarity and consistency in the interpretation of the contract documents.

## Pay–If–Paid and Pay–When–Paid (Contingent Payment Clauses)

If there is a list of risky terms you must pay attention to, these two are at the top. Let's start with a short scenario to set the scene. Let's pretend you are negotiating a subcontract for a large project. The owner is a large investment firm, and the contractor is well-established on the Outer Banks. You have worked with this contractor on similar projects over the years, and you are often invited to their annual Christmas parties.

While reviewing the subcontract, you notice it differs from the subcontracts you have signed previously. Furthermore, you see the following clauses:

> **Paid if Paid**. The Contractor's obligation to make payment to the Subcontractor is dependent on the Contractor receiving payment from the Owner first; the Subcontractor fully understands and accepts the risk of nonpayment from the Owner.

And

> **Payment Bond.** Subcontractor shall not seek payment from the payment bond provided by Contractor for any amounts due if the Owner has not paid Contractor for such amounts.

And

> **Payment**. As compensation for fulfilling its responsibilities under this Agreement, the Subcontractor shall receive the amount specified in the Purchase Order. Subcontractor will be paid within 30 days of the Contractor receiving payment from the Owner for the Work.

While reviewing the contract, you notice your customer's obligation to pay you is directly tied to their receipt of payment from the owner. Okay, let's take a moment to explain what these terms mean, although the language in the example clauses defines them. A pay-when-paid clause only controls the timing of when your customer will pay you and typically provides a fixed period. This clause is not as scary, but it may affect your cash flow. If the owner fails to pay your customer, your customer still must pay you within a reasonable period.

The paid-if-paid clause shifts the risk of the owner's nonpayment from your customer to you. If your subcontract contains a paid-if-paid clause, your customer has no duty to pay you unless and until the owner pays him. Does this seem like an acceptable amount of risk?

Let's jump back into our scenario. You have accepted the paid-if-paid and paid-when-paid clauses without modification and signed the subcontract. You made this decision based on your previous relationship with your customer, and you are confident that you and your customer can work together and resolve any issues that may arise. Halfway through the project, you discover problems with the owner's site survey. As a result, you build the foundations in the wrong place. Does this sound like a claim situation?

While preparing your change order requests, your customer provides you with a written directive to take the necessary corrective actions. Your customer also asks you to mobilize additional crews to keep the project on schedule. You comply and finish the project in record time! While working on the project, you provide proposals to your customer for the rework, and your customer issues you signed change orders. Do you have any worries yet?

You're now at the end of your project, and you've got a list of change orders in your change order log that your customer still needs to pay. You submitted all the documentation (i.e., payment applications, lien waivers, and project documents) over 90 days ago. When you ask your customer, he advises that they submitted the payment requests (that included your payment requests) but have yet to receive approval or payment from the owner. Okay, now it's time to start getting concerned!

After a few weeks, you receive a call from your customer. He tells you the owner denied your portion of their payment application and they will not be paying you. Wow, now it's time to get very worried!

What recourse do you have in this scenario? Maybe lien rights? Maybe make claims against a payment bond? Can you issue a stop-work notice if you are still performing? Although a few states have invalidated the paid-if-paid clauses, they are largely enforceable by court decisions or statutes. It would be best if you did not rely on your customer's verbal good-faith assertions that you will be paid and should consider consulting an attorney who practices claims litigation. This scenario is scary, and if you are a small business, it may result in you losing everything. You should consider not accepting paid-if-paid clauses and walk away from a potentially bad deal.

## BEST PRACTICES

"Paid-if-paid" clauses should be scrutinized thoroughly as they pose a significant risk of non-payment. These clauses, which are often hidden under unrelated headings or worded differently, essentially state that your payment is contingent upon the owner paying the contractor.

> Redlining any reference to "paid-if-paid" is a good practice. Vigilantly monitor your change order log and avoid accumulating a large number of unpaid change orders, as this could exacerbate the impact of a paid-if-paid clause. Remember, protecting your financial interests is paramount.

## Price and Payment

This clause is crucial, as it dictates when, how, and under what conditions you'll be paid. It also outlines how payment disputes will be handled. Let's consider this example:

> **Payment Terms**. As full consideration for the satisfactory completion of the work outlined in the Purchase Order, Subcontractor shall be paid in USD, in accordance with the payment terms outlined in this Agreement. Subcontractor shall be paid within thirty (30) calendar days of Contractor receiving payment from Owner for the Work. Any disputes regarding payment shall be resolved through the Dispute Resolution process outlined in Article 19. As a condition for the first payment, Subcontractor shall provide Contractor with the following: a fully executed original of this Agreement, including all exhibits; a completed preliminary schedule of values (if applicable); a completed Federal Taxpayer Identification Number Form and W-9; any performance or payment bonds outlined in the Purchase Order; certificates of insurance; and an executed lien waiver (Exhibit C).

But what if you're not paid as agreed? This is where things get tricky. If your contract contains "paid-if-paid" or "pay-when-paid" language, your payment is tied to the owner paying the contractor. Non-payment or withholding payment for valid reasons, such as defective work, are other possibilities.

If you face non-payment, review your contract carefully. If the contractor lacks a legitimate reason for withholding payment, they may be in breach of contract. You might have the right to stop work or even terminate the contract, but only after issuing a written notice and allowing an opportunity to cure the default.

Consider the following termination clause:

> **Termination for Default**. If one party materially does not fulfill their responsibilities outlined in the agreement and does not correct the issue within sixty (60) days of receiving written notice, the other party has the right to terminate the agreement immediately with written notice. If the breach in question involves nonpayment, the party in breach will only have one chance to correct the issue before the agreement can be terminated without a 60-day cure period.

Remember, termination should be a last resort. Consult an attorney before taking such drastic action. During contract discussions, negotiate to include clauses allowing you to suspend work due to non-payment.

If facing non-payment, explore options like mechanic's liens (for private property), claims against payment bonds, or initiating dispute resolution. Always communicate with your customer and document all interactions before taking any action.

## BEST PRACTICES

During contract negotiations, establish a solid foundation by including clauses that allow you to suspend or stop work if you aren't paid, and to terminate the contract if non-payment persists for a specified period. This proactive approach safeguards your interests and provides leverage in case of payment disputes.

## Records Retention

Most contracts include a record retention clause. It should go hand-in-hand with your organization's record retention policies and auditing procedures. Let's explore the following example clause:

> **Record Retention**. Contractor must maintain accurate and comprehensive financial records that comply with generally accepted accounting principles and practices, and that support all invoices related to the Contract. Owner or their representative has the right to review, inspect, and copy these records, vouchers, and their source documents, upon giving five (5) days' written notice ("<u>Audit</u>"). This applies to all compensation, except for compensation that is specified in the Contract as firm-fixed-pricing. These documents must be available for review, inspection, and copying for three (3) years after the completion or termination of the contract.

This clause, along with your company's record retention policies and auditing procedures, is vital for project management. It mandates proper record-keeping and allows for audits by the owner. Consider how you'll store these documents, whether physically (requiring space and vulnerable to damage) or electronically (more secure but with potential security concerns).

As a contractor, ensure your internal policies align with contract requirements and the owner's security needs. Develop a plan to guarantee compliance and readability of records, even decades later. Regardless of the storage method, ensure these documents remain accessible and usable over time.

## BEST PRACTICES

It is common for companies to retain signature pages separate from the contract. Consider this point. If you send a 50-MB file to your customer, it will probably be rejected or overload their e-mail server. In this sense, only sending the signed signature page is understandable, but this is a bad practice. Signature pages often get filed on someone's hard drive, e-mail files, or misfiled and never get attached to the contract.

## Scope of Work

The Scope of Work clause is your contract's roadmap. It outlines your duties, the work to be performed, and how it will be completed. Often, it also addresses unforeseen events, work quality, and how contract documents will be interpreted.

Let's look at a typical example:

> **Scope of the Work**. Subcontractor shall perform the work ("the Work") described in Schedule A to this Subcontract, as well as any additional work that is necessary or reasonable to complete the project. This includes providing all necessary labor, project management, supervision, quality control, materials, tools, equipment, supplies, services, and other items to construct the work safely and properly, in compliance with all applicable laws and the requirements outlined in the Contract Documents. Subcontractor must perform this Work in accordance with the terms of this Subcontract, and to the satisfaction of Contractor and Owner. This summary is not intended to limit the scope of the Subcontractor's Work, which is fully defined in the Contract Documents.

While this clause defines your responsibilities, it's crucial to remember that it's just a summary. In this example, the full scope of your work is detailed in the contract documents.

A comprehensive scope of work is crucial to avoid disputes and ensure project success. It's worth dedicating time and resources to develop a clear and thorough scope during contract negotiations. Remember, a well-defined scope sets the stage for smooth project execution and minimizes the risk of misunderstandings or disagreements down the line.

## Set-off

The "set-off" clause can be a significant risk for contractors. It grants your customer the right to unilaterally withhold payments or offset any liability they owe you, even across different contracts, in case of default.

Let's look at a typical example:

> **Set-off**. If Contractor fails to fulfill any of their obligations outlined in this Contract, Owner has the right to reduce, subtract, or make other adjustments to any payments made under this Contract or any related contracts with Contractor or any of its affiliates, without any prior notice or request. This action does not constitute a breach or excuse for non-performance on Contractor's part.

This broad language can be problematic. The phrase "any obligation" is vague and could be interpreted to include even minor issues. It's also concerning that the clause bypasses notice requirements and allows the customer to reach across multiple contracts and projects.

To mitigate this risk, consider modifying the clause during negotiations. Replace "any obligation" with a list of specific, material breaches that warrant a set-off. Limit the customer's right to set-off to the specific contract and project in question. Additionally, define a clear timeframe for the set-off period.

While having a strong set-off clause may be advantageous for a contractor, keep in mind that it can strain subcontractor relationships. It's sometimes reasonable to limit the events triggering a set-off to maintain healthy working relationships.

## Severability

This clause belongs to the same boilerplate bucket category as the previous ones covered in this guidebook. I need to emphasize that just because something is in that category doesn't mean it's something you can gloss over quickly. The term severability isn't frequently used in everyday conversations and can be confusing without opening a legal dictionary. I'll try to define it and demonstrate how it relates to your contracts. Before I tell you what it is, let's start with a short scenario to add context to this clause.

Imagine you are a hardworking executive tasked with negotiating a voluminous contract with a new customer and you are under pressure to turn it around quickly. To make your boss happy, you have been up every night this week researching, redlining, and commenting on terms in the contract. You also spent considerable time during the day trying to wrap it up so you could move on to other things on your plate.

You are frustrated because negotiating the terms has taken much longer than you anticipated, and you are now receiving calls from your boss. However, you finally reach the finish line, and the contract is signed. While you are reviewing the finalized contract, you discover a problem with one clause. Specifically, you find a grammatical mistake that changes the meaning of the clause. After giving this problem some thought, you remember inserting the following severability clause into the contract:

> **Severability**. The parties agree that, to the extent allowed by law, any clause or part of this agreement that makes it invalid or unenforceable will be separated and modified or cut off as needed to prevent it from being invalid or unenforceable. This will be done in a way that most closely maintains the intended benefits for both parties under this Agreement.

You confirm that it is included in the contract and feel relief. However, this is short-lived. You realize that the court may find the clause invalid, rendering the entire agreement null and void, resulting in losing money, time, and resources, among other dire consequences. But you start to think about the severability clause. It ensures the remaining terms and conditions in the agreement will be preserved if the court rules that a particular clause is invalid or otherwise unenforceable.

Theoretically, this sounds like a lifesaving clause you want to consider adding to your contracts. However, I want to caution you about assuming that one size fits all when considering a severability clause. Just because you insert a severability clause into your contract doesn't mean it will salvage and sustain its overall objective and purpose.

### BEST PRACTICES

Upon discovering any ambiguities, conflicting terms, or errors and omissions in the contract, promptly document your findings through a formal notice letter or a request for information, seeking clarification from the other party. Begin by thoroughly reviewing the relevant terms to understand your obligations and identify any inconsistencies that need to be addressed.

## Survival

The "survival" clause in a contract means certain obligations continue even after the contract ends. This means that even after finishing the work, some of your responsibilities may extend far beyond project completion. For instance, indemnification, warranties, and confidentiality obligations could remain in effect.

Let's take a look at an example clause:

> **Survival.** The parties acknowledge that certain provisions of this Agreement, which are meant to remain in effect even after the Agreement ends, will survive regardless of the reason for the Agreement's termination.

This clause can have far-reaching implications, so it's important to understand the potential risks. Always carefully review the contract to identify which provisions survive termination.

## Special Terms and Conditions

Special terms and conditions, also known as supplemental or additional terms, are often referenced in contracts. They can significantly impact your obligations and should never be overlooked.

Consider this common clause:

> **Incorporated by Reference.** The terms and conditions outlined in the Supplemental Terms and Conditions are now included in this Agreement and will be binding for both parties. These Supplemental Terms and Conditions can be found on the company's website.

As someone responsible for the project's execution, review the supplemental terms and conditions alongside the contract to understand your obligations.

You may find that the supplemental terms and conditions contain contractual language or obligations that should be in the scope of work. You may find additional requirements or that it incorporates other documents by reference (e.g., code of conduct, safety, and quality).

> **BEST PRACTICES**
>
> If your contract includes any reference document, such as the prime contract, you have the right to review it thoroughly. Some clients may omit these documents due to their size or other reasons, but this shouldn't deter you from requesting them. It's essential to fully understand the terms and conditions that apply to your work, regardless of whether the referenced documents are readily available.

## Suspension

Due to disruptions like COVID-19 impacting the global supply chain, suspension clauses in contracts have become increasingly important. These clauses typically allow either party to temporarily halt work without breaching the contract, outlining conditions for recovery of costs and potential termination.

Some clauses, on the other hand, may allow the owner to suspend work without incurring any costs. Let's look at two examples:

> **Suspension of Work**. In addition to any other rights Owner may have under the Contract or by law, Owner can, at any time, by sending a written notice to Contractor with the suspension's effective date, ask Contractor to stop the work temporarily, or any part of it, without incurring any costs for Owner.

And

> **Suspension**. Owner has the right to temporarily halt the work under this Agreement for a period of thirty (30) days after providing written notice to Contractor. If the suspension lasts for more than 90 consecutive days or 120 days in total, and it is not caused by a Force Majeure event or Contractor's or its subcontractors' fault or negligence, Contractor has the option to terminate the Agreement by providing 14 days' notice. In this case, Contractor would be entitled to the compensation outlined for termination for convenience. If Owner suspends the work, Contractor can request a change order to recover costs related to the suspension, including demobilization and remobilization costs, and an additional 25% for overhead and profit. Contractor would also be able to claim any retention withheld from previous payments.

Notice the stark difference. The second clause offers greater protection for the contractor, requiring written notice and allowing termination under certain conditions. It also allows for cost recovery through change orders.

Remember, written documentation is crucial whenever your customer directs actions that may affect the project cost or timeline. Upon receiving a suspension notice, promptly notify your subcontractors and suppliers to avoid complications and ensure everyone is on the same page.

## *Insight Story: Unanticipated Suspension*

A suspension shouldn't turn adversarial, but it's common for the suspended party to feel uneasy. Consider this scenario: You're subcontracted to fabricate and install custom stairways in a hotel. You mobilize after your supplier delivers most materials. You complete one stairwell. You receive the following notice from your customer:

> Sent Via Electronic Mail and Courier Service
>
> Dear John,
>
> We just received notice from our local county inspector, who noted some significant defects in the work that another subcontractor is performing. We have suspended most of the work on the site until these defects can be remedied. Please demobilize your crew and equipment and take any necessary action to protect the in-progress work. I anticipate this suspension will last five weeks. I will let you know once I have a clearer picture of the schedule.
>
> Jake

You acknowledge the notice, which includes a reservation of rights. You instruct your workers to protect the materials before demobilizing. You remember the implied obligation to mitigate delays and damages during suspension, so you return rented equipment early and reassign your crew.

Weeks pass without updates. Around week seventeen, your customer asks you to remobilize. You can't reassign your workers, and your customer threatens delay damages. This scenario, while unfortunate, is not uncommon.

You consult the contract's suspension clause, realizing you could have terminated the contract. However, you'll find replacement workers. They face delays and increased costs, doubling your initial estimate. You start preparing a claim for damages.

In a similar situation, review the contract's suspension clause. Conduct a schedule delay analysis, assess demobilization/remobilization costs, idle crew costs, and other damages.

## Term of Contract

The "term of contract" clause defines the lifespan of your agreement—its start and end dates. It's essential to pay close attention to this clause, especially its duration and any renewal provisions.

Consider this example:

> **Term of Contract**. The duration of this Agreement shall be for a period of one (1) year, with the possibility of renewing it for up to four (4) additional years on the same terms and conditions as the original contract, unless either party sends written notice to the other party sixty (60) days prior to the end of the current term indicating their desire not to renew.

For contractors and suppliers, long-term contracts or those with automatic renewal clauses (evergreen clauses) can pose risks. If the contract lacks provisions for cost escalation, you might be locked into pricing that becomes unprofitable over time.

Therefore, before signing, carefully assess the contract duration and any renewal terms. If necessary, negotiate for the inclusion of clauses that allow for price adjustments to protect your profit margins over the contract's lifespan.

## Termination for Convenience

Most contracts include a termination for convenience clause, which allows ending the contract without a breach. This can be advantageous as it simplifies the termination process and reduces potential disputes. However, it also comes with disadvantages. The clause typically limits compensation for the terminated party, potentially leaving them with less than they anticipated.

Let's consider a scenario: You're a contractor building a convenience store and hire a local subcontractor for tiling. Despite several discussions, their work quality remains substandard. During the project, you meet another subcontractor with impressive references and experience. You decide to hire them, but how do you handle the existing subcontractor?

Given the situation, terminating the current subcontractor for convenience might be the best option. This eliminates the potential complexities and costs of a default termination, which could lead to disputes and even court battles.

Here's an example of a termination for convenience clause:

> **Termination for Convenience**. Contractor has the right to terminate the services and work of Subcontractor at any time and for any reason, by providing written notice to Subcontractor. Upon receiving the notice, Subcontractor must immediately discontinue the work and stop placing orders for materials and supplies, unless the notice specifies otherwise. Subcontractor must also make an effort to cancel any existing orders or contracts in a way that is satisfactory to Contractor or, if Contractor chooses, give Contractor the right to assume those obligations directly, including all benefits. Subcontractor will only be entitled to payment for the work that has been completed and an additional 10% for overhead and profit. Any payments that Subcontractor has already received will be deducted from this amount. Subcontractor will not be able to claim any additional compensation or damages in the event of termination for convenience and payment. However, Subcontractor will still be responsible for any obligations and duties that would usually survive completion, including warranty obligations and duties to indemnify and insure risks.

This clause outlines the terms of termination, including compensation for completed work and the subcontractor's continuing obligations. While terminating for default might seem like a better option, it could lead to higher costs and potential liabilities. As a result, despite its limitations, choosing a termination for convenience can often be a more predictable and less risky path.

Remember: When facing situations like this, carefully review your contract, assess the risks, and consult with legal counsel if needed to make an informed decision.

## *Insight Story: New Flooring*

You are a project manager building a new convenience store. To install floor and wall tiles throughout the store and in the bathrooms, you need a subcontractor. Local businesses are busy, and their proposals lack the experience and quality you need. You were desperate to start the project, so you awarded the subcontract to My Best Friend Subcontracting. However, their work quality is subpar, despite repeated discussions with their project manager, Pete.

Meanwhile, another subcontractor approaches you, apologizing for not submitting a proposal earlier. Impressed by their references and past work, you decide to hire them under a time and materials contract if they agree to your budget.

Now, you have a problem: How to handle the existing contract with My Best Friend Subcontracting. Terminating for default is an option, but the evidence might be insufficient. Instead, it could be easier to terminate for convenience.

You meet with Pete to discuss the situation.

"Pete, I appreciate you coming out to discuss this," you begin. "Unfortunately, we've decided to go in a different direction with the tiling work."

Pete looks surprised. "What do you mean, John? We have a contract!"

"I understand," you reply, "and I'm prepared to compensate you for the completed work, plus 10% for overhead and profit. This aligns with the termination for convenience clause in our agreement."

Pete frowns. "But this isn't fair! We were doing the work as agreed."

"I disagree," you say, "but this is the most efficient solution. It's better than a legal battle over termination for default. Let's part ways amicably."

Pete sighs, but ultimately agrees. Terminating for convenience might incur some costs, but it's often more predictable and less risky than termination for default, which could lead to costly disputes.

The termination for convenience clause in your contract with My Best Friend Subcontracting reads:

> **Termination for Convenience**. Contractor has the right to terminate the services and work of Subcontractor at any time and for any reason, by providing written notice to Subcontractor. Upon receiving the notice, Subcontractor must immediately discontinue the work and stop placing orders for materials and supplies, unless the notice specifies otherwise. Subcontractor must also make an effort to cancel any existing orders or contracts in a way that is satisfactory to Contractor or, if Contractor chooses, give Contractor the right to assume those obligations directly, including all benefits. Subcontractor will only be entitled to payment for the work that has been completed and an additional 10% for overhead and profit. Any payments that Subcontractor has already received will be deducted from this amount. Subcontractor will not be able to claim any additional compensation or damages in the event of termination for convenience and payment. However, Subcontractor will still be responsible for any obligations and duties that would usually survive completion, including warranty obligations and duties to indemnify and insure risks.

This clause outlines the terms, making it a known risk you can negotiate beforehand. In contrast, a default termination could result in unknown liabilities and be overturned in court. Carefully considering the specific contract terms and risks of each option is crucial before making a decision.

## BEST PRACTICES

Terminating a subcontractor or supplier for convenience requires following specific steps. First, adhere strictly to the notice requirements outlined in your contract. Second, ensure both parties conduct a thorough inventory and inspection of any partially or fully completed work, documenting acceptance of the work.

To finalize the termination, consider having an attorney draft a settlement agreement that clearly outlines the terms agreed upon by both parties. This helps prevent future misunderstandings or disputes and provides a clear closure to the subcontract. While it might seem like an additional expense, the investment in a settlement agreement can save you from costly legal battles down the line.

Finally, remember the golden rule: document everything. Keep detailed records of all communications, agreements, inspections, and payments. This documentation will be invaluable in the event of any future disagreements or claims.

## Time is of the Essence

The "time is of the essence" clause, often found early in a contract, carries significant implications for both parties. It means that meeting deadlines is a crucial contract obligation, and any unexcused delays could be considered a material breach. This could lead to termination of the contract and potential damages.

Here's a typical example:

> **Time is of the Essence**. Supplier must adhere to the quantities and delivery schedule ("Delivery Schedule") specified in the Purchase Order and make Deliveries to the designated location. If Supplier anticipates any deviation from the Delivery Schedule, they must promptly notify the Contractor in writing, providing reasons for the delay and proposed solutions. If the delay is caused by Supplier, they are required to take all necessary steps to expedite delivery without seeking additional compensation from Contractor.

While this clause seems straightforward, the legal interpretation of "time is of the essence" can vary. Some courts may view project schedules as guidelines, while others may consider significant delays as a breach even without this clause.

As a subcontractor, it's wise to mitigate this risk during negotiations. Changing the language to "time is important" or "time is critical" can soften the legal implications and reduce potential liability.

If the clause is non-negotiable, remember that most courts allow for a "cure period" where delays can be rectified before a contract is voided or damages are awarded.

For contractors, including this clause in subcontracts and supplier agreements is a good practice. It reinforces the importance of timely performance and provides a clear basis for recourse in case of delays. However, remember that its interpretation can vary, so it's crucial to understand the specific legal context of your contract and seek legal advice if needed.

## BEST PRACTICES

Even without explicit wording, time can be considered "of the essence" depending on the nature of your contract. To ensure you have the right to exercise all contractual remedies in case of delays, explicitly include the "time is of the essence" clause in your subcontracts. This provides clarity and strengthens your position in enforcing deadlines.

## Title and Risk of Loss

The "title and risk of loss" clause is a crucial aspect of contracts involving the sale of goods or equipment, especially in international transactions. It outlines when legal ownership (title) and responsibility for potential loss or damage transfer from the seller to the buyer.

Here's a typical example:

> **Title and Risk of Loss**. Upon delivery of the goods by Supplier to the carrier, ownership of the goods and any risk of loss will be transferred to Contractor. Contractor will be responsible for making any claims for losses or damages directly to the carrier.

In simpler terms, this means the buyer takes ownership and responsibility for the goods once the seller delivers them to the specified location or carrier. However, there are exceptions, such as when the seller retains a security interest:

> **Reservation of Security Interest**. The Equipment and any proceeds from it shall remain the property of the Supplier until Contractor has made full payment. Supplier retains a security interest in the Equipment and proceeds as collateral until the payment is complete.

This clause allows the seller to retain ownership until full payment is received, even after delivery.

The risk of loss typically transfers upon delivery, but if the seller breaches the contract, the buyer can reject the goods, and the risk remains with the seller. This rejection should be communicated through a phone call and a written notice detailing the reasons for rejection.

Remember, the transfer of title and risk of loss can have significant consequences. It's essential to understand the specific terms of your contract, especially if it involves international trade and utilizes Incoterms©, which define the precise point of transfer.

## BEST PRACTICES

The transfer of title and risk of loss can happen simultaneously, but you can specify different times and places in the contract. You can address the risk of loss either explicitly in the contract or by using an Incoterm. If you choose the latter, avoid using additional terms or similar language in the contract to prevent any confusion or conflicts regarding ownership and risk of loss. This clarity ensures a smooth and transparent transaction.

If you opt to explicitly address the risk of loss, clearly state in the contract the exact moment the title to the equipment transfers from you to your customer. This leaves no room for ambiguity and helps both parties understand their responsibilities regarding ownership and potential risks. Remember, a well-defined clause regarding title and risk of loss protects both parties and minimizes the risk of disputes arising from misunderstandings.

# Warranty

A warranty clause should be simple and easy to understand. It should clearly state the remedy (repair, replacement, or refund) if the product or service doesn't meet the promised standards.

Let's examine this example:

> **Warranty**. Supplier warrants to Contractor that the Products will be free from material and workmanship defects ("Warranties") for a period of twelve (12) months from the date of delivery to the location specified in the purchase order (the "Warranty Period"). During this time, Supplier also warrants that any services performed will be done in a good and workmanlike manner and will comply with the purchase order. If Contractor informs the Supplier in writing of any breach of the Warranties before the end of the 12-month period, Supplier may choose to repair or replace the Products, reperform the services, or refund the purchase price. Supplier also warrants that any repaired components or units of the Products will be free from defects for the remaining portion of the original Product's warranty or 90 days, whichever is longer. These warranties do not apply to Products not manufactured by the Seller or Products made to the Contractor's specifications. Contractor's remedies are limited to those offered by Supplier and the warranty is subject to Contractor making full payment, providing written notice of the defect within 10 days of discovery, following storage, installation, operation, and maintenance instructions, maintaining proper records, and not making unauthorized modifications or repairs.
>
> THE ONLY WARRANTY PROVIDED BY SUPPLIER IS THE ONE EXPLICITLY STATED IN THIS AGREE-

MENT, AND ANY OTHER IMPLIED WARRANTIES SUCH AS MERCHANTABILITY AND FITNESS FOR A PARTICULAR PURPOSE ARE NOT INCLUDED. SUPPLIER'S LIABILITY IN THE EVENT OF A CLAIM IS LIMITED TO THE ACTUAL AMOUNT PAID BY CONTRACTOR FOR THE PRODUCT OR SERVICE IN QUESTION.

While this clause outlines the warranty terms, it's lengthy and complex. To improve it, consider using simpler language and breaking it down into smaller, more digestible sections. For instance:

- Warranty Period: The warranty covers defects in materials and workmanship for 12 months from the delivery date.
- Remedies: If a defect is found, the supplier will repair, replace, or refund the purchase price at their discretion.
- Limitations: The warranty doesn't cover products not manufactured by the supplier or made to the contractor's specifications.
- Conditions: The warranty is valid only if the contractor makes full payment, provides timely written notice of defects, follows instructions, maintains records, and doesn't modify or repair the products without authorization.
- Disclaimer: The warranty provided is the only one offered, and implied warranties like merchantability and fitness for a particular purpose are excluded. The supplier's liability is limited to the amount paid for the product or service.

Breaking down the warranty into these key points makes it easier for both parties to understand their rights and obligations. Remember, a clear and concise warranty clause fosters trust and minimizes the potential for disputes.

## BEST PRACTICES

A well-structured warranty clause is crucial for both protecting your business and fostering trust with your customers. Here's a breakdown of key considerations:

Scope and Timing:

- Clarity is Key: Clearly define what your warranty covers and, equally important, what it doesn't. Be specific about the products, services, or workmanship included.
- Start Date: Ensure your warranty period commences upon delivery, completion, or client approval of your work. This shields you from extended warranty periods caused by delays beyond your control.

Financial Considerations:

- Proposal Inclusion: If you offer an extended warranty, explicitly outline its associated costs in your initial proposal.
- Honor Your Promise: A warranty is a contractual obligation. Failure to uphold it could lead to a breach of contract.

Drafting Checklist:

1. What's Covered: Specify the exact products, services, or workmanship under warranty.
2. Warranty Period: Clearly state the duration for products, spare parts, and any extended warranty options.
3. Responsibilities: Define each party's obligations if a warranty claim arises (e.g., who covers repairs, shipping).
4. Exclusions: Explicitly list situations where the warranty is void (e.g., misuse, unauthorized modifications).
5. Logistics: Outline requirements for removal, repair, replacement, and who bears these costs.

6. Access: If repairs require site access, ensure that the client is obligated to grant it.

7. Ownership: Clarify who retains ownership of returned defective equipment.

8. Return Process: Detail the steps for returning faulty items.

9. Incoterms: If applicable, specify the Incoterms governing international transactions.

10. Shipping Costs: Indicate who is responsible for shipping and handling expenses.

11. Factory Assistance: If provided, describe the services offered and their availability.

12. Theft: State whether the warranty covers theft or loss.

13. Conditions: Disclose any conditions for warranty validity (e.g., original packaging, proof of purchase).

14. Clarity and Disclaimers: Make sure the clause is easy to understand, with disclaimers prominently displayed.

Express vs. Implied Warranties:

- Express: Clearly stated promises about product performance or quality.
- Implied: Laws automatically arise, such as the implied warranty of merchantability.

To prevent ambiguity, expressly waive implied warranties in your contract, as shown in the example clause.

***Key Takeaway:***

A well-crafted warranty clause not only safeguards your business but also demonstrates your commitment to customer satisfaction. Invest time in creating a comprehensive and transparent warranty to ensure a successful and mutually beneficial transaction.

## *Insight Story: Who is to Blame?*

Let's rejoin John as he embarks on a new chapter in his career, stepping into the world of manufacturing. As John navigates the challenges of his new role, we'll uncover valuable lessons about the intricacies of warranties and the importance of proactive communication in customer relationships.

John's first day on the job began with a mix of anticipation and nerves. The night before had been restless, his mind buzzing with thoughts of the company's investment in him and the unfamiliar territory of manufacturing. Eager to make a good impression, he arrived early at his new office. Before he could even settle in, the phone rang—a customer requesting a copy of the company's standard warranty. John jotted down the details, promising to follow up promptly.

With the customer's inquiry fresh in his mind, John headed down the hall to seek guidance from Karen, a familiar face from his introductory tour of the manufacturing floor. As he knocked on her door, Karen rose to greet him with a warm smile and an outstretched hand.

"Karen is certainly proactive," John thought to himself. "Is this a good time to chat?" he asked aloud.

"Absolutely," Karen replied, gesturing towards a chair across from her desk. "I was hoping to catch up over coffee at the local shop and discuss how we can best support each other's work."

"That sounds great," John responded, taking a seat. "Just let me know when you're free."

"How can I help you today?" Karen inquired, her smile inviting and genuine.

"I just received a call from a customer inquiring about our warranty terms, and I'm not sure where to start," John admitted.

Karen turned to her computer and quickly pulled up the relevant file, sharing her screen with John. As she searched, she provided a brief overview of the customer and their intended use for the gearbox—a critical component of an industrial mine's conveyor belt system.

"Here it is," she exclaimed, locating the document. "I'll email it to your company address."

"Thank you so much," John said, relieved.

"If they're asking for the warranty, they're likely serious about placing an order," Karen observed. "Would you like me to reach out and answer any questions they might have?"

"I appreciate the offer," John replied, "but I'm eager to learn, and there's no better way than diving right in." He flashed a confident smile.

John, back in his office, quickly located the file Karen had sent and promptly called the customer to discuss the warranty terms and gearbox specifications. Confident that the chosen model was well-suited for the customer's operating conditions, he ended the call feeling reassured.

After reviewing the warranty language and checklist, John meticulously noted any potential concerns in his journal. A few days later, the customer responded, agreeing to most of the warranty terms but proposing a change to the start date. They requested the warranty period begin after commissioning rather than upon delivery to the site. Recognizing that his company didn't control the installation timeline, John consulted with the executive leadership team. Despite the inherent risks involved, they agreed to accommodate the customer's request.

Fast forward 24 months, and John received a warranty claim letter from the customer. The gearbox, installed by a third party eight weeks earlier and seemingly operational during substantial and final completion, suddenly malfunctioned, causing a costly plant shutdown. The installation crew discovered failed bearings, necessitating the gearbox's removal and return for repairs. The customer asserted that John's company was liable for all damages incurred due to the shutdown.

John carefully reviewed the contract, confirming that the warranty period had indeed commenced at commissioning, meaning they were now two months into the warranty. As he sifted through his notes and e-mails, a series of troubling questions began to gnaw at him.

"Why did the bearings fail?" John pondered. "And why didn't the customer contact us sooner when they first noticed an issue?"

Determined to address the situation promptly, John scheduled a meeting with the executive team to inform them of the claim and formulate a plan.

Later that afternoon, John appeared at my office door. "Got a few minutes?" he asked, a hint of concern in his voice.

"Absolutely," I replied, motioning him in. "What's going on?"

"I just received a warranty claim, and I could really use your help," John explained. "I've scheduled a meeting with the team and would appreciate your input. Are you free to join us today?"

"I'll be there," I assured him.

In the meeting, John provided the executive team with a comprehensive overview of the project, the gearbox itself, and the customer's background. He distributed copies of the warranty claim letter and the relevant contract for everyone to review.

After quickly scanning the letter, I raised a crucial question: "John, before we dive deeper, has an engineer been dispatched to the site for a visual inspection and documentation of the gearbox's condition? We need to get someone out there before the customer alters or attempts to remove it."

The room fell silent momentarily. However, the lack of tension reassured John.

"No," he admitted, "I just received the notice and wanted to gather the team's input before taking any action."

I turned to Pete, the CEO, and voiced my concerns: "Pete, we need to conduct a thorough root cause analysis of this failure. As it stands, we have no defense against this claim. The customer is asserting liability for consequential damages, but I believe we excluded those in our limitation of liability clause. I'll need to review the contract to confirm."

Pete turned to Bill, the VP of Operations. "Bill, get one of your engineers to the site as soon as possible. Ensure they take plenty of photos and videos."

"Jose will be there this week," Bill assured him.

Turning back to John, I asked, "Do you have a few minutes after the meeting? There are a few more things I'd like to discuss."

The meeting concluded swiftly, and John and I returned to my office to delve into the contract details.

As I flipped through the pages, thoughts and questions tumbled out: "Okay, we negotiated and signed this contract 24 months ago, and our standard warranty is 12 months." I looked up at John, puzzled. "Why are we dealing with this now? Shouldn't the warranty have expired?"

John reminded me of the earlier decision to align the warranty period with substantial completion, which had occurred just eight weeks prior.

"Ah, right," I acknowledged, my memory refreshed. "Let me review the contract. We need the results of the root cause analysis before we can assess our risk exposure and potential options. For now, I'll send the customer a letter acknowledging receipt of their claim."

"Shouldn't we deny any responsibility in the acknowledgment?" John questioned.

"Not at this stage," I explained. "The acknowledgment letter is simply to confirm that we've received their claim. We don't want to prematurely agree or disagree, make arguments, or accept responsibility. Let's gather all the facts before we make any assertions."

John nodded in understanding and headed for the door. Just then, his phone rang with an unfamiliar number. It was Jose calling to share his travel arrangements.

A few days later, a virtual meeting invite from Jose landed in everyone's inbox. As team members gathered in the conference room, Jose shared a series of images on the monitor, highlighting specific areas of concern in red.

A few days later, the team members received a virtual meeting invite from Jose. Most team members gathered in the conference room, and Jose displayed a handful of pictures on the monitor with specific areas highlighted in red.

Jose began the meeting. "Thanks for joining on such short notice. I wanted to share my observations with everyone as soon as possible."

He used a pointer to highlight a set of bearings within the gearbox displayed on the monitor. "Can you all see the shape of the bearings and the rust?" he asked. "They're not round; they're deformed. We usually don't see this kind of damage unless the customer has neglected the required maintenance."

As the group started asking questions, I turned to the warranty exclusions section of the contract. It stated, in pertinent part:

> This warranty and remedy are only valid if the Products are stored, installed, operated, used and maintained in accordance with the instructions provided by Seller in the operation and maintenance manuals, a copy of which the Buyer acknowledges receiving and to which Buyer agrees to be bound. If Buyer does not follow these instructions and as a result replacement parts are needed, Buyer will be responsible for paying the full cost of the replacement parts.

"Jose," I interjected, "do you have a copy of the customer's operation and maintenance manuals?"

"Yes, I do," he confirmed.

"Since the gearbox sat idle for almost two years," I continued, "were there any maintenance requirements during that period, and most importantly, can you determine if they were performed?"

"Can everyone see my screen?" Jose asked, sharing his computer display.

A chorus of "Yes" echoed through the room.

"The manual states that the customer must rotate the gearbox's bearings every six months and top off the oil while it's in storage or idle," Jose explained.

"Excellent. Can you confirm that the customer fulfilled these requirements?" I inquired.

"The documents they provided don't indicate any maintenance was performed on the gearbox," Jose replied.

"So, it's safe to assume that the lack of bearing rotation caused the deformation?" I pressed. "Why is that the case?"

"Several factors contribute," Jose clarified. "Essentially, the weight of the gears inside the gearbox constantly presses down on the bearings. Rotating them prevents this deformation."

"What about the rust?" I asked.

"The gearbox was low on oil when I opened it," Jose responded. "There's a gauge on the outside to check the oil level."

"And the purpose of the oil?" I probed.

"It coats and seals the bearings and the gearbox from moisture," Jose explained.

Jose then shared a relevant section of the operation and maintenance manual:

The equipment requires maintenance (to the shaft and bearings) to be performed bi-annually if the equipment is idle for more than six months. Maintenance is to be performed on an annual basis if the equipment is in continuous use.

"How can we be sure the equipment didn't arrive in this condition?" I asked.

"We have rigorous quality control measures in place," Bill interjected. "Each gearbox is thoroughly inspected, tested, and certified before it leaves our facility."

I thumbed through the contract, locating the section on inspections and acceptance:

> **Inspection**. Buyer is responsible for inspecting the Products within seven (7) days after receiving them (the "Inspection Period"). If no issues are reported during this time, the Products will be considered accepted by Buyer. However, if Buyer finds any issues with the Products, they must notify Seller in writing and provide any necessary documentation or evidence to support their claim.

I began to feel optimistic about resolving the claim swiftly. The customer's failure to perform the required maintenance seemed to offer a strong defense. However, I still wanted to understand the potential risks in case our argument proved unsuccessful. I turned to the limitation of liability clause, which excluded consequential damages and capped our liability at the purchase order price:

> **LIMITATION OF LIABILITY**. SUPPLIER SHALL NOT BE LIABLE FOR ANY INDIRECT, SPECIAL, CONSEQUENTIAL, MULTIPLE OR PUNITIVE DAMAGES, OR ANY DAMAGES DEEMED TO BE OF AN INDIRECT OR CONSEQUENTIAL NATURE, ARISING OUT OF

OR RELATED TO ITS PERFORMANCE UNDER THIS AGREEMENT, WHETHER BASED ON BREACH OF CONTRACT, WARRANTY, NEGLIGENCE, OR ANY OTHER THEORY OF LIABILITY, INCLUDING STRICT LIABILITY. THIS LIMITATION OF LIABILITY APPLIES EXCEPT IN CASES OF DEATH OR BODILY INJURY RESULTING FROM SUPPLIER'S NEGLIGENCE OR WILLFUL MISCONDUCT. ADDITIONALLY, THE TOTAL CUMULATIVE LIABILITY OF SUPPLIER, ITS SUBCONTRACTORS, OR VENDORS OF ANY TIER, WHETHER IN CONTRACT, WARRANTY, TORT, OR OTHERWISE, FOR THE PERFORMANCE OR BREACH OF THIS AGREEMENT SHALL NOT EXCEED THE PURCHASE ORDER PRICE.

"Jose," I requested, "please send me copies of all the photos and videos you've taken. A detailed description of your observations and findings would also be helpful."

Turning to Pete, I concluded, "I think we're all in agreement about the cause of this issue. I'll draft a formal letter detailing our denial of the warranty claim and circulate it for everyone's feedback."

As the meeting dispersed, I returned to my office and began drafting the letter. Over the next few days, I shared the draft with sales, engineering, and the executive team, incorporating their feedback. Once the letter was finalized and ready to send, I called John to my office.

"John, the letter is complete," I explained, "and I've attached the photos and relevant sections of the contract and manual. However, I'd like you to call the customer before we send it. We don't want to blindside them or escalate the situation. Offer to meet with them after they've had time to review our findings."

"I agree," John replied. "I'll contact them today and give them a heads-up."

Later that day, John spoke with the customer, who ultimately conceded that they had neglected the required gearbox maintenance. The story had a surprisingly positive outcome: John was able to upsell the customer, securing a purchase order for a second gearbox as a spare. The original gearbox was repaired and returned, with the company covering the shipping cost as a goodwill gesture. This experience underscored the power of open communication and proactive problem-solving in maintaining positive customer relationships.

## Waiver and Release forms and Contract Language

To ensure you receive payment for your work, it's crucial to understand your two most powerful tools: mechanic's liens and payment bond claims. These are separate rights, each offering unique protections you should never unintentionally waive.

Think of it like this: a mechanic's lien is your safety net, securing your payment directly to the property you improved. It's a powerful way to incentivize the property owner to pay up.

A payment bond claim, on the other hand, is your insurance policy. It taps into a fund specifically set aside to guarantee payments for projects like yours. If the property owner doesn't pay, the bond issuer steps in to cover the cost.

Both tools are essential, and you should never give up these rights without fully understanding the consequences. To illustrate the importance of this, let me share a brief story.

## *Insight Story: Getting Paid!*

John, his brow furrowed as he juggled multiple screens, spoke into his headset to his subcontractor's owner, "James, we just wrapped Phase I—payment request is going out today. But listen, those punch list items need to be done by Friday, no exceptions."

James' voice crackled with urgency, "John, I can't stress this enough—if that check isn't in my hands by Friday close of business, I'll have to look at all my options, you understand?"

A bead of sweat formed on John's temple. "I hear you, James. Loud and clear. I'll push this through as fast as humanly possible."

As the call ended, John's eyes darted to an old email. "Construction Claims Management Workshop," he muttered, clicking it open. "Alright, let's see what we've got here."

The phone's shrill ring cut through the silence. It was Jason, the owner.

"John, payment's ready," Jason's voice boomed through the speaker, "but I need that lien waiver. Original, unmodified. Today."

John's stomach tightened. "Jason, submitting it like that leaves us exposed on unresolved claims."

"John," Jason interrupted, his tone unwavering, "we agreed on this during negotiations. The contract is clear. I need that waiver today to release the funds."

John hesitated, "I need to discuss this with my contracts manager. I'll get back to you by end of day."

John hung up, the contract's waiver clause burning into his mind. The weight of the decision—potentially forfeiting their $200,000 claim for the sake of this payment—made him physically ill. He found the following language in the contract:

> Contractor and all its subcontractors, Contractor Personnel, and other individuals providing labor and materials for the work covered by this Agreement, waive any right to file mechanics' liens or other liens for labor or materials furnished. They also agree that all labor and materials furnished, any improvements or structures they are incorporated into, and any

land they are ancillary to, will always be free and clear of any such liens.

John read the guidance on lien waivers and decided to modify the wording that excludes pending claims and change orders that have not been resolved [bolded here for emphasis]. He also excluded delay damages and retention and added language to protect his company if his customer's check bounces.

> **Lien Waiver Form**. Subcontractor certifies that they have been fully compensated in the amount of $_____ for all labor, services, equipment, and materials provided to \_\_\_\_, **except for those listed in Attachment A – Additional Work and Pending Claims**, up until the date of \_\_\_\_\_ for the project located at \_\_\_\_\_. By signing this document, Subcontractor releases any right to claim a mechanic's lien, stop notice, or any other claim against the project up to this date. **This waiver and release does not apply to any delay damages or retention, or any labor, services or materials provided after the date of the payment application/invoice for which this payment applies. The release is only valid upon receipt of the specified payment in the form of cleared funds, otherwise this release is null and void.**

John suddenly became more anxious and started thinking about a pending claim that hadn't been resolved. He walked down to my office. While knocking on my door, he stuck his head in and looked around.

"Do you have a minute?" he asked.

"Sure, I have a few minutes, but you must make it quick. I have another meeting down the hall." I started gathering the papers to take to the meeting. "So, what's up?"

John sat down on the seat where I gestured. I offered John a cup of coffee in a Styrofoam cup. I had a flashback to the mugs he kept in his office, which were permanently stained black from years of use. I could tell he was more anxious than the last time we discussed a problem. I knew when people come into my office, it's almost always to help them dress a wound that's bleeding profusely.

"I have a question, but I'm afraid I already know the answer. I want you to give me a sanity check and ensure I am on target," John said.

"Okay," I replied with a smile on my face.

He took a deep breath and continued, "We just completed phase I and are working through the final punch list. We may have one or two more weeks of remaining work, and we will immediately start phase II." He took a sip of coffee and continued, "I submitted my Payment Application and a modified Partial Lien Release form to the owner today. I modified the form to ensure I wasn't inadvertently waiving my rights to pursue any outstanding claims, delays, or retention. I got a call from the owner, and he's now holding the payment hostage unless we sign the Partial Lien Release form without any modifications." He shook his head, worry written on his face. "I'm afraid to sign it because we would be giving up our rights. I need your help resolving this."

John handed me the form and contract with the waiver clause circled. I examined the form and read the language.

"So, for curiosity's sake, what is the payment amount?" I asked.

"It's only 100K, but the claim will be upwards of 200K. I don't know the exact amount yet, and I am still getting invoices from our suppliers," John replied.

I nodded. "That's substantial, and I'm unsure if they are acting in good faith."

John looked puzzled and asked, "What is that? I've heard you use that term before, but I'm unsure how that applies here."

I leaned back in my chair and gave it some thought, not because of John's question but thinking about how to explain it clearly and concisely.

"Every contract has an implied promise of good faith and fair dealing. It means each party will not do anything to interfere unfairly with another party's right to receive the benefits of the contract. We completed the work required by the contract, but our customer is asking us to provide a blanket waiver of our rights to submit a claim for extra work we performed, among other things. I'm not convinced they are acting in good faith. You are doing the right thing by not signing that form and elevating this to me," I said.

The light dawned on John's face, and he felt a sense of relief, even if it was for a moment.

After suggesting drafting a formal letter and some suggestions for the content of the letter, I said, "John, if you decide on this option, float the letter by legal counsel and me before sending it out. She may want to review the local and state statutes, and I want to see if we can recover attorney fees and penalty interest. She may have some input and add some additional language to your letter," I said.

"Okay, what is option two?" John asked.

"John, any time you get into a legal letter-writing campaign, it usually doesn't end well. People get defensive and stubborn, and I have learned that calmer heads prevail," I said.

John nodded and smiled.

Seeing he understood, I continued, "I suggest you consider other approaches. Maybe draft an e-mail outlining why you can't agree to it. Blame it on me too. You can say your contracts manager won't allow you to send the form without it being modified." I shrugged, smiling.

"Another approach is to elevate it to the executive team. I've seen things like this resolved by a simple phone call to the customer's CEO," I said.

"But let me say you are doing the right thing. Don't sign that form unless you have your change orders and claims excluded from the waiver," I paused for a moment, considering how to reassure him.

"John, this problem is common in the construction industry, and most contracts will require you to execute a partial or final lien release form as a condition precedent to receiving payments," I said. "It's hard to tell the customer's intentions, but it's better to be defensive and not agree to things like that."

**Commentary**

Ideally, these forms should be reviewed and negotiated before signing a contract. However, we know this doesn't always happen. As in our example, the owner was technically correct: signing a contract often means agreeing to its terms, even if certain forms were overlooked or not provided during negotiations.

The takeaway? If you're asked to sign any form that waives your right to compensation, claims, or mechanic's liens, scrutinize it carefully. Understand exactly what rights you're relinquishing.

Let's revisit the language John found in the contract:

> Contractor, its subcontractors, Contractor Personnel, and all individuals . . . hereby waive any right to file mechanics' liens or other claims for payment. . . . They also agree that all labor and materials furnished . . . will always be free and clear of any such liens . . . . Contractor will take necessary steps . . . before performing any construction . . . that could result in the filing of a lien.

This language is problematic. Here's a modified version that's more favorable:

> Contractor, its subcontractors, Contractor Personnel, and all individuals... upon receipt of the check or funds (cleared funds) and excluding the items listed in the Request for Payment Application form, hereby waive any right to file mechanics' liens . . . .

With this change, payment becomes a prerequisite to waiving lien rights. We've also removed the requirement to execute a lien waiver before starting work.

## Lien Waivers and Claim Release Forms

These forms, often attached to contracts, warrant closer examination:

- Partial Lien Releases: Release the general contractor from liability for payments made up to a certain point.
- Full Lien Releases: Release the contractor or owner from all issues, including claims, change orders, and disputes, up to the date of the release.

Cautionary Tale:

Imagine you submit a $200,000 payment application, but $38,000 is in dispute. You receive $142,000 and are asked to sign a partial lien release. If you sign without noting the disputed amount, you could waive your right to it.

### BEST PRACTICES

- Insist on payment before signing any lien waiver.
- Make sure the waiver is conditional on the check clearing.
- If a dispute exists, add exclusion language to the release (e.g., "excluding items in Attachment A").

Remember: A release is broader than a lien waiver. Waiving lien rights doesn't necessarily forfeit your right to a breach-of-contract lawsuit.

Final Note:

Lien waiver laws vary by state. Always seek legal counsel to navigate the complexities and protect your rights.

## Conclusion

In this chapter, we've explored a wide array of contract terms and conditions, each with its own unique implications for risk management and project success. From payment terms and change orders to warranties and dispute resolution, we've delved into the nuances of these provisions, offering insights into their potential pitfalls and strategies for mitigating them. By understanding the interplay between different clauses and their impact on your rights and obligations, you're now equipped to navigate the complexities of contract negotiations and protect your interests.

In Chapter 6 we'll delve into the power of documentation in safeguarding your projects and minimizing potential disputes. We'll explore how meticulous record-keeping, clear communication, and proactive documentation practices can serve as your shield against misunderstandings, delays, and costly claims. From daily logs and meeting minutes to change orders and correspondence, we'll uncover the essential documents that form the backbone of effective project management. Get ready to discover how proactive documentation can transform your approach to risk management, empowering you to anticipate challenges, resolve issues efficiently, and ultimately, achieve project success.

# 6

# RISK MANAGEMENT THROUGH PROJECT DOCUMENTATION

Having thoroughly examined the complexities of contract structures; we now shift our focus to a cornerstone of successful project execution: documentation[9]. Project documentation is an essential part of project management[10]. While previous chapters touched on this vital aspect, we will now delve deeper into the specific types of documentation that should be meticulously created and maintained throughout your project's lifecycle.

Project documentation serves as a comprehensive record of a project's journey, from inception to completion. It encompasses everything from project plans and risk assessments to meeting minutes and change orders. This meticulous record-keeping is essential for several reasons:

---

9  William Vidogah and Issaka Ndekugri, "Improving the Management of Claims on Construction Contracts: Consultant's Perspective," *Construction Management and Economics* 16, no. 3 (1998), https://doi.org/10.1080/014461998372385.

10  Amirali Shalwani and Brian Lines, "Using Issue Logs to Improve Construction Project Performance," *Engineering, Construction and Architectural Management* 29, no. 2 (2021), https://doi.org/10.1108/ecam-12-2020-1089.

- Alignment and Communication: It ensures all stakeholders, from team members to management, are on the same page regarding project goals, timelines, and progress, minimizing confusion and miscommunication.
- Risk Mitigation: By documenting potential risks and their impact, project managers can proactively develop strategies to address them, safeguarding the project from unforeseen setbacks.
- Performance Evaluation and Learning: It provides a valuable historical record for evaluating project performance, identifying areas for improvement, and informing future projects.
- Compliance and Legal Protection: It helps demonstrate adherence to industry regulations and standards and can serve as crucial evidence in legal proceedings.

## What Exactly is Project Documentation?

Essentially, project documentation is the comprehensive collection of information generated throughout a project's lifecycle, from initial concept to final delivery. It serves as a meticulous written record, capturing every facet of your project's journey. While the depth and breadth of documentation may vary depending on the project's complexity and scope, its core purpose remains unwavering: to provide a dependable reference point and a historical account of the project's evolution[11].

This documentation can include a wide array of materials, including:

- Proposals
- Scopes of Work
- Project Management Plans

---

11 Seng Hansen, "Developing a Model of Construction Contract Management Competency in a Developing Country: Quantitative Approach," *Journal of Legal Affairs and Dispute Resolution in Engineering and Construction* 13, no. 4 (2021), https://doi.org/10.1061/(asce)la.1943-4170.0000504.

- Risk Mitigation Plans and Risk Registers
- Change Order Plans and Change Order Logs
- Communication Plans and Stakeholder Registers
- Financial Plans (Profit and Margin Tracking)
- QA Plans
- Safety Plans
- Meeting Minutes
- Agendas
- Photographs
- Videos
- e-mails
- Notice Letters
- Site Diaries
- Journals
- Certificates of Final Acceptance
- Lessons Learned

This list is far from exhaustive, but it illustrates the breadth of documentation that can contribute to a project's success. Each document plays a unique and indispensable role, and as a project manager, mastering the creation and maintenance of these materials is essential.

## The Power of Documentation

Project documentation is more than just a historical record; it is also a powerful tool for safeguarding your project from potential claims. It provides a treasure trove of reference materials in case you need to prove damages. Furthermore, these documents form the backbone of your presentations to executive teams during project review meetings or monthly status reports.

For executives, project documentation offers a window into the project's overall health. When examined in greater detail, it reveals the intricacies of its performance. To illustrate the critical importance of documentation, let's delve into a real-world scenario that highlights the power of even the simplest document: the agenda.

### Insight Story: *The Crooked Subcontractor*

John walked into my office without knocking and sat in the chair in front of my desk holding a cup of coffee. He leaned back in his chair, raised his arms above his head, and smiled at me. Over the years, I learned to recognize this smile and knew this conversation would be interesting. John was recently promoted as a lead project manager. Still, he's continuing to play the roles of assistant project manager, scheduler, safety manager, and coordinator. He worked his way up through the ranks, and I see he has the potential to advance to the top. Since this was his first gig as the lead project manager, all eyes were on him. It was a big deal for him, and our company tossed him into the fire to see if he had what it took to do the job.

"John, how are you doing?" I asked, knowing the answer.

"Man, I am just living the dream!" John bellowed.

"What's going on?" I asked. "You have this look on your face."

"You know, we are just getting started on this project, and I already have subcontractors complaining and submitting change orders. I think this project will do me in for good," John said, still wryly.

I smiled and replied, "That's why the company pays you the big bucks."

John laughed. He explained some problems he was encountering. They stemmed from the lack of resources, or, as he said, "warm bodies" to do the work.

"Okay, tell me about the change orders," I said, nodding.

"The change orders I can manage, but I need your help with a claim," John said.

John took a sip of coffee and handed me a one-page claim letter.

"I just got this claim for $90,000 from our subcontractor we contracted to erect the utility building," he said.

I read the letter and noted it was written with little thought taken on the letter's structure, grammar, and punctuation. In the subcontractor's letter, they claimed damages for our failure to give them access to the project site. According to what I read, our crew denied the crane operator access to the construction area, but no names or other specific details were provided. They claimed the crane was parked on the public road for two days, waiting for us to give them access. The subcontractor also claimed they had received the crane company's invoice (which wasn't attached to the letter).

"Interesting," I said as I placed the letter on my desk and reached for my coffee.

John smiled and said, "Not for me! I spoke to my crew, and no one recalled the crane. We have a lot of pieces of heavy equipment going back and forth and about four other subcontractors driving piles, pouring concrete, and digging trenches."

"So we don't have any documentation showing when they arrived on-site? Surely the security shack has a record of people coming and going?" I asked.

He paused for a moment, considering the question, "Yeah, that's in our scope to provide security, but I haven't awarded that subcontract yet. So the security shack was empty."

"John, this is a significant security issue. If someone wanders onto the site and gets hurt or killed, our liability could be limitless," I said pointedly, hoping he understood the severity of the consequences.

"I know, I know." He nodded. "I will get a company on-site today."

I picked up the claim letter and reread it again.

"There has to be some record of who was on-site and what they were working on," I thought.

"John, did you have your assistant project manager or a safety manager on-site?" I asked.

"Yes, they were on-site," John said.

"Did they fill out site records like a site diary or daily report?" I asked.

"No, I checked, but they didn't fill anything out," John replied.

"John, this is also problematic. We need to know who is on-site and where they are working. Do you require your subcontractors to give you daily site reports?" I asked.

I didn't mean to seem like I was scolding him; instead, I wanted to show him my concern for things I believed were more than minor infractions. These are basic reporting requirements and may play a significant part in our defense if an event happens on the project site.

"John, without documentation, it comes down to that same old argument, 'he said, and she said'," I added.

John's frustration showed on his face. "Quite honestly, I don't have the time to document everything that's occurring on my projects and manage the project simultaneously. If I spent as much time documenting everything as you have suggested, I would never leave the site trailer," John exclaimed.

"John, I understand, but let's consider this claim from your subcontractor. As it stands, it is difficult to determine whether this claim is valid. If we had a site report of who was on-site, we might be able to determine whether it's valid," I said, checking on my tone.

"I know, sorry. It's my fault, and I hate it when I forget to do something," he said, sighing.

I was shocked and relieved he was receptive to criticism and self-reflective on his faults. These are two outstanding qualities in any good manager. Throughout my career, I have learned no one is perfect, and we all falter, but if we are open and self-reflective, we can learn to change our behavior.

"John, no worries," I reassured him. "Let's think about this problem some more. What do we have that can help us determine if this claim is valid?" I asked.

John sat there for a minute and said, "I have pictures."

"Okay, I'm intrigued," I said. "Tell me more."

"We have a camera mounted on a pole over the middle of the site, and it takes pictures every 15 minutes. I also make my safety manager walk the site every hour and take random pictures of the crews working," John said.

"Perfect; where are the pictures?" I asked.

John stood up and started walking out of my office. He turned back and said, "I'm going to send you a link to the project folder with the pictures."

A few minutes later, I received an e-mail notification from John with a link. I wasn't feeling confident we would find anything useful. I clicked on the link and opened the file. I looked at the date on the claim letter and the dates in the metadata of thousands of pictures in the file to get a ballpark range. And lo and behold, there it was! I was surprised to see the site safety manager had taken a random picture capturing a crane on the concrete pad where the utility building was in the process of being erected. Around the crane was a crew of five people staging the steel and wearing reflective vests with the subcontractor's name imprinted on the back. The picture's date and time stamp were in bold red in the lower left-hand corner of the picture. I picked up the letter to confirm the dates on which the subcontractor claimed our project team denied the crane access to the site, as well as the date and time stamp on the face. The date on the face of the picture was the first day of their claim. I picked up the phone and called John.

"John, come down to my office. I have a few questions," I said.

I met John at my office door and stood in the hallway.

"John, tell me about the camera your site safety manager uses," I said.

"I bought it right before the project started. Actually, I bought three and a video recorder," he replied.

"Who set up the cameras when you bought them?" I asked.

"I did," John said.

"Are the dates and times correct on the pictures?" I asked.

"Yes, I have my team check them every day before they're used," he said.

"Perfect," I said excitedly. "Let me show you what I found."

We walked into my office, around the back of the desk, and looked at my computer screen.

"John, I found a picture of the crane on the concrete pad the day they claimed we didn't give the crane access to the site. With this picture, we can deny their claim," I said.

"Man, this is perfect! I have my bi-weekly meeting tomorrow, and I thought I would have to explain this hit to my project's margins," John exclaimed. "What's our next step?" he asked.

"I'll prepare a letter, attach the picture, and deny their claim," I said.

"Great, can we get it out today?" John asked.

"Sure, but I am worried about this subcontractor. It appears they are lacking in the integrity department. I'll get you the letter, but you should hand deliver it, and while you are at it, have a heart-to-heart with them. I'm afraid this will become a routine with them," I said.

I prepared the letter, attached the picture, and denied their claim. John did have a long discussion with them. As expected, they were shocked and blamed it on their crane operator.

## BEST PRACTICES

Having progress photos and videos is incredibly useful for future reference if any unexpected issues arise. The benefit is that this documentation can be kept on file and utilized if necessary. Despite taking a short time to create, it can save a significant amount of time and effort in identifying the cause of a problem without having to damage finished surfaces. You keep the photos for your own convenience and protection and do not provide them to your customer unless your contract requires otherwise.

## Commentary

This story may have ended differently if John couldn't produce the pictures. The story is a good teaching tool and illustrates the importance of project documentation. As a construction claims manager, I rely heavily on the project's documentation to start an analysis, prosecute a claim, or defend against a claim. To build a picture of the events, I collect the facts and present it chronologically. It's important to recognize the facts are only as good as the evidence that backs them up. Let's be clear about one thing, and I hope you'll take this to heart. When a project is delayed or suspended, or there are warranty claims or other subcontractor claims (and change orders), it's typical for the party with the most thorough documentation to win most arguments, and they will have a tremendous advantage over the other party.

When preparing a claim or defending against one, I often rely on notices, e-mails, photographs, videos, change orders, daily reports, site logs, requests for information, plans and specifications, agendas, meeting minutes, cost reports, schedules, and other relevant documents. The project's history is inevitably revealed in all of these documents. So why is this so important? We use these documents to verify claimed statements, help us to form arguments, oppose claimed statements, verify schedule impact dates/scope in time impact analyses, and confirm any dead-end theories.

John mentioned in the previous story that he has limited bandwidth and needs more time to document events. I get it. I hear the same complaints in my workshops. I understand it's incredibly time-consuming, but it's necessary. I can remember a time when I had a similar viewpoint. Most project managers are fixated on all their other responsibilities and view these documentation requirements as unnecessary and a waste of time and resources. When these arguments arise, I always ask, "Who is responsible for the profit and loss on your project?" I will also try to argue a few other points, like "Let's assume you receive a claim from a subcontractor. How will you evaluate it if you don't have the proper documentation?"

If you fail to document the day-to-day events on your project, you may be exposing it to risk. Now that I have expressed the importance of project documentation (and photographs), let's move on to other types of paperwork you should incorporate into your project plan.

## The Agenda: A Small Document with Big Impact

An agenda may seem like a mundane pre-meeting formality, but its significance cannot be overstated. This unassuming document sets the stage for productive meetings, outlining topics, introducing participants, and fostering effective time management. By creating an agenda, you not only demonstrate professionalism but also contribute to the project's written record.

Often, the importance of an agenda becomes apparent only when problems arise. Let's follow John, a project manager, as he navigates a challenging situation, and discover how this seemingly simple document can make a world of difference.

### *Insight Story: We are Having Problems Now*

Cruising down the coastal highway, I was making my rounds through the Southeastern project sites. As I pulled away from John's project near Wilmington, my phone buzzed.

"Hey, just missed you this morning," John's voice crackled through the speaker, a hint of urgency in his tone. "Got a minute?"

Sure, I'm all ears for the next hour," I replied, glancing in the rearview mirror.

John launched into his predicament. "Remember, we're the electrical sub on that JCCC Contracting job? They've got a bunch of local subs on this one, and the drywall guys are causing us major headaches. They're flying through their work, not giving us enough time to get our electrical conduits in. It's not impacting the overall schedule yet, but it's starting to eat into our profits."

"Is this the same crew you had issues with on that last project?" I inquired.

"Nope, different guys," John sighed. "I've got a project review meeting with everyone tomorrow, though."

I couldn't help but shake my head, even though he couldn't see me. "John, you know the drill. We need to loop in the general contractor (GC) on this."

"I know, I know," he conceded. "But it's not a change order situation yet, so I was hoping to handle it internally."

"Fair enough," I said, "but at the very least, they need to be aware of the coordination issues. It could snowball into something bigger."

"Right, right. Should I draft a notice letter?" John asked.

I paused, considering the options. "Not yet. See if you can get this added to tomorrow's agenda. With everyone in the same room, you might be able to hash it out then and there. If not, we can escalate it next week."

"Sounds like a plan," John agreed.

We hung up, and as I continued down the highway, I couldn't help but feel a sense of relief. John was a proactive guy, and I knew he'd handle the situation with professionalism.

## Commentary

By taking this proactive approach, John has achieved several key objectives. Firstly, he has documented the issue within the project's official record, creating a time stamped reference point. Secondly, he has alerted the GC to the problem without resorting to a formal notice, allowing for a potential informal resolution. Thirdly, and perhaps most importantly, he has given the GC, who has a contractual relationship with the drywall subcontractor, the opportunity to address the issue directly. It's crucial to remember that without a direct contractual link (privity), we cannot enforce actions upon the drywall subcontractor.

Let's consider the possible outcomes of the upcoming meeting. The coordination and scheduling problems may be resolved, or they may not. However, the essential takeaway is this: regardless of the outcome, a clear record now exists, detailing the companies and individuals involved, the date, time, location, and most importantly, the specific issues raised. This documentation not only informs the GC but also serves as a valuable reference point should further action be required.

## Effective Meeting Facilitation:

When leading the meeting, encourage open dialogue and active participation from all attendees. Allow others to suggest additional discussion topics and voice any concerns they may have. Remember, effective communication is a two-way street. By fostering an inclusive environment, you can gain valuable insights and address a wider range of issues.

## Important Note for General Contractors:

If you are the GC in this scenario, be vigilant about managing expectations during project meetings. It's essential to prevent subcontractors from viewing these meetings as a platform for submitting change orders or claims. If a changed condition arises during discussions, direct the subcontractor to adhere to the formal change order process outlined in their contract.

Following the meeting, promptly distribute a concise meeting summary and detailed minutes to all participants. This ensures everyone is on the same page and reinforces transparency throughout the project.

## The Project Management Plan

Crafting a comprehensive project management plan is akin to laying the foundation for a successful construction project. It acts as a roadmap, guiding the project team through the intricate phases of execution, ensuring alignment with objectives, and mitigating potential risks[12]. As a project manager, your role in developing this plan is pivotal, requiring meticulous attention to detail and a deep understanding of the project's unique requirements.

The project management plan serves as a single source of truth, providing a reference point for all stakeholders involved[13]. It outlines the project's scope, objectives, timeline, budget, resources, communication strategies, and risk management approach. By consolidating all this information into a well-structured document, you establish a clear framework for decision-making and problem-solving, fostering a collaborative environment where everyone works towards a common goal[14].

Sections of a Project Management Plan:

- Executive Summary: This section provides a concise overview of the project, highlighting its purpose, objectives, key stakeholders, and expected outcomes. It serves as a quick reference for executives and decision-makers.

- Project Scope Statement: This section delineates the project's boundaries, outlining what is included and what is excluded. It clarifies deliverables,

---

12 Albert Lester, "Project Management Plan," in *Project Management, Planning and Control* (n.p.: Elsevier, 2021), https://doi.org/10.1016/b978-0-12-824339-8.00014-6.
13 Butković, "A New."
14 Harvey Maylor et al., "Mind the Gap: Towards Performance Measurement Beyond a Plan-Execute Logic," *International Journal of Project Management* 41, no. 4 (2023), https://doi.org/10.1016/j.ijproman.2023.102467.

acceptance criteria, and constraints, preventing scope creep and ensuring everyone is on the same page.

- Project Schedule: This section details the project timeline, including key milestones, activities, dependencies, and deadlines. It often includes a Gantt chart or other visual representation of the schedule, facilitating progress tracking and resource allocation.

- Project Budget: This section outlines the project's financial plan, including estimated costs, resource allocation, and contingency reserves. It ensures financial viability and enables effective cost control throughout the project lifecycle.

- Resource Management Plan: This section identifies the resources required for the project, including personnel, equipment, materials, and technology. It outlines roles and responsibilities, staffing plans, and resource allocation strategies.

- Communication Plan: This section establishes communication channels, frequencies, and formats for sharing information with stakeholders. It ensures transparency, collaboration, and timely decision-making.

- Risk Management Plan: This section identifies potential risks that could impact the project and outlines strategies for mitigating and responding to them. It includes a risk register, which documents each risk's probability, impact, and mitigation measures.

- Quality Management Plan: This section defines quality standards and processes for ensuring that deliverables meet or exceed expectations. It outlines quality control measures, inspections, and testing procedures.

- Procurement Management Plan: If applicable, this section outlines the procurement process for acquiring goods or services from external vendors. It covers supplier selection, contract negotiation, and performance monitoring.

- Stakeholder Management Plan: This section identifies project stakeholders and their interests, outlining strategies for engaging and managing their expectations throughout the project.

Remember, the project management plan is a living document that should be reviewed and updated regularly to reflect changes in the project environment. By meticulously crafting and maintaining this plan, you set the stage for a successful project outcome, ensuring clear communication, effective resource management, and proactive risk mitigation[15].

## The Value of Meeting Minutes:

In our ongoing scenario with John, the project meeting successfully addressed the coordination issues, and all parties committed to collaboration to prevent further delays. So far, so good. However, the real test lies in whether the drywall subcontractor fulfills their promises. This is where meeting minutes prove their worth.

Meeting minutes serve as a critical piece of documentation in case the situation deteriorates. Ideally, John would have reviewed the minutes upon distribution to ensure they accurately reflected the discussions and any agreed-upon corrective actions. This is crucial because these minutes can later be referenced in formal notice letters, demonstrating that the GC was aware of the problem but failed to adequately address it.

## Discrepancies in Meeting Minutes:

What if John discovers that the meeting minutes don't align with what was actually discussed or decided? In this situation, immediate action is required. He must promptly request corrections, as silence could be interpreted as agreement. If the GC refuses to amend the minutes, John has the option to create his

---

15 Ofer Zwikael and Jack Meredith, "Evaluating the Success of a Project and the Performance of Its Leaders," *IEEE Transactions on Engineering Management* 68, no. 6 (2021), https://doi.org/10.1109/tem.2019.2925057.

own version or issue a rebuttal. Can he send an email outlining his objections? Yes! The important point is that it is captured in the project documentation.

Remember, meeting minutes should be a collaborative effort, representing the perspectives of all participants[16]. Accurate documentation ensures transparency and protects all parties involved in case of future disputes or claims.

## *Insight Story: That's Your Interpretation!*

The phone rang not long after John's meeting. He sounded frustrated. "Hey, just got off a call with the GC. They're refusing to include my comments in the meeting minutes."

"What do you mean?" I asked, concerned.

"They said my version is unacceptable and want me to change it," John explained, a sigh escaping his lips. "But I just documented the events and issues we've been dealing with, nothing more."

"Are you sure your minutes accurately reflect what was discussed?" I probed.

"Absolutely," John insisted. "I'm just stating the facts."

"In that case," I advised, "send an email back. Keep it simple. Just say that it's your interpretation of the meeting and you stand by your account."

## Commentary

This situation raises an important question: what if the GC had simply deleted John's comments from the minutes? Would that hold up in a dispute? While it depends on the specific circumstances, it's generally unwise to rely solely on agendas or meeting minutes as the basis for a claim. They are valuable "supporting documents" that provide context and a timeline, but a formal notice letter outlining the events and referencing these documents is crucial.

---

16 Jaques van Niekerk, Jan Wium, and Nico de Koker, "The Value of Data from Construction Project Site Meeting Minutes in Predicting Project Duration," *Built Environment Project and Asset Management* 12, no. 5 (2022), https://doi.org/10.1108/bepam-03-2021-0047.

Remember, the key is to build a robust written record that accurately reflects the project's history. This record can prove invaluable in protecting your interests should any disagreements or disputes arise.

## Project Review Meetings

We have covered some of the project documentation you should use throughout your project's life. But we haven't covered the importance of holding *internal* pre-proposal, project kick-off, biweekly, and quarterly project review meetings. Project review meetings are an essential aspect of project management and play a critical role in ensuring that a project is completed on time, within budget, and to the satisfaction of all stakeholders. These meetings provide an opportunity for project managers, team members, and stakeholders to review the progress of a project, identify any issues or risks, and make any necessary adjustments to the project plan.

One of the primary benefits of project review meetings is that they provide a structured forum for communication between all parties involved in the project. This helps to ensure that everyone is on the same page and that any issues or concerns are addressed in a timely manner. For example, team members can raise concerns about delays or obstacles they are facing, while stakeholders can provide feedback on the progress of the project and suggest any changes that may be needed. Project review meetings also play a vital role in risk management. By regularly reviewing a project's progress, project managers can identify potential risks and take steps to mitigate them before they become major problems. This can include revising the project plan, allocating additional resources, or implementing new strategies to overcome any issues that may arise.

Another important aspect of project review meetings is that they help project managers stay up to date on project progress and ensure that the project is on track to be completed on time and within budget. Regularly reviewing the project schedule and budget allows project managers to identify any delays or cost overruns and take steps to get the project back on track. Additionally, project review meetings can help ensure that the project meets the stakeholders' needs and that any necessary changes are made to the project plan. Project review meetings can also be an opportunity to recognize and celebrate the project team's success. This can help to boost morale and motivation among team members, and it can be particularly useful during the final stages of a project when the team is working hard to complete the final deliverables.

Project review meetings should be scheduled regularly throughout the project, such as at the end of each phase or at specific milestones. The frequency of these meetings will depend on the project's size and complexity, but they should be held frequently enough to ensure that progress is made and that any issues or concerns are addressed in a timely manner. Let's explore why this is so powerful in this scenario.

## *Insight Story: The ICW Project Kick-off Meeting*

John received a call from Kevin, his program manager, congratulating him on getting the hospital construction project.

"John, make sure you pack your swimsuit because the site is close to the Intercoastal Waterway. You can walk down there every day and jump in," Kevin said and chuckled.

"I'm excited and ready to jump in!" John said.

"I just sent you the invitation to the project kick-off meeting, and I want you to take Brayden. He's a new project manager, and he's never been to one of these types of meetings. Walk him through it and show him the ropes," Kevin said.

A few days before the meeting, John printed a copy of the contract and related documents, e-mailed them to Brayden, and attached a quick note. He said, "Come by my office when you have a few minutes."

John started thinking about how much he liked working there. There was a sense of camaraderie, and people genuinely cared about each other and the company's success.

"It wasn't always like this," he thought.

In the recent past, the company focused on cost savings and eliminated many of the risk assessment meetings. That is, until a project went wrong and cost them several million dollars. They quickly saw their value and implemented policies requiring project kick-off meetings before each project started. He also liked mentoring junior people moving up in the company. He was in a position to influence them, show them the right way to manage their projects, and provide them with someone who would listen to them and guide them when things went wrong.

The next day, Brayden stopped by John's office.

Poking his head in the door, he asked, "John, is this a good time for you?"

"Sure, give me a minute to clean the conference table," John said.

John brushed aside the project management magazines, supplier catalogs, and brochures of boats.

"Have a seat," John said as he gestured for Brayden to sit down.

Brayden sat down, and they introduced themselves. Brayden previously worked as a coordinator but decided to join our company as an assistant project manager. This career path was common for most project managers, allowing them to learn from the ground floor up.

"Kevin has assigned me as a mentor to you," John said. "I get the concept, but what does that mean? Are you going to check my work each day?" he asked.

"No, unless that's what you want me to do," John said.

John got up, poured a cup of coffee into a Styrofoam cup, and offered it to Brayden. Brayden held up his hand and gestured that he wasn't interested. John sat back down and started sipping the coffee.

"Brayden, my job as a mentor is not to be your boss but to show you the ropes and give you the knowledge and teach you the skills necessary to be good at your job," John said. "I am here to answer your questions and advise you about your career path. For this relationship to work, we need to be open and honest with each other. I promise to be responsive when you need help, and you need to promise me that you will come to me and ask questions," John said.

Brayden laughed and said, "It sounds like we are saying our wedding vows."

John leaned back into his chair and laughed.

"Yeah, it does sound a lot like that, but there's a reason behind the madness. Often, new project managers do not know they need help, where to get help, do not take the initiative to seek it, or do not know what questions to ask. Think of me as a member of your support network," John said.

"Thank you, and I will call you," Brayden said, nodding.

"No, Brayden, I need more commitment from you. Let's schedule a call each Friday afternoon to discuss how you are doing and what you've experienced that week." He paused for a second and then continued, "Again, I'm not your boss, but if we leave it up to you to occasionally call me, you won't benefit from having me as a mentor."

"Okay, I'll schedule it each Friday," Brayden said.

"Let's move on to discussing the hospital project. They haven't officially named it yet, so we need to create one," John said.

"I see it's over where Taylor's Creek and the Newport River meet," Brayden said.

"The name needs to be short and memorable, and I don't want to make my hand sore writing it," John said.

"Okay, how about the ICW Junction Project?" Brayden asked.

"I like that a lot!" John exclaimed.

John jotted down the name and opened the scope of work. "We have a project kick-off meeting scheduled in three days. It's our job to review our proposal, the scope of work, and the contract to ensure we understand what we are doing before the meeting. Since you are attending the meeting, I expect you to read these documents and be prepared to ask questions," John said.

"I attended kick-off meetings at the last place I worked, but they were just an informal document turnover from the proposal team, and I didn't have to ask questions. How is this any different?" Brayden asked.

John nodded, acknowledging a difference from the normal operations of other companies. "Our proposal team does perform their risk assessment during the proposal phase, but it's not as in-depth as the kick-off meeting. The contract hasn't been finalized during the proposal phase, and the scope may have been just a thought." He paused, thinking, "Think of it this way. The proposal meeting determines how to win the job, while the kickoff meeting determines how to execute it. Well, it's not that simple, but it's close."

"I don't understand why you need the meeting if you have the scope of work ready. Doesn't that give you everything you need to know?" Brayden asked.

"Well, yes and no. Let's think through this for a few minutes." He leaned forward to make sure he had Brayden's attention. "In the kick-off meeting, you have everyone from all the functional groups in our organization, including engineering, contracts, finance, safety, and sales. Each of these groups has a part to play. For instance," he held up a finger to indicate each group, "contracts will provide you with an overview of the contract and the terms that present risk to the project. Typically, they will give you a term sheet with all the clauses you should be aware of, including notices, claims, change orders, warranty, and safety. Finance may provide the payment terms and any potential issues. The Environment Health and Safety (EHS) manager may provide an overview of the contract's safety requirements, and engineering will give you an overview of nuances to complete the project. Sales may give you a rundown of 'who's who at the Zoo,' so you understand the key stakeholders. We may also invite trusted subcontractors or suppliers to the meeting. Another important point is that it allows you to learn who the subject matter experts are and whom to call when you have a question or problem. This is the real power of these meetings," John said.

"It seems like we could review the contract and upload these reviews into a shared folder," Brayden said.

"Yes, we ultimately do that, but not until the end of the meeting. Have you ever heard someone say that two minds are better than one?" John asked. "This meeting pulls in the subject matter experts from each discipline and puts them in the same room. The meeting is typically facilitated by an outside person or someone within our company that isn't attached to the project, but you have to be careful in selecting the person in your company to facilitate the meeting," he said.

Brayden looked up from the papers in front of him and asked, "Isn't getting an outside facilitator just an added expense?"

"Yes, it is, but we have learned over the years that if you have brass in the room, the facilitator may not ask the right questions, and the team won't become fully engaged. The team shuts down, or if the executive team member says something, whether right or wrong, the team comes down with a case of 'groupthink.' This is what we are trying to avoid," John said.

"Can you give me a rundown on what I can expect during the meeting?" Brayden asked.

"Okay, we are going to bring in an outside facilitator. This meeting should last between six and eight hours, but I've seen these meetings last several days. The facilitator will bring about five posterboards and tape them to the wall. Each poster board is labeled with a specific aspect of the project. For instance, one may say 'risks.' Another one may have 'schedule' written on it," he continued. "The facilitator will break the participants into three or four teams. Each team has about 25 minutes to collaborate and discuss the topic written on the poster board. For instance, if it covers 'risks,' the team may start identifying and discussing the known risks, such as narrow bridges leading onto the site or the potential of hurricanes slowing down the shipment of equipment. The team will list potential steps that may be taken to reduce the risks for these scenarios. Once that's done, each team member will list each item in order of severity or potential," he said.

John got up, made another cup of coffee, and sat back down. He grabbed a piece of paper and drew a crude outline of the conference room. The paper showed five poster boards and an easel, and the chairs were lined up on the back of the wall. Each of the poster boards was labeled.

"Where is the conference room tables, and why are the chairs like that?" Brayden asked.

"We take them out. There's no sitting, and it's a standing room only. No, just kidding," he chuckled. "You won't stand all day, but you will be up and down all day. The facilitator gives each group time to discuss each topic, and then you will move to the next poster board and continue until you have visited each one. After everyone has had the opportunity to visit each poster board, we discuss each topic together as a group. If you added a comment to the poster board, such as that you believe that permitting may be a challenge, you would be allowed to express your concern and the risk. After working through all the comments on the poster board, the group would collectively itemize and number the risk as low, medium-low, medium-high, and high into a 4x4 risk matrix. Once we identify and understand the risks and their potential, we can begin discussing ways to mitigate them," John said.

While John was talking, Brayden started jotting down questions to ask.

"What happens afterward? Is it just filed away and not seen again?" Brayden asked.

"No, this is just the start. After the meeting, I will return to my office and start drafting the project's plans. For instance, I'll use the stakeholder information from sales to develop my communication plan, and I may use the information from our suppliers to create our internal project schedule. The plans aren't just filed and forgotten. We have to pull them out during our bi-weekly and quarterly project reviews, perform a sanity check, and ask, are we on track?" He paused to make sure Brayden understood. "At the end of the project, I have to host a project closeout meeting that covers lessons learned. We will look at what we believed the risks were during the project kick-off meeting and compare it to how we did. It's a powerful learning tool, enabling us to improve with each project," John ended.

"I've never been involved in something like this, and it seems to be expensive tying up everyone," Brayden said.

John nodded in agreement. "Yes, it can be ridiculously expensive, especially when the project is located in another state or country. But what is the cost of not doing it? I believe it sets the tone for the project and allows our executive team to show how important an investment it is. It is an investment in your team."

"How is this an investment if the company flips the bill for hotels, lunches, and dinners?" Brayden asked.

"I have learned that we all learn from each other. Some people learn by seeing; others learn by doing; and others learn by listening. A kick-off meeting covers all three aspects of learning. I am visual, but I also learn by listening. If I hear a question, problem, or scenario, I tend to remember it when I encounter similar situations. My argument is that it pays dividends in this specific kick-off meeting and future meetings. It may not be worth much for a small project, but for large complex projects, like this hospital, it is more than worth our investment," John said.

John stood up and stuck his hand out for Brayden. "I've run out of time and need to jump on a call. Let's connect later, but make sure you read the contract and scope of work before the kick-off meeting." Brayden stood up and shook John's hand. "I appreciate what you are doing for me."

The meeting came and went as predicted. John asked Brayden to help him prepare for the biweekly meetings that went into more detail about the financial and schedule risks. John had to create a PowerPoint with an overview of the project and its status, along with the change order log and risk register. The quarterly meeting was more intense and required more preparation. John would be required to present to the entire executive leadership team the same things he had to present in the biweekly meeting, but in greater detail and with more scrutiny.

## The Critical Role of Letters and Correspondence:

Throughout this guidebook, we will repeatedly emphasize the significance of notice letters and provide guidance on their proper drafting. The key takeaway is this: when delays, disruptions, or other issues arise on your project, it's imperative to document these events meticulously (as previously discussed) and issue timely notices as warranted.

You might wonder, "When exactly should I send a notice?" A good rule of thumb is to do so whenever you anticipate a problem, are currently experiencing one, or—if the issue was unforeseen—immediately after its occurrence. Never succumb to the temptation to ignore problems, hoping they will resolve themselves. They rarely do, and more often than not, they escalate if left unaddressed.

Written notices serve multiple purposes: they clarify the situation, ensure all parties are informed, and provide a comprehensive account of the issue. Furthermore, your contract likely mandates the submission of such notices, which is often essential to preserving your legal rights and remedies.

## Responding to Correspondence:

Equally important is your response to any notice letters or other correspondence you receive. While you needn't admit fault or immediately resolve the matter, a timely response is crucial. Failing to respond can be construed as tacit agreement with the contents of the letter, even if they are inaccurate or misleading.

**Strategic Use of Notice Letters:**

Be aware that some companies may use notice letters strategically to bolster their position for potential claims. They might embellish facts, omit crucial details, or portray themselves as victims. If you receive a notice letter containing inaccuracies or misrepresentations, it's vital to respond with a clear and concise rebuttal. Remember, your silence can be weaponized against you.

Whether you agree with the contents of a notice letter or not, a response is always necessary. This response can range from a simple acknowledgement of receipt to a detailed refutation, depending on the situation. Here's an example of a response letter:

> Dear Ms. Subcontractor:
>
> This letter serves as an acknowledgment of your correspondence dated August 14, 2025. We are currently evaluating the details provided in your letter.
>
> We will respond once we have completed our evaluation.
>
> Thank you for your patience.

By actively engaging in written communication, you protect your interests and maintain transparency throughout the project.

## Journals: The Unsung Heroes of Project Documentation

I recently stopped by John's project to catch up. The project was wrapping up, and John was visibly relieved.

"Just a few punch list items left," he said as we strolled the site. "Then it's off to the mountains for a well-deserved break."

"Sounds fantastic," I replied, a twinge of envy in my voice.

As I continued my site visits, I reflected on how valuable these in-person check-ins were. Building relationships with project teams is key, but it takes time and effort. Initially, it felt like everyone was putting on a show for the "corporate guy," but over time, trust developed, and the real picture emerged.

One of the first initiatives I implemented when I started these site visits was to provide each team member with a project journal. While project managers are usually diligent about collecting daily reports from subcontractors, they often need help documenting their observations and experiences. I always ask them, "If you were called to testify in court years later, would you remember the details of what happened today?"

Our memories are fallible, and details fade with time. This is where journals become invaluable. They allow team members to record project-specific information like meeting notes, phone conversations, site observations, and any other relevant details. I always advise them to document verbal conversations in writing—what seems crystal clear today can become hazy months later.

However, it's important to exercise caution when using these journals. They should be strictly project-related information. Personal notes, grocery lists, or venting about your day have no place in a project journal. In a legal context, anything you write could be discoverable and used as evidence against you. Imagine being grilled by opposing counsel about snarky comments you made in your journal!

**Key Takeaway:**
Journals are a powerful tool for capturing the day-to-day realities of a project. They serve as a reliable reference point and can be crucial in resolving disputes or claims. Just remember to keep them professional and focused solely on project-related matters.

## Daily Site Reports: The Backbone of Project Tracking

While we've touched on the value of personal journals, daily site reports are equally crucial and complement the information captured in those journals. These reports serve as a snapshot of each day's activities on the project site, recording details such as:

- Visitors to the site
- Weather conditions
- Personnel present (both your team and subcontractors)
- Work performed and its location
- Materials delivered
- Progress achieved
- Bottlenecks or delays encountered

From a project management perspective, daily site reports are invaluable. They provide a real-time overview of the project's status, enabling you to track material deliveries, monitor work completion, and plan the next day's tasks. These reports also help identify potential roadblocks and delays, facilitating proactive decision-making and resource allocation.

You might initially view daily site reports as just another administrative burden. However, as a construction claims manager, I can attest to their immense value in dispute resolution. They offer a wealth of objective information, cutting through the "he said, she said" arguments that often arise. Once completed, these reports become part of the project's permanent record and can be a lifesaver in litigation or arbitration, potentially saving your company significant sums of money.

Fortunately, numerous online resources offer free daily site report templates. I encourage you to find one that aligns with your project's specific needs and make it a mandatory practice for your team and subcontractors to complete them daily. Consider it an investment in your project's long-term success and smooth operation.

## RACI Matrix: A Powerful Tool for Defining Roles and Responsibilities

The RACI (Responsible, Accountable, Consulted, Informed) matrix is a valuable tool typically employed during the proposal development phase. After reviewing the client's requirements and specifications, and as you contemplate the scope of work, developing a RACI matrix can be immensely beneficial. This matrix clearly delineates each party's role and responsibilities, ensuring everyone understands who is responsible for what.

If you haven't yet integrated the RACI matrix into your proposal process, I strongly recommend doing so. Its power should not be underestimated, as it can prevent misunderstandings, streamline decision-making, and ultimately save your company significant time and money.

Considered a best practice in project management, the RACI matrix effectively charts and documents project activities and deliverables. While you'll find various interpretations of this matrix, they can all be adapted to suit your specific project needs. By clearly defining who is responsible for each aspect of the project, you can confidently develop your project schedule, outline goals, allocate resources, and craft a comprehensive scope of work.

## *Insight Story: A Case of the Missing Requirements*

On a clear morning, the Cape Lookout Lighthouse can be seen from Beaufort to Atlantic Beach, from Cedar Island to Shackelford Banks. On cloudy days, the light is visible almost 18 miles offshore, warning ships of the treacherous sandbars. These sandbars constantly shift with the ocean's tides and are unpredictable, having claimed countless seaworthy ships, including Blackbeard's pirate ship, the Queen Anne's Revenge. They say the wild horses on the barrier islands originated from the Spanish galleons that ran aground on those sandbars.

John couldn't see the lighthouse from his house, but on calm days, when the ocean wasn't in an uproar, he could hear the inlet's fog buoy tolling. It seemed to ring louder in protest as each successive wave passed by on its way to the shore.

When John woke up, he rolled out of bed and headed into the kitchen to pour a cup of coffee. As he pulled out the coffee and filter, he heard the fog buoy ringing and looked outside to see the Carolina blue skies. John noted that the wind was blowing from the south, resulting in beautiful weather today.

Sitting at his dining room table, he peered outside at his wife's bird feeder and thought about his day. He expected a formal acknowledgment from his customer stating the project's second phase was considered complete. The second phase was completed in record time, and he maintained most of his margins. He started daydreaming, reliving the memory of his program manager congratulating him during a project review meeting last quarter. That was a good day, and he believed that once he finished this project, he would move on to the hospital project scheduled to start construction next year.

"That would be a career maker," John thought to himself.

John made the short drive over to the project site. Before starting the project, he had ordered his office trailer and office equipment. The trailer barely had enough room for him and three others. It did have a large conference room table and a widescreen monitor mounted on the wall. Behind the conference room table were a couple of large printers, a sink with a countertop, and a small coffee pot.

His office was relatively small and didn't have many amenities, but it did have a bookcase filled with half-empty binders to collect the massive amount of paperwork his project generated. In his walk-in closet were his hard hat and safety vest. John grabbed his hat and vest and headed to his customer's trailer. He found himself almost skipping with excitement thinking about his next project. He then thought to himself that everyone was watching him, and he calmed down.

John walked across the site and saw Tom, the customer's project manager, standing outside the newly constructed control building.

"John, this is amazing. It looks like a plain utility trailer from the outside, but when you go in, it looks like something you would see at a NASA facility in Florida. This is magnificent work," Tom said.

"I don't know if you remember, but we added a large kitchen and a bathroom with a shower. We also installed our supplier's largest backup generator, which is much larger than the generator in the specifications. You could live in there comfortably for an extended period," John said, smiling.

Tom replied, "I know, and we designed it to accommodate our crews when hurricanes roll around. But the added kitchen and shower will make our crews feel better about leaving their families and positively affect morale."

"Tom, do you have a few minutes?" John asked. "I would like to discuss the next phase of the project."

"I have about five minutes, and then I need to leave," Tom said.

Tom and John turned toward Tom's trailer. The walk to Tom's trailer forced them to walk through part of the construction site that resembled prehistoric wetlands. It was adjacent to the Neuse River, and sometimes a layer of water covered it after an exceptionally high tide. John avoided the part of the site after his crew complained of cottonmouth snakes hanging from the trees, waiting to fall on unsuspecting prey, John avoided the area. Whenever he walked in that area, his leather boots seemed to soak up the water like a sponge. Tom stopped and turned to John.

"When will your crew start working in this section of the yard?" he asked.

John looked at him with surprise. "Tom, we are waiting on your crews to do the excavation."

"We aren't responsible for the excavation. I believe that's in your scope," Tom replied.

"Can we look at the contract documents together today?" he asked.

"I'm tied up in meetings today on the other side of the river, but we can schedule something later this week," Tom said. "Send me an invite for Friday. I'll make some adjustments to my calendar, and I'll make it work."

Tom and John separated, and each turned and headed in a different direction. John couldn't wait to get out of the area. Once he sat down at his desk, he tapped his pen while turning the pages in his scope of work. He wasn't concentrating on the text; instead, he was trying to digest his discussion with Tom and, more importantly, its implications.

"To complete the excavation could cost over $300,000. That's on a good day," John thought to himself.

"Jane, can you come in here for a minute?" John asked.

Jane was the document controller for the project. She was short and soft-spoken, but she was intelligent and knew how to do her job. John learned early that Jane would make his life easier, and he was right. She was the glue of the operation, and everyone knew it, including him.

"Sure, what can I help you with?" she asked.

"I need a complete copy of our proposal and the contract," John said.

"Just those documents?" she asked.

"Let's start with those, and I will let you know," he said. "Also, can you clear my calendar today?"

That day, John devoted time to researching this potentially huge problem. He thought it was more important than his routine day-to-day work, which he could catch up on by staying late. John poured through the scope of work and couldn't find any reference or requirement for his company to do excavations.

"Jane, can you dig up the specifications?" John asked. "On second thought, bring me the entire binder," he said.

John looked through the specifications for earthworks and found that his customer was responsible for the "clearing and grubbing," but the specifications were silent about the excavation. John closed his eyes to think but found he had lost his ability to concentrate on the words he was attempting to read.

"I'll give it more thought later. My stomach is letting me know it's lunchtime," he thought.

While John was driving to pick up lunch, his thoughts went back and forth between fear and failure.

"I have two choices: do the work and let my company's executive team know there is an added cost or push back and refuse to do the work. Neither one of those options is good," John thought.

As John was passing the future site of the hospital, he remembered that Logan, the company's lead business development guru, had led the proposal team's efforts. He picked up lunch, rushed back to the office, and started making phone calls.

"Logan, is this a good time for you?" John asked.

"How have you been, John?" Logan asked.

"I'm just living the dream," John replied. He continued, "Hey, I'm down here working on the Neuse River Project, and I have run into a problem I'm hoping you can help me fix. Do you remember the foundations in our scope on the site's east side? You know, the area that looks like a swamp?"

"Yes, I remember. I think that's in phase three of the project, right?" Logan asked.

"That's right. I am finishing phase two and briefly touched base with the customer's project manager today. He believes we are responsible for the excavation. I checked our scope of work and the specifications, and I don't see any reference to it," John said.

"That's a problem. I remember having a couple of engineers review the bid documents and draft the scope of work we included in our proposal. Still, I don't recall who is responsible for it," Logan said.

"Okay, I'll spend some time going through our proposal. Thanks for your help," John said.

John and Logan said their goodbye. John opened his browser and looked for the proposal. After searching for what he thought was an endless amount of time, he found the file with the proposal. He felt a sense of trepidation pour over him like a giant wave, knocking him down.

Based on what he saw, he thought his company had missed pricing in a sizable portion of the scope. John hit the print button, walked to the coffee pot, and poured a cup of two-day-old coffee. He thought, "As long as it's still hot." John picked up the printed proposal and then headed back into his office.

John realized that the day had passed quickly and sensed that the sun was setting. He heard Jane moving around the office.

"John, I'm getting ready to head out. Is there anything that you need before I go?" she asked.

"No, I'm good," he replied, shaking his head with dread.

John read every word in the proposal and didn't see anything related to excavation. He turned to the back of the proposal and looked at the exhibits, then he saw it. John leaned back and laughed. A sense of relief washed over him when he saw a RACI matrix in their proposal. It outlined in great detail the specific work requirements, deliverables, and a list of those responsible for completing those portions of work.

At the top of the RACI matrix, he saw a column containing excavation. On the left-hand side, he saw the rows listing portions of the work and the site location. It provided either the customer or others would complete the excavation in that column. John saw that the proposal's Assumptions and Exclusions section expressly stated that his company would not be responsible for excavation but that an estimate would be supplied upon request.

John thought, "Well, that answers that question."

But that feeling of anxiety came rushing back when he thought about the scope of work.

"Why didn't the scope of work reference the RACI matrix? Why didn't the contract reference the RACI matrix? Either of them would have helped to clarify this early," he thought.

John thought about what he had learned in one of the construction claims workshops and gave me a call.

"I'm glad I caught you before you left the office. I hope you can help me work through a problem I'm having," John said.

"Sure, I'm all ears," I said.

While I was on the phone, John filled me in and sent me the documents.

He said, "I'm hoping I can resolve this quickly. I need to get started on phase three, but until this is taken care of, I can't look for subcontractors."

"Okay, there's no reference to the excavation requirements in the scope of work, but we did include an exclusion in the RACI matrix, which was part of our proposal. Is that correct?" I asked.

"Yes, that sums it up," John replied.

"Okay, now the question is, did we include our proposal in the contract?" I said it out loud as I perused the contract.

John overheard my question and said, "I looked. I didn't see any reference to our proposal in the contract. I'm not quite sure where to look."

"Okay, let's look at the order of precedence and then the entire agreement clauses. The quickest and dirtiest way to do this is by a word search to see if anything comes up," I said.

I shared my computer screen with John and began a word search for a proposal. We found it in the entire agreement and order of precedence clauses, which surprised me, but the proposal was ranked at the bottom.

I leaned back in my chair and started thinking, "Okay. We know that we excluded the excavation in our proposal, and our proposal was included in the contract's order of precedence. We now need to determine if any excavation requirements were referenced in any of the other contract documents with a higher order of precedence."

I briefly told John what I was thinking and started a search for excavation in the contract and other documents referenced in the order of precedence.

"John, it doesn't look like there are any references to the excavation requirements, and I feel confident it wasn't part of our scope. The RACI matrix says that others would perform the excavation, and we expressly excluded it in the proposal's assumptions and exclusions section. It may be a misunderstanding, and your customer missed this scope entirely and failed to subcontract it out," I said.

"This helps to support our position. It hasn't turned into a disagreement yet, and I think I will be able to show Logan that we aren't responsible for the excavation," he said.

"Great, I'm glad I could help," I said.

We said our goodbyes and hung up the phone. John looked out his window and saw the sun had set. The streetlight flickered and started buzzing loudly outside his window.

After hearing a loud noise, John became startled and thought, "What is that? Is that a bat?" John cautiously opened the trailer's front door and headed out, but decided to walk around the site to see if anyone else was still working. "Yes, that was a bat!" he thought. "Glad they are eating all of these mosquitoes."

While walking around the site, he took mental notes for his discussion with Logan and the lessons learned portion of the project closure. The following day, when he arrived at the site trailer, John asked Jane to print the contract, scope of work, and their proposal, and he headed over to Logan's trailer. Logan arrived and welcomed John into the trailer. John explained what he had found and showed Logan the documents with highlighted sections, supporting his assertion that the excavation wasn't part of his scope.

Logan answered, "John, I can't say that I agree, and I need my legal team to look at this for a determination. I know you are anxious about getting started, and I will issue you a directive to start the excavation. I promise we will resolve this as quickly as possible. When can you give me a quote for doing the excavation?" Logan asked.

By the middle of the following week, John received an email from Logan informing him that his legal department agreed that the excavation was not part of their scope and that he needed a change order request with the pricing.

## Commentary

This story helps to illustrate the power of the RACI matrix and its use in your proposals, scope of work, and contracts. This scenario could have cost John's company hundreds of thousands of dollars without this document. If you do not include it in your proposal or it isn't part of the contract, you should ask for it to be included in your scope of work or contract as an exhibit.

### BEST PRACTICES

Once the contract is signed and handed over to you, take the following steps to set your project up for success:

1. Schedule a Project Kickoff Meeting: Gather your project team as soon as possible for a comprehensive review of the project management plan and the contract. This meeting is essential for aligning everyone's understanding of the project scope, deliverables, timelines, and contractual obligations.

2. **Review the Contract Together:** Don't just distribute the contract for individual reading. Walk through it as a team, clarifying any questions or concerns. Pay special attention to key clauses like payment terms, change order procedures, and dispute resolution mechanisms.

3. **Discuss Roles and Responsibilities:** Ensure each team member understands their specific responsibilities as outlined in the contract. Discuss communication channels and reporting structures to ensure smooth collaboration.

4. **Highlight Potential Risks:** Identify potential risks and discuss mitigation strategies based on the contract terms. This proactive approach can help you avoid costly surprises and delays later in the project.

5. **Establish a Change Management Process:** Review the contract's change order procedures and develop a clear process for managing any changes that arise during the project. Emphasize the importance of documenting all changes in writing to avoid disputes.

By following these best practices, you'll create a shared understanding of the project's contractual framework, foster a collaborative environment, and lay a solid foundation for successful project execution. Remember, a well-informed and prepared team is more likely to deliver on time, within budget, and to the satisfaction of all parties involved.

Project managers have a variety of tools and methods at their disposal to help them successfully plan, execute, and close out projects. Some essential tools and methods for project management include:

- Project management software, such as Asana, Trello, or Microsoft Project allows project managers to create project plans, assign tasks, track progress, and communicate with team members.

- Gantt charts, which provide a visual representation of a project's schedule and help project managers to identify potential conflicts and delays.
- Agile methodologies, such as Scrum or Kanban, are designed to help project managers manage complex, fast-paced projects and adapt to changing requirements.
- Earned value analysis, which helps project managers to track project progress and identify potential cost overruns or schedule delays.
- Risk management techniques, such as SWOT analysis and contingency planning, help project managers identify and mitigate potential risks to the project.
- Communication and collaboration tools, such as email, instant messaging, and video conferencing, help project managers stay in touch with team members, stakeholders, and other key parties throughout the project.

## Change Order Logs

Change order logs are an essential element for successful project management. They serve as a meticulous record of any modifications, additions, or deletions to the original project scope, acting as a single source of truth for all stakeholders.

For project managers, change order logs are indispensable tools. They help track the evolution of the project, providing a clear audit trail of decisions made and their impact on the budget, timeline, and resources. By documenting change orders, project managers can maintain transparency and accountability, ensuring everyone is informed and aligned with the project's current status.

Additionally, change order logs are critical for risk management. They enable project managers to assess the potential impact of changes on the project's overall success, allowing for proactive adjustments and mitigation strategies. This helps prevent scope creep, budget overruns, and schedule delays, safeguarding the project's profitability and timely completion.

In essence, change order logs are more than just administrative documents; they are strategic assets that empower project managers to navigate the complexities of project execution, ensuring smooth sailing even in the face of unexpected changes. By embracing change order logs as an integral part of their toolkit, project managers can enhance communication, mitigate risks, and ultimately steer their projects towards triumphant outcomes.

## *Insight Story: The Ghosting General Contractor*

My phone vibrated insistently on the desk, the screen flashing "John." A knot tightened in my stomach as I answered.

"Hey, John. What's going on?"

His voice crackled with tension. "Can you swing by the high school site? Need a fresh pair of eyes on something."

An hour later, I found John pacing amidst the rising steel beams, his brow furrowed with worry.

"What's the problem, John?" I inquired, taking in the sprawling construction site.

"The GC's been ghosting me," he muttered, kicking a loose pebble. "Months of change orders, over half a million bucks outstanding, and he won't even return my calls."

I let out a low whistle. "Half a million? That's serious. Have you alerted the executive team?"

With a stubborn glint in his eyes, John shook his head. "Nah, I've dealt with this kind of thing before. Usually, I can smooth things over directly with the GC."

"And in those situations, were you able to recover the full payment due?" I probed gently.

"Well. Not exactly," he admitted, looking away. "There's always some compromise involved, right?"

"John," I said, my voice hardening, "trying to resolve open change orders at the end of a project is like playing Russian roulette with your profit margin. You're leaving money on the table."

"But I've emailed him, sent calendar invites," John protested. "He just ignores them."

"E-mails are easy to ignore," I countered. "You need to get him on the phone. Tell him that your company conducted an audit and determined that these unresolved change orders were a significant financial risk. Say your contracts manager is demanding action and threatening to escalate the issue to the executive level if it's not resolved immediately."

John's face paled. "That means involving the CEO. Maybe even lawyers?"

"Exactly," I affirmed. "The GC needs a wake-up call. He needs to understand the gravity of the situation."

A few days passed. Then, John's name flashed on my phone again. This time, his voice boomed with newfound confidence.

"He's agreed to a meeting!" John exclaimed. "Said he wants to avoid any 'unnecessary complications' with the higher-ups."

The negotiation was tense, but John managed to secure a significant portion of the outstanding payments for change orders. It wasn't the full half-million, but it was enough to satisfy the company's leadership.

"Thanks for the advice," John said later, grinning. "Sometimes, you gotta rattle a few cages to get things moving."

"Just remember, John," I cautioned, "this shouldn't be your default strategy. Addressing issues early is always the best way to avoid these high-pressure situations. Send the GC your change order log each month and press to get it cleared."

He nodded, the lesson sinking in. John's experience at the high school site served as a powerful reminder: sometimes, the most effective negotiations are the ones you threaten to have, not the ones you actually end up having.

## Risk Register

A project risk register is a living document that serves as a central repository for identifying, analyzing, and managing potential risks that could impact a project's success. It's a critical tool for proactive project management, enabling teams to anticipate and mitigate potential threats before they become major issues[17].

The importance of a risk register lies in its ability to:

1. Enhance Project Visibility: By documenting potential risks, teams gain a clearer understanding of the project landscape and the challenges they might face.

2. Facilitate Proactive Planning: With identified risks, project managers can develop mitigation strategies and contingency plans to address potential problems before they escalate.

3. Improve Decision-making: A risk register provides valuable information for making informed decisions, allowing teams to weigh the potential impact and likelihood of risks.

4. Foster Collaboration: The risk register serves as a communication tool, ensuring all stakeholders are aware of potential risks and the actions being taken to manage them.

---

17  Hafnidar A. Rani et al., "Risk Management Planning by Risk Register in Building Construction Project," *IOP Conference Series: Earth and Environmental Science* 1303, no. 1 (2024), https://doi.org/10.1088/1755-1315/1303/1/012034.

5. Protect Project Objectives: By proactively addressing risks, teams can minimize the likelihood of delays, cost overruns, and other negative impacts on project goals.

A typical risk register includes information such as:

- Risk Description: A clear and concise explanation of the potential risk.
- Impact Assessment: The risk's potential consequences if it occurs.
- Probability Assessment: The likelihood of a risk occurring.
- Risk Owner: The individual or team responsible for managing the risk.
- Mitigation Strategy: Actions to be taken to reduce the risk's probability or impact.
- Contingency Plan: Steps to be taken if the risk arises despite mitigation efforts.

By regularly updating and reviewing the risk register, project teams can stay ahead of potential threats and ensure the project stays on track for success.

## Lessons Learned

A lessons learned log is a vital tool in a project manager's arsenal. It serves as a repository of knowledge gained from past project experiences, both successes and failures. This log can be used to identify patterns, anticipate potential pitfalls, and refine strategies for future projects. By documenting lessons learned, project managers can foster a culture of continuous improvement within their teams and organizations.

Maintaining a comprehensive lessons learned log involves recording not only the challenges encountered but also the solutions implemented, along with their effectiveness. This information can be invaluable for future PMs, providing them with a roadmap to navigate similar obstacles and make more informed decisions. It's also important to regularly review and update the log to ensure its relevance and usefulness.

Continuing training is equally important for future PMs. The project management landscape is constantly evolving, with new methodologies, technologies, and best practices emerging regularly. Engaging in ongoing professional development activities such as workshops, webinars, and certifications can help PMs stay abreast of these changes and enhance their skills.

By combining a robust lessons learned log with continuous training, organizations can create a learning environment that empowers PMs to grow and develop, ultimately leading to more successful project outcomes. This approach not only benefits individual PMs but also contributes to the overall knowledge base and expertise of the organization, fostering a culture of innovation and excellence.

## Conclusion

In the intricate world of project management, documentation emerges as an indispensable ally, safeguarding your endeavors and paving the way for triumph. It's not merely about archiving information; it's about creating a living testament to your project's journey, a treasure trove of insights that can illuminate the path to success. From agendas and meeting minutes to change order logs and risk registers, each document plays a pivotal role in fostering transparency, accountability, and effective communication. Remember, the power of documentation lies not just in its creation but in its strategic utilization.

In the next chapter, we will explore the art of crafting impactful notice letters and e-mails, essential tools for effective claims management. Having established the significance of notices, we now delve into the components of a notice letter and other correspondence. Letters offer a tangible, permanent record and are particularly valuable when conveying critical information. They serve as a testament to your professionalism and commitment to clear communication.

# 7

# CLAIMS MANAGEMENT: DRAFTING NOTICE LETTERS AND ELECTRONIC MAIL

Previous chapters have firmly established the significance of notices in project management. Now, we shift our focus to the practical aspects of crafting these crucial communications. In this chapter, we will delve into the specific components that make up a well-structured notice letter and other forms of correspondence. We will explore the nuances of language, formatting, and delivery methods, providing you with the tools to communicate effectively and professionally in any project scenario.

Letters offer a tangible, permanent record and are particularly valuable when conveying critical information.

Carefully collect and assimilate information.

1. Think through the message you want to say.
2. Tailor your message to a specific individual or about an event.
3. Avoid misunderstandings.

## How to Write an Effective Letter

Project managers are trained in the art of managing projects, and most are exceptionally good at their jobs. However, over the years, I have found that drafting formal letters is one area that needs improvement. I'm not talking about letters filled with legalese; instead, I am referring to letters often required by your contract. You need not draft a letter that sounds like a lawyer wrote it. However, keep in mind that it may be read aloud in court.

Whatever approach you take, please keep it factual, professional, simple, clear, and concise! You are judged on your ability to communicate well. The letters you write directly reflect your skills, knowledge, and abilities. You must accurately provide the appropriate content and structure to ensure your message is understood in its interpretation. However, do not second guess yourself; send e-mails or letters when the situation warrants it. If whatever you write gets lost in its interpretation, let the lawyers argue it out in court.

## Parts of a Notice Letter

As we work through this chapter, I assume your letter has a preprinted letterhead with your company's name and address at the top or in the footer. If you are not using a preprinted letterhead, include your address (e.g., street address, city, and zip code) at the top of the letter. You should not print your name or title here. This information will be included in the letter's closing below your name.

## The Manner of Sending the Letter

As I mentioned, most official letters (e.g., notices, claims) that you are required to send to your customer require specific methods for delivery. Review the contract's relevant clause to determine the requirements for your letter. For instance, the notice clause may require you to send it by courier service. Start your letter out with the following:

## Sent by e-mail and Courier Service

If the notice clause requires you to send it by another method, note it here. I often include the statement "Sent by e-mail." Before sending any official letter, let the other party know they should expect it by sending them an e-mail or phone call. Don't ever blindside the other party! Since time is of the essence, you can get the information through e-mail to your customer quickly and before the courier service can deliver it. Whatever the process for delivery, document the tracking number, delivery time, and date and attach it to the letter.

### *Date*

Including the correct date in your letter is important. However, this is one area that requires correction on many letters. The project manager may fill it out manually once, and the date still needs to be updated after several revisions. Please consider using the date and time function. Once you select the "insert the date function," you should select "update automatically." The letter's date will automatically be updated with each revision.

What date format should you use for letters? In the US, use the format "June 11, 2025." One of my biggest pet peeves is seeing letters with the date "06/11/2025." Is there anything wrong with using this approach? No, it's just a personal preference. Place the month, year, and day about 2 inches above the top of the page. You can either right-justify or tab to the center and type the date.

### *Inside Address*

When drafting notice letters, you must review the contract's notice clause to determine the names and addresses of the recipients. What if they aren't included? In that case, use the address in the contract's introduction section and the name of the person signing the contract. You may also need to address the letter to one or more individuals. Consider using the appropriate pronoun (if you know it) when addressing someone. When you address someone in some correspondence, use contractions (e.g., Mrs., Ms., or Mr.). If you're unsure about the preferred way to address a woman, you can use Ms. If you think the person to whom you are writing might be a doctor or have another title, then use that title.

### Subject Line

The subject line lets the reader know what your letter is about immediately. There are a few standard methods to distinguish the subject line from the body of the letter:

- Use "Subject: . . . " or "Re: . . ."
- Type the subject in capital letters and bold the text.

Example:

SUBJECT:NOTICE OF DELAY IN RECEIPT OF DRAWINGS

Salutation

Use the same name as the inside address, including the personal title. For example:

Dear Dr. Lewis:

Leave one line blank after the salutation.

If you don't know a reader's gender, use a nonsexist salutation, such as their job title, followed by the receiver's name. If you can't determine gender, using the full name in a salutation is also acceptable. For example:

Dear Logan Johnson:

## The Body of the Letter

It is acceptable to leave a single space in block and modified block formats and to justify each paragraph within the letter's body. You can leave a blank space between each paragraph. In the first paragraph, consider a friendly opening and a statement about the main points. The following paragraph should justify the main point's importance. Next, add background information and supporting details to the justification. In the closing paragraph, reiterate the purpose of the letter and, in some cases, request action.

That's how I like my letters. Again, this is a personal preference. If you are unfamiliar with the following terms or how to set up the template, use the search box in Microsoft Word.

- Font: Times 11
- Line Spacing: Exact, 15
- Paragraph Spacing: 6 pt for the body of the letter
- Alignment: Justified

What does a paragraph look like in a letter?

> This letter serves as a formal request for dispute resolution. We would like to schedule a meeting between our company's executives, who can make binding decisions, within thirty (30) calendar days of this letter. Please provide the name(s) of your executives that will attend the meeting, a suggested location for the meeting, dates and times, and an attendees list. Once we receive this information and finalize the meeting, we will provide an agenda and attendees list.

This approach gives our letter "curb appeal" (for a lack of better words) and makes it easier for the reader to absorb the letter's message and content.

## Closing

You should capitalize the first word only (e.g., Thank you, Best wishes, or Regards) and leave enough room under it for your signature.

### *Carbon Copy (or Courtesy Copy)*

Insert cc: and copy any required individuals. Your contract may require you to send notification letters to a legal firm or company.

*Enclosures*

If you have referenced any documents, listing them in your letter helps clarify the information you are presenting. A basic rule of thumb is that if you refer to it in your letter, it should be referenced as an enclosure and physically attached to the letter.

    Encl.:    Engineer's Report

                 Project Schedule

                 As-builts

If you have Microsoft Office, the software's Letter Wizard may be used to eliminate some of the guesswork and manual work in formatting notice letters. I will include several examples of notice letters and other correspondence for you to understand how I do it throughout this guidebook. You can also find a lot of templates and resources on the Internet. Use what you have available!

## Navigating Authority in Project Management

Misunderstandings about authority can lead to costly disputes and unpaid work. It's a common scenario in project management: a customer's representative, like an engineer, instructs you to make changes. You get verbal approval, do the work, and then—surprise!—your change order gets rejected. Why? Because the engineer didn't have the authority to authorize those changes in the first place.

Imagine this: You're deep into a project when the customer's engineer requests a major modification. You submit a proposal, get the green light verbally, and proceed with the work. But when you submit your invoice, the customer's project manager slams on the brakes, stating the engineer wasn't authorized to approve the changes. Upon reviewing your contract, you discover a clause like this:

    **Authorized Signatures**: Any modifications to this Agreement must be made through a Change Order and signed by a vice-president or higher-ranking corporate officer of Customer.

Oops. Now what?

## Understanding Authority: The Key to Avoiding Costly Mistakes

This scenario highlights the importance of understanding the different types of authority that individuals within an organization may hold. There are two primary types:

1. **Express Authority:** This is the authority explicitly granted to an individual, either in writing (like in a contract or job description) or verbally by their employer. It's black and white, leaving no room for interpretation.

2. **Implied Authority**: This authority isn't spelled out but is inferred from the person's position or actions. For example, a project manager might have implied authority to approve minor changes within a certain budget, even if the contract doesn't explicitly state it.

The distinction between express and implied authority is crucial. A customer's representative might be knowledgeable and experienced, but that doesn't automatically mean they have the power to bind the company contractually. Failing to recognize this can lead to significant financial losses, project delays, and damaged relationships.

## Protect Yourself: Verify Authority Before You Proceed

To avoid getting burned, always verify the authority of the person requesting changes before you start any work. Ask for written confirmation of their authority, especially for major modifications. If the contract specifies authorized signatories, make sure any change orders are signed by those individuals.

By being proactive and understanding the nuances of authority, you can protect yourself from potential disputes and ensure your projects run smoothly.

In the following sections, we'll dive deeper into this topic, exploring different types of authority clauses, strategies for verifying authority, and tactics for navigating situations where authority is unclear.

## Miscommunication

It's common knowledge that e-mail encourages poor communication and makes it too easy to react negatively. It often lacks context, and it's impersonal. As we read it, we can't observe the expression on someone's face or the reflection in their voice, and this may lead to miscommunication or the message becoming distorted. A few years ago, I read a book suggesting we should smile or laugh as we write because we use words or convey the message positively. Maybe or not. I'm not in that camp, but words do matter, and how you structure your message can affect the way the reader interprets your message. To avoid conveying a thoughtless message, you should make sure that your message is clear and concise (and be aware of your communication skills).

## Best Practices for Managing Change Orders

In the world of contracts, managing change orders effectively is crucial for protecting your company's interests and avoiding unnecessary disputes. Here are some best practices to follow:

1. **Create a Risk Register:** The risk register is a cornerstone for effective change order management. By systematically identifying, assessing, and prioritizing potential project risks, it empowers project managers to proactively develop mitigation strategies. This foresight minimizes the likelihood and impact of unexpected challenges, ensuring that change orders are handled efficiently while safeguarding project scope, budget, and timeline.

2. **Create an Issue Log**: While change orders often result from multiple complex issues that impact project timelines and budgets, proactive issue management can prevent these problems from escalating into formal

change requests. Project managers should implement a detailed log to track issues and address them early and often.

3. **Create a Change Order Log**: A project's change order log is a crucial document that meticulously records all modifications to the project's scope, schedule, and budget. It serves as a cornerstone for tracking changes, fostering transparency and accountability among stakeholders, and empowering project managers to maintain control over the project's trajectory. By providing a detailed record of each change order, the log facilitates effective communication, aids in dispute resolution, and supports comprehensive project evaluation and auditing. It's crucial that project managers address and resolve open change orders promptly and avoid deferring negotiations to the end of the project.

4. **Know Your Contract:** Thoroughly review your contract to identify the individuals specifically authorized to direct changes. Look for clauses titled "Authorized Representatives" or "Change Order Procedures." If the contract is silent on this matter, formally request a list of authorized individuals from the other party.

5. **Verify Express Authority**: Remember that express authority is typically granted through a written document, such as a contract or power of attorney. Before acting on any change requests, confirm that the person making the request has express authority to do so. Ask for written confirmation if needed.

6. **Be Cautious of Implied Authority**: Implied authority can be trickier to identify. It arises when someone's words, actions, or position suggest they have the authority to act on behalf of their company, even if it's not explicitly stated. While a project manager might seem like the go-to person for change requests, don't assume they have the authority to bind the company without verifying it first.

7. **Document Everything:** Always get written confirmation for any changes, even if they seem minor. This could be in the form of a formal change order, a written directive, or even an email. This documentation serves as proof of agreement and protects both parties from misunderstandings down the line.

8. **Protect Your Interests**: If you're unsure whether someone has the authority to authorize changes, don't hesitate to ask for clarification. It's better to be safe than sorry. Remember, your primary responsibility is to protect your company's interests, and that means ensuring that any changes are made in accordance with the contract.

Let's revisit the scenario we discussed earlier. If a project manager—who isn't explicitly listed as an authorized representative—directs you to make changes, what steps should you take? First, politely but firmly request written confirmation of their authority to approve the changes. If they are unable to provide this, escalate the issue to a higher-ranking official within the company.

Remember, a few extra steps now can save you from a world of trouble later. By following these best practices, you'll be well-equipped to navigate the complexities of change orders and ensure your projects stay on track and within budget.

## *Insight Story: Where is the Scope Creep?*

A few years ago, I received a call from John. He was juggling a major construction project and a team of eager junior engineers. He was clearly frustrated. "I'm dealing with major scope creep on this project," he confessed, "and I need your help figuring out where it all went wrong. The client's PM just denied my change order request."

I asked John to gather his project team in the conference room, where I could assess the situation firsthand. As everyone settled in, I began, "Thanks for meeting with me on short notice. Let's talk about the equipment we're developing for the research facility."

I scanned the room, gauging reactions. "Have the deliverables changed since the initial proposal?"

A brief silence hung in the air before a young engineer named Paul spoke up, "Yes, they've changed quite a bit since we started." Others nodded in agreement.

"How so?" I asked, leaning forward.

Paul explained how he'd been meeting regularly with the client's engineer, who'd requested numerous modifications to the equipment, requiring additional design hours and components. "I kept providing quotes, and he always said they were approved," Paul added, pulling out his site journal as evidence.

The room fell silent again. I reassured Paul, "We're not here to blame anyone. We're just trying to understand how the scope changed. Was the client's project manager aware of these modifications?"

Paul shook his head. "I don't think so. The engineer acted like he had the authority to approve them."

I thanked the team and asked them to return to their work. Then I turned to John, who remained seated. It was clear that Paul felt terrible for relying on the engineer's verbal approvals, but he also acknowledged he should have kept John informed.

"John," I said, "I have to be honest. It's unlikely you'll recover all the costs for these change orders. I've seen similar situations play out in both directions. Sometimes the client agrees to partial payment, other times it leads to a legal battle."

John's shoulders slumped. "I know, it's my fault. I should have established clear guidelines with the team at the start of the project." He paused, then continued, "It's easy to see mistakes in hindsight. I didn't communicate our scope or contract terms effectively. How can I hold Paul accountable if I didn't explain our change management process?"

"You're right," I agreed. "Let's treat this as a learning experience for everyone. You and your team have gained valuable insights from this situation."

John visibly relaxed. "I'm going to revisit our project plan and meet with the team this week," he said, a renewed sense of purpose in his voice. "Would you be willing to stop by and discuss the contract terms with them?"

"Absolutely," I replied. "Just let me know when."

This incident highlighted the critical importance of clear communication, thorough documentation, and a shared understanding of the contract from the very beginning. By learning from these mistakes, John and his team were able to course-correct and prevent similar issues from arising in the future.

## Communication Skills that Aren't Taught but Learned

The last twenty years have given us new ways to communicate and transfer massive amounts of information. Cell phones, text messaging, videoconferencing, and e-mail have revolutionized how we communicate. This technology has been mostly positive and helps us to manage our work effectively. For instance, as a tool, e-mail has simplified our jobs by allowing us to communicate with people anywhere in the world at the click of a mouse. Features, such as an email contact list, allow us to send an email instantly to a specific individual or a large group of people. More importantly, it provides us with a written record. Yet, with all the positive attributes of e-mail, it presents several problems. Let's discuss some of these problems and consider solutions.

### *Insight Story: The Message in the e-Mail*

John left his house early in the morning. He noted it was bright, sunny, and unseasonably warm when he stepped outside. He enjoyed being in North Carolina but found it could be sunny one moment and torrential downpours the next. The weather followed the coast up from South Carolina. John decided today would be a great day to ride his bike to work and clear his mind. Twenty minutes later, he made it to the site trailer. Once settled in at his office, he heard his assistant project manager and safety manager making fun of his vest and helmet.

"Doesn't he look cute? I'm sure his wife dressed him today," they said.

"Whatever. At least I'll outlive the both of you," John shouted.

John decided he couldn't put off a problem he was having with a customer any longer. He picked up the phone and hit the speed dial button for my number.

"What's up, John?" I asked.

"Do you want an excuse to get out of the office today?" he asked.

"Absolutely! I am always looking for an excuse," I said.

"Well, I need your help. I'll buy lunch today if you get here early," John offered.

While driving to the project site, I noticed the morning walkers on the sidewalks.

"I love it when it starts warming up," I thought.

When I arrived, John met me at the front door. I noticed he was carrying a file. He handed me a hard hat and safety vest and gestured for us to walk the project site.

"We are about to wrap things up around here," he began, "and I'm having a problem clearing my change order log. My program manager is on my ass now, and I don't know what to do."

We walked through the site and into the gravel parking lot.

"I think it's about lunchtime," John said.

I turned to him. "John, it's only 11 o'clock."

"Is that a problem?" he asked.

"No, it's never a problem. I can eat all day long," I said, chuckling.

John pointed toward a Mexican food truck.

"Best fajitas in town," John said.

We sat at a picnic table with our order, and John talked while building a fajita.

"I had a phone call with my customer's project manager this morning, and he informed me that he is denying payment for all the open change orders I have on the project," John said. "I also just received this e-mail and want you to look at it."

John opened the file he had been carrying and handed me a few sheets of paper with e-mail correspondence.

As I thumbed through, I asked, "How much money are we talking about?"

"It's about $400,000 now, and I have a few change orders I am working on," John said.

"That's a lot of money," I said, surprised.

"All these change orders were approved and signed by my customer's project manager," John said.

John then handed me the change order log. As we ate, we reviewed each line item and discussed its scope and status.

"John, he didn't give you any reason other than he wasn't paying you?" I asked.

"No, just that he wasn't going to pay me," John said, shaking his head and taking another bite.

"Send me the contract and all the signed change orders when we get back to the trailer. Do you know if you have anything else in writing that relates to the change orders?" I asked.

He replied, "I have some meeting minutes from a few months back where we discussed the unpaid change orders."

"Okay, send those to me as well," I requested.

We finished our lunch and walked back to the trailer. The conversation shifted from business to the boat John was planning to purchase.

"It's not much, but it's what my wife wanted. I want something I can dock in Wrightsville and spend the night in," John said.

"Man, that sounds amazing. I'm jealous. But call me, and I'll be happy to let you spend your money on gas chauffeuring me around," I said, laughing.

John laughed, and we made it back to the trailer. I jumped in my car and drove back to the office. When I arrived, I found an e-mail from John with the contract. Before opening the contract, I read the chain of e-mails. In the first e-mail from six months ago, John asked the customer about payment for the last change orders. The second and third e-mails were follow-ups to the original e-mail. The customer's project manager insisted that the payments were being processed in response to John's follow-up e-mails. In the latest e-mail exchange, the customer's project manager stated:

> "I have reviewed your request for payment of the change orders, and I have denied them all. I consider this matter closed."

I looked but didn't find any more e-mail exchanges between John and his customer's project manager, but there were two exchanges between his customer's project manager and his executive boss, Williams Biggs. Here is the exchange:

Customer's Project Manager to His Executive Boss:

> "I needed them to complete a lot of additional work outside their original scope. I asked them to give me quotes for doing the extra work, and we agreed on the pricing. I approved the work and issued them signed change orders. The change orders are valid, and we need to pay them."

Williams Biggs—Executive Boss to the Customer's Project Manager:

"This project is out of money, and significant cost overruns have occurred. I don't care if their change orders are valid. Don't pay them!"

After reading this exchange, I sat back in my chair and laughed. They just violated rule number one (which was good for us!). The rule is—don't forward any internal e-mails unless you have reviewed them for content! That day, I drafted a lovely demand for payment letter and stop work notice, sent it to John to send out to his customer's project manager, and asked him to copy the executive boss too. Oh, I also included a copy of the e-mail as an enclosure. Here is a copy of the letter:

> SENT BY E-MAIL AND COURIER SERVICE
> December 12, 2025
> My Company, Inc.
> 157 Evens Street
> Morehead City, NC, 28557
>
> Best General Contracting, Inc.
> Attention: Johnny B. Good, PMP
> 111 Atlantic Circle
> Atlantic Beach, NC 28512
>
> SUBJECT: DEMAND FOR PAYMENT OF APPROVED CHANGE ORDERS AND STOP WORK NOTICE
>
> Dear Mr. Good:
>
> This letter serves as a (1) demand for payment letter for previously approved change orders and (2) stop Work notice. As

you are aware, My Company, Inc. ("My Company") and Best General Contracting, Inc. ("BGC") entered enter an agreement dated January 2, 2024 (the "Agreement") for the performance of specific Work and the supply of materials on the Beach Circle project (the "Project").

On July 10, 2025, My Company provided BGC with a change order log (Exhibit A) containing a list of previously approved change orders totaling $405,231.00. In addition, My Company provided copies of the approved change orders (Exhibit B). However, BGC has ignored My Company's repeated requests for payment and failed to provide a valid reason for such delay.

All attempts by My Company to resolve this issue have not been fruitful. Under the terms of our Agreement, My Company will stop Work on the Project on December 18, 2025. Section 5 (b) provides in pertinent part:

In addition to all other remedies available to My Company (which My Company does not waive by the exercise of any rights hereunder), My Company may suspend the delivery of any Products or stop Work if BGC fails to pay the amounts when due and the failure continues for five (5) days following BGC's receipt of notice thereof. BGC may not withhold payment of any undisputed amounts due and payable as a set-off of any claim or dispute with My Company.

BGC has decided to withhold payments for approved change orders without the contractual right to do so. Furthermore, BGC continues to ignore My Company's requests for payment even though it acknowledges that the changes to the scope of Work were authorized and BGC's project manager signed the change orders. In the e-mail (see the attached e-mail exchange dated December 11, 2022, between BGC's project manager and William Biggs), BGC's project manager stated:

"I needed them to complete a lot of additional work outside their original scope. I asked them to give me quotes for doing the extra work, and we agreed on the pricing. I approved the work and issued them signed change orders. The change orders are valid, and we need to pay them."

Unless BGC makes a good-faith effort to resolve this issue in a timely manner, My Company will stop Work and will evaluate its rights and remedies under applicable contract law.

If you have any questions or wish to discuss these matters further and work towards a mutually acceptable resolution, don't hesitate to contact me at (999) 555-1111 or e-mail me at projectmanager@mycompany.com. My Company reserves all rights and remedies in this matter.

Regards,

John Hardy, PMP

My Company, Inc.

cc: Dondi M. Day, Contracts Manager (sent via e-mail)
Williams Biggs, BGC Executive (sent via e-mail)

Encl.: Exhibit A – Change Order Log
Exhibit B – Change Orders
Exhibit C – e-mail Correspondence, dated December 11, 2025

# Commentary

About a week after John sent the letter, he received payment for all the approved change orders. While this story worked in our favor, I must caution you. This is a double-edged sword. Here are the important lessons: (1) You must review any e-mails for content if you forward them, and (2) You must be careful not to include anything that can be viewed as accepting responsibility for anything. Rule 2 applies even if you are to blame. Let the lawyers fight that point in court!

## *Knee-jerk Reactions*

I'm sure there has been a time in your career when you received a text message, letter, or e-mail that made you mad. Your first guttural response would be to scream, followed by the impulse to respond immediately. I would like to ask you a question: how often have you misunderstood the content of the text, letter, or e-mail after you responded? I've learned hard lessons over the years about taking knee-jerk reactions. If I get a text, letter, or e-mail that upsets me, I have learned to put it aside or leave a note and follow up the next day. Once I return to the text, letter, or e-mail, I often find that I interjected my thoughts or feelings into it and reacted to some perceived notion I later found to be wrong. We all do this unintentionally. We all have different worldviews, and our emotions are often tied to those perceptions. With that said, we all must recognize that there is always the possibility of miscommunication and distortion.

> **BEST PRACTICES**
>
> When you receive emotionally charged communication, learn to set it aside. Depending on the urgency or nature of the letter, you can wait to open it for a day or two and then respond to it. You may find you misinterpreted it. All e-mails should be stored in your project file.

## Other Considerations about e-Mail

Over the years, I've discovered that the best teaching tool is to convey lessons learned the hard way through storytelling. When you hear a horrible story (life-changing or career-ending), you may empathize with the other person and take mental note of what not to do. Here is one of those lessons, and it is relatively simple: never open your e-mail program and create a draft e-mail as a placeholder for your message. Why? As you draft your e-mail, your ideas, comments, and thoughts are still unvarnished. Your e-mail may need additional work for your message to be precise.

Let's put this into the proper context. Let's pretend you just received an e-mail from a colleague that upset you. The entire organization was copied in the e-mail; you believe it was filled with misinformation, and you feel personally attacked. You open your Outlook program and start pounding away at your keyboard. You intend to set the record straight. While you are halfway through your response, you realize it is lunchtime. You decide to return to it later. You start closing all your open programs, and you accidentally hit the send button, or worse yet, when you first opened the original e-mail, you hit reply all. You need to ask yourself: Was my message clear? Was it professional? Do you need to start looking for a new job?

I always use Microsoft Word to compose my first communication draft. Consider drafting your response in Word and then leaving it. Come back later that day or the next day. You may be surprised that your response could be more precise or has an unprofessional tone. Once you have it ready to send, please check your spelling, grammar, and punctuation. Consider sending it to a colleague or someone unaware of the situation and asking for a sanity check. It is always wise to have someone do a third-party review.

## Other Considerations about Letters

When drafting letters, recognize that people may perceive that you are attacking them personally. For example, you might have a subcontractor performing poorly for reasons beyond their control, and they may even be waiting for information from you. You believe that, by sending them a notice letter, which may be required under your contract, you insert the project manager's name instead of neutralizing the letter by writing in the third person ("Subcontractor"). This may leave the project manager feeling like you are attacking them personally, which can have a negative impact on the project and relationship. Here are some final considerations and thoughts.

- You can't control the conditions under which an individual reads your message or how they will interpret and react to it. It's always best to meet face-to-face to discuss problems, but not when you are emotionally charged.
- Under no circumstances should you communicate negative emotions through a text, e-mail, or letter. If something needs to be discussed, schedule a time to meet with that person, but only after you have had time to reflect on what you want to say. A coffee shop is a great place for this type of meeting!
- Remember, once something is written down and sent, it becomes permanent. It may also be open to discovery in litigation!

## Summary

The art of crafting impactful notices and e-mails is a cornerstone of effective claims management. By mastering the nuances of language, formatting, and delivery methods, you can ensure that your communications are clear, concise, and professional. Remember, the key is to be proactive, timely, and thorough in your documentation. By establishing a robust written record and fostering open communication channels, you can mitigate risks, resolve disputes efficiently, and protect your company's interests.

In the following chapter, we'll delve into the art of developing your subcontracting skills. We'll explore strategies for effective subcontract negotiation, emphasizing the importance of preparation, communication, and collaboration. We'll also discuss the significance of post-award activities, such as project kick-off meetings and ongoing subcontract administration, in ensuring project success and mitigating potential risks. By the end of this chapter, you'll be equipped with the knowledge and tools to navigate the complexities of subcontract management and build stronger, more successful relationships with your clients and partners.

# 8

# PROJECT-SPECIFIC SUBCONTRACT MANAGEMENT

The success of any project hinges on the performance of those involved. When specialized tasks arise that are beyond your team's expertise or budget, subcontractors become essential partners. But choosing the right subcontractor is like finding the perfect puzzle piece – it needs to fit seamlessly into your project's vision. Their skills, reliability, and shared goals can make all the difference between a project that soars and one that stumbles.

In this chapter, we'll explore the ins and outs of managing subcontractors on your projects. We'll break down the process of finding the right fit, from checking their qualifications to ensuring their financial stability. We'll also emphasize the importance of clear communication, teamwork, and proactive risk management. By the end of this chapter, you'll be equipped to navigate the world of subcontractors, ensuring they contribute to your project's success.

## Vetting Your Subcontractors

Picking the right subcontractor is crucial. The wrong choice can lead to delays, budget blowouts, and even legal headaches. So, how do you find the perfect match? It starts with thorough research and careful evaluation.

Before you sign on the dotted line, dig deep into the subcontractor's background. Check their references, look into their safety record, and make sure they're financially sound. Don't be afraid to ask around in the industry or even request resumes of their key people.

There are companies that offer pre-qualification services, but you can also find free resources and checklists online. The key is to start this process early, so you're not rushed into a decision you might regret.

And remember, the lowest bid isn't always the best. Some subcontractors might try to win the job with a low price, only to make up for it later with change orders and claims. Do your homework and make sure you're getting a reliable partner, not just a cheap one.

Even if you've worked with a subcontractor before, don't skip the due diligence for new projects. Things change, and you need to make sure they're still a good fit. Also, keep an eye on your client's financial health and how they handle change orders. These factors can also impact your project.

Finally, create a clear process for evaluating subcontractors and document everything. Keep track of your observations, both good and bad. This will help you make informed decisions and protect your company if any issues arise down the line.

## Recommendations

The following recommendations to guide you in making informed decisions and building strong, mutually beneficial relationships with your subcontractors:

1. Establish Evaluation Criteria: Define clear and specific criteria for evaluating subcontractors, including experience, qualifications, financial stability, safety record, past performance, and references.

2. Request for Information (RFI): Issue an RFI to gather initial information from potential subcontractors, including their capabilities, experience, and interest in the project.

3. Request for Proposal (RFP): Develop a detailed RFP outlining the project scope, requirements, and evaluation criteria. Invite qualified subcontractors to submit proposals based on the RFP.
4. Proposal Review: Carefully review the proposals received, comparing them against the established evaluation criteria. Assess technical qualifications, proposed solutions, pricing, and overall value proposition.
5. Reference Checks: Subcontractors provide contact references to confirm their past performance, reliability, and professionalism. If necessary, consider conducting further background checks, including litigation searches.
6. Interviews: Conduct interviews with shortlisted subcontractors to discuss their qualifications, experience, approach to the project, and ability to meet your specific requirements.
7. Financial Assessment: Evaluate the subcontractor's financial stability by reviewing their financial statements, credit reports, and bonding capacity. Ensure they have the financial resources to complete the project successfully.
8. Site Visits (Optional): If feasible, visit previous projects completed by the subcontractor to assess the quality of their work, safety practices, and overall professionalism.
9. Risk Assessment: Identify potential risks associated with each subcontractor, such as their experience with similar projects, capacity constraints, or potential conflicts of interest.
10. Decision and Award: Based on the evaluation results, select the subcontractor that best meets your project's needs and offers the most value. Ensure the contract clearly outlines the scope of work, payment terms, and performance expectations.

## Insight Story: I've Had It. Let's Terminate Them Today!

In the coastal town, the sun beat down on John as he prepared for his new project. "Office with a view, here I come," he muttered, eyeing the prime spot in front of the town hall the town had allocated for his site trailer. With the boardwalk bustling in the distance, he meticulously positioned the trailer to capture the perfect vista. Excitement coursed through him; this was his project to manage, and initially, it seemed straightforward. But John, a seasoned veteran, knew Murphy's Law was always lurking.

And so it was, as my phone buzzed early one morning with John on the other end. "I've had it with these guys!" he barked; his usually calm demeanor replaced with raw frustration. It was the subcontractor's performance that was abysmal.

"Hold on, John," I said, trying to temper his anger. "Let's not jump to termination just yet. We need to understand the issues fully, explore all our options, and discuss this with the executive team."

"I'm on my way," he replied, the tension palpable in his voice.

John arrived at my office; his agitation barely contained. "What's going on?" I asked, motioning him to a seat.

He launched into a detailed explanation of the project and the subcontractor's failings. "I need to see the contract and any project documentation you have," I said. "Anything to bring me up to speed."

John smirked. "Seems like I'm getting better at anticipating your needs," he said, a touch of humor returning to his voice. "I've documented everything in my site journal, dates, times, conversations, the works. Before leaving the trailer, I e-mailed you a synopsis of the contract and other documents. It's all there."

"Excellent, I see it," I replied as I was opening the email. "Give me a couple of hours to review everything, and I'll call you."

As John left, I leaned back in my chair, pondering the all too common scenario playing out. The construction industry was cutthroat, especially in the current economic climate. Companies were bidding low, sometimes barely breaking even, just to keep their crews employed. Unexpected project issues could cripple small businesses, resulting in change orders and claims that strained finances to the breaking point.

My mind raced, formulating the next steps and necessary precautions to avoid wrongful termination liabilities. Questions filled my notes: Do we have a vetted subcontractor ready to step in? What are the potential costs and delays? What other risks are we facing? Have we discussed this with the executive team and John's client?

The thought of terminating a subcontractor was daunting. It required solid justification and a thorough examination of all angles, including potential personality clashes or other underlying issues.

Opening John's meticulously organized synopsis, I was impressed. His proactive approach and attention to detail were evident, making my job easier. It amused me that he thought he had my expectations figured out. Perhaps it was time to shake things up a bit. With a renewed focus, I delved into the synopsis, ready to unravel the intricacies of the problem at hand.

## SYNOPSIS

Project's Name: Crystal Shores Water Meter Project

Location: Town of Crystal Shores ("Town")

Project Manager: John Hardy, PMP

Subcontractor: Mark Stewart & Son's Mechanical Contracting Company

Type of Services: Installation Subcontractor

Project Start Date: February 2, 2025

Substantial Completion Date: February 2, 2026 (365 Calendar Days)

On February 2, 2025, we were awarded a contract (Attachment 1) to install 4,354 water meters and new water main lines. Our work included removing the existing water meters and installing new water mains in recently annexed locations. The substantial completion date was February 2, 2026, or 365 days from the contract award. The contract contains liquidated damages of $1,000 per day for each day the project is late. There is no cap on the liquidated damages.

Before we signed the contract with the Town, we received a limited notice (Attachment 5) to select subcontractors and purchase the water meters.

We received four bids from local subcontractors to install the water meters during the bidding process. Most subcontractors were on the Town's approved vendor list. Once we received all the bids, we saw a significant disparity in pricing. The highest bid was $55,000 over the lowest bidder's pricing, and the remaining two were in the upper middle of the bid range.

On February 16, 2025, we awarded the subcontract for removing and installing the water meters to Mark Stewart & Son's Mechanical Contracting Company ("Stewart") based on their pricing. We negotiated and signed the subcontract (Attachment 2) with flow-down terms and conditions, specifically the liquidated damages. The scope of work (Attachment 3) required Stewart to complete their scope within 252 business days. It required Stewart to install 172 water meters per week. We estimated the average time to remove one water meter and reinstall a new one was 30 minutes. We also estimated it would take each crew of four people to install 24 water meters daily. Our estimates did not include weekend or holiday work.

We estimated that Stewart would need three crews, one safety supervisor, and one site manager to oversee the installations. We left the means and methods of performing the work up to Stewart.

Before we awarded Stewart the subcontract (while we were waiting for internal reviews and final approval), we issued a notice of intent to award a purchase order (Attachment 4). Later that week, we issued them a limited notice to proceed (Attachment 5), allowing them to hire and mobilize their crews. We were under demanding time constraints and had this conversation with Stewart. We also told them they needed to mobilize quickly to meet the substantial completion date. We anticipated they would immediately mobilize or have their crews on site the day we signed the subcontract.

On March 3, 2025, they mobilized one crew. The period between February 16 and March 3 created a two-week delay. I called Stewart's project manager (Jimmy Johnson) about the delay, and I followed up with an e-mail asking for his reassurance they would make up for the lost time. I am still waiting to hear from him.

On March 4, 2025, I called Stewart's owner, Mark Stewart. He said they are having difficulty finding qualified people, but he assured me they could compensate for the lost time. A few days later, another crew arrived and started working, but they were still down one crew.

On March 15, 2025, I called Mark after reviewing their daily site reports. The reports reflected that they only installed half the meters required to be installed each week. I also expressed my concern that he has only two crews working. Mark blamed the delays (again) on problems finding qualified people. He also said his crews were having problems with the water meter couplings, which had slowed down the progress of their work. I called Mark, and I jotted down our conversation:

"Mark, do you have a few minutes to talk about the Crystal Shore project?" John asked.

"Yes, I have a few minutes," Mark responded.

"Mark, you've been on site for a while. Why haven't you called me sooner about these problems you noted in your daily site reports?" John asked.

"John, my proposal didn't include the additional labor that I need to hire, and it didn't include the couplings and other materials required to install the water meters," Mark said.

"Mark, your scope included removing and reinstalling 4,354 water meters. The Town Manager has noticed problems, and I am getting calls. If we don't get the project back on schedule, I'm afraid we will be assessed liquidated damages. You have the same damages in your subcontract," John said.

"John, you don't have to threaten me. I know we are behind. We need to discuss giving me more money to cover the changes," Mark said.

"What changes?" John asked.

"I will submit a change order request for the couplings, other materials we didn't include in our proposal, and the extra costs related to labor. I expect it to be approved, or I may have to consider pulling my crew off the project," Mark said.

"Mark, if you believe you are entitled to more money, submit the change order request, and I will look at it, but I need you to get more people on the project and get back on schedule," John said.

"I will see what I can do, but I'm not promising anything," Mark said.

"Mark, I spoke with my contracts manager this morning, and he wants me to send you a notice letter. It doesn't change anything, and I will continue to work with you. It's a formality, so when you get it, call me if you have questions," John said.

"Okay," Mark said.

On March 16, 2025, I sent a formal notice letter to Mark (review Attachment 6).

On March 17, 2025, I received a call from the Town Manager, Jake. He said he has been getting calls from the people in the Town complaining of low water pressure or no water.

"John, I'm sending you a list of people with low water pressure or no water now. I took a look at your installation list from last week. The houses where the meters were installed appear to be the same ones experiencing problems. We sometimes get calls about low water pressure after working on the water mains. I checked this morning, and we haven't done any work on those lines in over a year. I sent my guys from our water department over to take a look. You're not going to be happy with what they found. They removed one of the meters where there was no water pressure, and they found that they were clogged with mud and rocks," Jake said.

"Thanks for letting me know. I will go down there today and personally inspect the water meters," John said.

On March 17, 2025, I went to the first house on the list and turned on the outside water valve; there wasn't any water flowing through the valve. I opened the water meter box lid and saw standing water in the pit. Also, the water register was not turning, so I turned off the water line and removed the water meter. There was mud and other debris inside the water meter. Once I removed it, flushed out the mud and debris, and reinstalled it, it appeared to function fine afterward. I'm not sure if the mud and debris damaged the water meter. On the same day, I returned to the office and called Mark. I told him that Jake had called and what I found when I went out to inspect the water meters.

"Mark, are your crews pumping out the standing water in the pit before installing the water meters? Is that correct?" he asked.

"Yes, and I don't appreciate your insinuation that we've done something wrong," Mark said.

"Mark, I am sending you the list I got from Jake. Pick a couple and let's go down together and inspect them today," he said.

"No, I don't have time today. Just send me the list, and I will send my crew back to see if they can figure out the problems," Mark said.

"Okay, I just e-mailed you the list. Please make sure your crews are pumping out the standing water. We will need to schedule a day late next week to inspect the water meters that Jake is saying aren't working right," John said.

Mark became noticeably irate on the phone and told me, "I am pulling my crew off the project unless you approve the change order request."

"What change order request? I still haven't seen it," John said calmly.

"It's on the way now!" Mark replied.

Later that day, I received a change order request for $60,000. It included additional labor, couplings, and materials for installing the water meters and anticipated rework associated with removing the debris from previously installed water meters. Their change order requests (Attachment 7) did not include supporting documentation.

On March 18, 2025, after reviewing their change order request, I responded to Mark (review Attachment 8 – Response to Change Order letter dated March 16, 2025). I found they failed to explain why we should pay the change order request and failed to provide supporting documents outlining how they arrived at their pricing. Furthermore, they claimed the rework for correcting the defectives was additional.

I called Mark and explained, "Mark, I can't effectively evaluate your change order request since there's no supporting documentation. You have indicated things as general line items with a dollar amount, but there isn't a description of the work or materials you are claiming as extra. You need to explain why you think you are owed the money and how you arrived at those dollar amounts. Once you resend the change order request with the supporting documentation, let's schedule some time to meet and review everything."

"I'll get you all that information tomorrow," Mark said.

Between March 19–22, 2025, Stewart's crew did not show up to start their work. I received an e-mail from Mark stating they would remobilize and complete the work once I approved the change order request. In his e-mail, "I provided you with everything you needed to evaluate the change order request yesterday. I expect the approved change order request by the close of business today. If not, we won't return to the site until it's approved."

### *Attachments:*

1. Contract with the Town of Crystal Shores
2. Subcontract with Mark Stewart & Son's Mechanical Contracting Company
3. Exhibit A – Scope of Work

4. Letter of Intent

5. Notice to Proceed

6. Formal Notice Letter

7. Change Order Request

8. Response to Change Order Request

After reading John's synopsis, I called and asked him to come to my office. I needed to ask him a few questions to see if we could get another subcontractor ready to work. Based on Mark's statements, I wasn't sure if we had any other option except to terminate Stewart's subcontract and hire another subcontractor.

"John, are you back in the office?" I asked.

"Just walked in," he replied. "Is now a good time?"

"Absolutely," I said.

"Be right there," John responded, a hint of anticipation in his voice.

A few moments later, John strode into my office and took a seat at the small conference table. I joined him, settling into a chair across from him.

"John," I began, "do you have a replacement subcontractor lined up?"

"Yes," he nodded, his tone assertive. "I have another one ready to go. We might incur some additional costs, but we can absorb them and back-charge Stewart. I've continued paying them, but I haven't approved their latest payment application since they abandoned the site. That should cover the extra expenses. I want to terminate their contract ASAP."

"I understand your urgency," I said, "but I need more time to review everything and consult with our executive team and legal counsel. We can't move forward without fully assessing our options and the potential risks."

"No problem," John replied, leaning back in his chair. "Just let me know what you need from me."

"I appreciate that," I said. "Would you be able to come back in about an hour?"

"Sure thing," John said, rising from his seat with a determined nod.

After John's departure, I reviewed all the documents he provided. Stewart's actions strongly suggest an attempt at extortion. It appears he intentionally underbid, planning to recoup losses through change orders.

Before we proceed with termination, it's crucial to address several key questions, likely to be raised by the executive team:

1. Notice and Corrective Action: Were proper notices issued? Was a corrective action plan requested? Was adequate time provided for rectification?

2. Documentation: Is there comprehensive documentation (photos, videos, drawings, reports, e-mails) of defective work and non-compliance?

3. Performance Bond: Was a performance bond required? Do we possess a valid copy? Can we file a claim?

4. Schedule and Replacement: Will termination impact the project timeline? How significantly? Are qualified replacement subcontractors readily available? Do we have quotes?

5. Cost and Risk Assessment: What percentage of work remains? What's the cost to complete with the current subcontractor versus a replacement? What are the risks associated with each option?

6. Scope Clarity and Communication: Is the scope of work unambiguous? Have we informed our client about the subcontractor's actions?

7. Additional Considerations: What other known and unknown factors might influence our decision?

To address these questions, I began with a thorough review of the scope of work. This document, often overlooked, is crucial for detailing the specifics of performance and can significantly impact project outcomes. A poorly defined scope often leads to increased change orders and claims.

"Project managers that invest less time putting this document together will pay for it in change orders and claims," I thought.

# Exhibit A – Scope of Work

1. **Work Description**. Subcontractor shall exercise reasonable skill and judgment in the performance of the work and shall provide all necessary equipment, material, tools, labor, and supervision ("<u>Work</u>") that are required to replace the existing water meters with new water meters. Specifically, Subcontractor's Work shall consist of but is not limited to, removing the existing water meters, installing new water meters (to be provided by Contractor), and repairing, replacing, or modifying the existing meter boxes and lids. Subcontractor shall complete the Work within 252 business days after the execution of the Subcontract ("<u>Project Schedule</u>").

   In addition to the foregoing, it is further understood and agreed that Subcontractor shall furnish all items completely, including all costs for labor, equipment, and materials, regardless of whether or not they are included in the Contract Documents. Drawings and detailed plans are provided for reference only and are not to be considered all-inclusive of the Contract Documents for the particular items referenced.

   *Section 1 – Work Description*

   The subcontractor must perform the following work:

   1. Remove the existing meters
   2. Reinstall the new meters
   3. Provide all labor, equipment, and materials
   4. Repair, modify, or replace meter box lids as needed
   5. Perform their work within 252 calendar days

   I noted the scope of work contained comprehensive language requiring Stewart to provide all necessary items, explicitly including labor, equipment, and materials, regardless of whether they were specifically listed in the contract documents. This holds Stewart accountable for all costs associated with the water meter installation, implying they should have anticipated and accounted for these expenses. Such all-encompassing language is commonly used to prevent contractors from claiming unforeseen costs.

### *Section 2 – Removal of Existing Water Meters*

The subcontractor must perform the following work:

1. Uninstalling the existing water meters
2. Document the account number, service address, serial number, water meter size, and the final reading from the meter's register

### *Section 3 – Installation of New Water Meters*

The subcontractor must perform the following work:

1. Install 4,354 – 5/8 x 3/4 residential water meters
2. Pump out all water from the meter box before installing the new water meters
3. Ensure a) the water meters are not damaged before or during installation and b) that standard industry installation practices are followed at all times
4. Provide all pipe fittings, couplings, flanged pipe spool pieces, nuts, bolts, washers, gaskets, and all required material for the installation of the water meters
5. Repair any leaks within three (3) feet of the water meter in either direction at their sole expense
6. Repair all leaks and related damage at no additional cost to the Town or Contractor for 180 calendar days after Final Acceptance

7. Immediately notify the Contractor and document any pre-existing conditions (e.g., existing leaks, damaged valves, damaged meter boxes or lids) and take photographs

I noted Section 3 explicitly states that Stewart is responsible for providing all pipe fittings, couplings, flanged pipe spool pieces, nuts, bolts, washers, gaskets, and all necessary materials for water meter installation. This directly contradicts Stewart's claim that supplying couplings wasn't part of their scope.

Additionally, this section mandates that Stewart adhere to standard industry installation practices for new water meters and pump out all water from the meter box prior to installation.

### Section 4 – Corrective Action for Non-Conforming Work

1. If the Work does not conform to the Contract Documents, Contractor shall notify Subcontractor of the non-conformance.
2. If Subcontractor states, or by its actions, indicates it is unable or unwilling to proceed with corrective action in a reasonable time, Contractor may accomplish the required corrective action by the most expeditious means available and back charge Subcontractor for its cost incurred.

After completing my review of the scope of work, I turned my attention to the subcontract, focusing on the notices and termination for default clauses. Notably, Section 4 of the Scope of Work does require us to notify the subcontractor of any non-conformance. Let's examine the specific notice clause within the subcontract for further clarification.

> **Notices**. Any notices required under this Agreement must be in writing and will be considered delivered when sent through mail with prepaid postage, return receipt requested, from the sender to the recipient at the addresses specified below or any

other addresses that may be designated by written notice in the future.

The decision to terminate a subcontractor is never taken lightly. As I sifted through Attachment 6, I noted that John had diligently sent the notice letter by certified mail, attaching a copy of the receipt for our records. His letter was clear, fulfilling our obligation to notify the subcontractor about the delays. However, the gravity of terminating a subcontractor weighed heavily on me. "Is this really the best route to the finish line?" I pondered, urging myself and John to strip any emotion from our decision-making and consider every possible angle.

I scribbled down some thoughts. John's synopsis mentioned Stewart's repeated complaints about struggling to find qualified workers. Rather than cutting ties, what support could we extend to them? Flexibility in this situation could be key. I turned to Stewart's change order request, presented on simple letterhead and listing only basic cost estimates for materials and labor.

Reviewing John's email response to the change order, it was evident he hadn't just rubber-stamped a decision; he had considered Stewart's claim thoroughly. "It's too easy just to send an email; we need a proper system to track these decisions," I mused.

Caught up in my thoughts, I considered the alternatives to outright termination. "Could we actually assist Stewart, perhaps supplement their team, or even partially descope their work instead of terminating them? What about a termination for convenience?" The options were numerous, but none without complications.

I dialed John. "Can you come by? We need to discuss some different strategies," I suggested.

Moments later, John was in my office, settling into the conversation quickly. "We have a few paths. We could bring in additional subcontractors to supplement Stewart's efforts, or we might descope their work, reducing their load in favor of another team," I outlined. "Terminating them for default is an option, but so is for convenience. Each carries risks, though."

John looked concerned. "What risks are we looking at if we supplement their work?" he inquired.

"When subcontractors bid, they assume control over their methods and aren't liable for others' mistakes. If we bring someone else in, who coordinates? Who ensures the work meshes seamlessly?" I explained.

"Could I just reduce their responsibilities and hire someone else for those parts?" Looking for simpler solutions, John asked.

"Descoping could sidestep the need for coordination, yes, but it doesn't solve all problems. You'd still face potential claims for the change order denial and even lost profits," I cautioned.

We both sat in silence, pondering the complexity. "Let's review the contract carefully before making any moves. Can you return later so we can finalize our strategy?" I suggested.

John agreed, and after a brief break to collect our thoughts and review the documentation, we reconvened.

"Should we just send a termination letter and move on?" John asked, clearly frustrated.

"No, that's too rash. We need to consider if Stewart could claim we breached the contract by denying their change order. Have you continued payments? This could complicate a termination," I advised.

John looked resigned but understood. "What's next then?"

"I've drafted a notice of default. It gives Stewart a chance to address the issues. It's tough, John, but sometimes easing off is cheaper than court battles," I said, handing him the letter.

John signed it reluctantly. "I suppose this is just the beginning of a longer conversation about their role in this project," he acknowledged.

"Exactly. We'll meet again tomorrow to see if termination for default is our best move," I confirmed.

As John left, I revisited his synopsis, impressed by his thorough documentation. That night, restless thoughts about our options kept me awake. At dawn, I reviewed the subcontract again, focusing on the termination clauses we might need to invoke. Each project brings its challenges, but navigating them carefully ensures we not only protect our interests but also strive for the most constructive outcomes for all involved.

I jotted down some of my thoughts. In the synopsis, John said Stewart complained several times about needing help finding qualified people to do the work. Instead of terminating their subcontract, what actions can we take to help them? Depending on the circumstances, you might have flexibility. I turned to Stewart's change order request. It was on their letterhead and only included a table with materials and labor cost estimates. I turned to Attachment 8 and found that John sent the following response to Stewart's change order request sent by e-mail (copy of the read receipt attached).

After reading John's letter, I believe John took the time to evaluate Stewart's claim. It's common for a project manager to check a box or handwrite on the change order request form and indicate that it was approved or denied with little or no explanation. I looked through the subcontract exhibits and didn't see we included a change order form.

Some project managers will send an e-mail when approving or denying a change order request. Is this the best approach?

"While it's quick and easy, it's not the right way to document the change order requests and their status," I thought.

I got caught up in my thoughts again. "Remember, the ideal thing is to persuade Stewart to perform. John's letter listed all the right reasons to deny the change order request, but it didn't leave any doors open for Stewart. Could we consider combining the threat of supplementing (i.e., hiring additional subcontractors to work with them), descoping (i.e., removing part of their subcontracted work and hiring other subcontractors), or threatening to terminate them for default? How about taking a wildly different approach? Could we terminate them for convenience?" I thought.

Our hands aren't as tied as we thought. There are additional options, but none are free or painless. I wanted to get John's thoughts on taking a different approach.

I called him and asked, "John, are you free now? I want to discuss some options with you."

"Sure, I'll be there in a minute," John replied.

John walked into my office and sat down. I quickly covered my questions and told him the risks associated with each option.

"John, our options are to supplement Stewart's work using other subcontracts, descoping them, or terminating them. We don't have to terminate them for default, and there's no reason for us not to consider terminating them for convenience. But none of these options are ideal, and each carries potential risk," I said.

I paused for a moment to see John's reaction.

"If we consider supplementing Stewart's work by hiring an additional subcontractor, we need to be prepared for change orders, claims, and disputes," I said.

"Why?" John asked with an incredulous look.

"When a subcontractor prepares a proposal, they assume many things. For instance, they assume they will control their means and methods (i.e., the techniques or procedures they will use to accomplish their work). They also assume they will not be responsible for another subcontractor's work. The glaring question is if we supplement their work, who will be responsible for planning, coordinating, and supervising everyone and ensuring the work is performed correctly?" I asked.

"Can I just descope part of their work and hire someone else?" John asked.

"Oh, now descoping them is a better option than supplementing their work. First, you don't need to ensure they are playing well together; second, it removes the potential for coordination-related claims. It does require you to hire another subcontractor and assign them a portion of the work. You still need to resolve the problems with Stewart. I am also willing to go out on a limb and say you will receive a claim for the change order you denied, as well as for lost profits. You may see them claim much more than that. In this situation, it's difficult to say which way it will go. Stewart may write off everything, and we will never hear from them again," I said.

I paused for a few minutes and thought about the steps we should take before we consider terminating Stewart. I wanted to take a few minutes, review the contract, and collect my thoughts.

"Can you come back in a little while, and we will continue our discussion?" I asked.

John returned an hour later.

"Is this a good time to continue?" John asked.

"Yes, come on in and take a seat," I replied and motioned to the small table.

"Okay, here is the gist of it all. We must ensure we have our bases covered and draft a few more letters," I said.

"Are these letters necessary?" John replied with a puzzled expression.

"Why can't we send a termination letter and get on with it?" John asked.

"Absolutely not! Let's consider these questions. Could Stewart argue that we are in breach of contract by not agreeing to pay their change order? Is this a potential payment dispute between us? Or is this an attempted extortion (for lack of a better word), or is it simply a matter of Stewart failing to live up to their obligations? Have you continued to make payments? If not, what gives you the contractual right to withhold payment? Let's take a look. As you can see, this is a complicated matter peppered with landmines," I said.

"Okay, what should I do?" John asked.

"John, I have prepared a notice of default letter (Attachment 9). This letter will help to show that our decision to terminate Stewart wasn't a knee-jerk reaction to them leaving the site," I said.

John took the letter and read it.

"All it needs is your signature and to send it certified. This letter will give Stewart three days to remobilize and provide you with a recovery plan," I said.

"Okay, we have now arrived at termination for default. Is this our best option? I'm not convinced, but before we discuss that option, we need to address other questions," I said.

"Stewart complained about the additional cost of materials not included in their proposal. Have you reviewed their proposal to see if those materials were included?" I asked.

"The contract says they will provide everything for installing the water meters," John replied.

"Okay, even though the subcontract and their scope of work require them to provide everything under the sun, did you take the time to evaluate their proposal and attempt to resolve it?" I asked.

"I did, but Mark is difficult to work with, and I didn't get the documents I needed. I am still at square one," John said.

I began, "John, you may not like what I am about to say but losing some of your margins to get Stewart to perform is better than the litigation cost you may incur. Remember, two of your goals are to complete the project on time and to make your customer happy."

John motioned acceptance and replied, "I understand. It's not personal, but Stewart's performance directly reflects on me with our executive team."

"John, I understand. You are in a tricky situation, and we must stop the bleeding. Do you believe terminating them for default is our best option?" I asked.

"I do. I want Stewart off this project and bring in another subcontractor that can do the work right!" John exclaimed.

"Okay, I need more time to review the termination for default language and prepare a letter," I said. "Can we meet tomorrow morning?"

He nodded. "Sure, I'll swing by around 9 o'clock."

John got up and left my office, and I continued to read John's synopsis. I stopped for the day and headed home.

That night, I woke up thinking about the subcontractor and the approaches we could take to resolve this problem painlessly. I rolled over and looked at the clock on my nightstand—four a.m. I had a few hours to kill before it was time to jump in the shower. I slowly got out of bed, went to my backpack, and pulled out the subcontract. I quickly looked at it for specific clauses that would help support our position in terminating the subcontractor.

"Most construction contracts and subcontracts contain a termination for default clause that attempts to establish how the parties will end their contractual relationship if things don't go as planned," I thought.

I discovered the termination for default clause and made a brief note at the top of the page. As I read the clause, I remembered discussing it in my last workshop, and I could almost recite its meaning word for word:

This clause allows the non-breaching party to terminate the contract in certain circumstances, such as a breach of specific contractual obligations (i.e., failing to make delivery on time, failing to pay as agreed, one party filing for bankruptcy) by giving written notice.

After teaching the courses a few hundred times, memorizing the slides and specific points I wanted to emphasize was easy.

I highlighted the termination for default clause and looked to see what events were listed:

> **Termination for Default**. The following actions by the Subcontractor shall be considered as a breach of this Subcontract:
>
> (a) Abandonment of the Work by the Subcontractor.
>
> (b) Unnecessary delays in the performance of the Work.
>
> (c) Any violation of any conditions of this Subcontract.
>
> (d) Executing the Work in bad faith or not in accordance with the terms of this Subcontract.
>
> (e) Failure to substantially complete the Work within the specified timeframe.

In the event of such a breach, Contractor may take over and complete the Work, either through another contract or by other means. Subcontractor shall be liable to Contractor for any damages incurred as a result of Contractor completing the Work.

I found this clause relatively straightforward.

"If Stewart abandons the work or refuses to perform (as in this case), we have the right to terminate their subcontract," I thought.

There were a few questions I needed to answer before jumping on that wagon, and I wrote them down in the contract's margins.

Since they essentially walked off the project site and expressly stated that they would not return unless we paid their change order, can we terminate them for anticipatory repudiation? In addition to the rights we may have under the contract terms and conditions, we have the common law right to terminate for a repudiatory breach.

"Stewart's actions demonstrate its intention not to be bound by the subcontract terms (i.e., putting down their tools and walking off the project site or refusing to mobilize to perform the remaining work)," I thought.

"Repudiation will not bring the contract to an end automatically. To terminate the subcontract, we need to affirm the subcontract or accept the breach and terminate it. Was this a repudiatory breach? Are we still required to send a notice of default and notice of termination letters since they walked off the project site?" I pondered.

While I know the answer to this question, I wanted to use it as a learning opportunity. I have found that, when in doubt, send it out. It's better to be proactive and overly cautious in situations like this.

"The subcontract states we must send a written notice of our intention to terminate the subcontract and offer to work with Stewart to develop a corrective action plan. Sending a notice outlining why they are in default and allowing them the time to cure shows you made a good-faith effort to work with them," I thought.

I turned the pages in the subcontract and found the notice and right-to-cure clause:

> **Notice and Right to Cure**. Both parties shall be notified in writing of any breach of contract (excluding non-payment, for which a ten-day notice will be given) and will have a five-day period from receiving the notice to rectify the breach before any remedies specified in this contract are exercised.

As I took notes and highlighted specific words in the clause, I remembered that I loved teaching through stories and roleplaying in my workshops. When we got to the termination for default clause, I would ask the participants to consider the following scenario:

"Let's imagine you work for a company that recently won a large road construction project connecting several major interstates. As of today, you are 65% finished, but you are incurring additional costs for materials you consider outside your scope of work. Furthermore, you can't find people who are not only qualified but willing to work long hours. You have been completing the work without any change orders, but suddenly, your customer notifies you that your contract has been terminated for convenience. To complete the remaining portions of the project, your customer replaces you with one of your competitors at a lower cost," I said.

"In this situation, you probably ask yourself: Is this fair? Can my customer terminate my contract for convenience, and if so, what compensation am I entitled to recover?" I asked.

This scenario would then lead to a discussion over termination for convenience.

"In the context of our subcontractor, while not ideal, terminating for convenience and making Stewart whole may be the best approach," I thought.

I turned to the termination for convenience clause and read:

> **Termination for Convenience**. Contractor may, at any time, upon thirty (30) day notice to Subcontractor terminate this Agreement for Contractor's convenience ("<u>Termination for Convenience</u>"). Upon receipt of a notice to terminate for convenience, Subcontractor shall (i) immediately discontinue such Work, (ii) place no further orders, and (iii) make every reasonable effort to obtain the cancellation of affected subcontracts upon terms satisfactory to Contractor and reasonably mitigate against any costs or losses. In the event of a Contractor's termination for convenience, Contractor shall pay to Subcontractor the following sums: all amounts due and not previously paid to Subcontractor for Work performed through

the date of termination; all costs reasonably incurred and fully documented by Subcontractor in obtaining cancellation of any subcontracts for Work so terminated. Subcontractor shall not be entitled to compensation for Work it has not performed, including any lost or anticipated profits or overhead on such unperformed Work.

I took a shower and headed to work. While driving, I called John to see if we could meet at this site trailer.

"I have a better idea. Let's meet at the coffee shop down the street from the trailer. Great coffee with a view," John said.

"Perfect. See you in 10 minutes," I said.

I pulled up next to the boardwalk that led down to the beach.

"I would love to take the day off, grab my beach chair, and find a spot," I thought.

I heard John's car pull alongside me. He grabbed something from his backseat and tucked it under his arm. Then he stepped out, closed his door, and opened mine with a big smile. We headed over to the coffee shop and found a table out front. The weather was amazing, and the sun felt good on my face. I opened the subcontract and started expressing my thoughts about our options.

"John, there are a few things wrong with terminating Stewart for default. You have the contractual right, but optics come into play and can leave a bad taste in everyone's mouth. Unless you have extraordinary reasons, you shouldn't remove a subcontractor to have the work completed by another subcontractor," I said.

"But I have reasons, and I can't get them to do what we subcontracted them to do," John said.

I shook my head. "John, I am not arguing with you or trying to convince you otherwise, but we must discuss the risks." I kept my tone steady, hoping to calm him. "Let me put it this way. A contract is simply a bargain between the parties. You can agree to anything if it isn't illegal, immoral, or against public policy (among other things). Under the terms of a contract, a party agrees to do or not do something, and the other party must pay for it. The parties entered the *bargain*, expecting to benefit from it. If either party later discovers it's a bad bargain, it cannot use the contract terms to escape from the bad deal. Again, we need to be clear about the optics and ensure it's not a matter of a *bad deal* or attempting to reduce our cost by terminating Stewart and replacing them with another subcontractor. The courts may view this as an act of repudiation, which would entitle Stewart to terminate the subcontract and claim a host of damages or payment for all the labor and materials it provided. Suppose we were to rely on the termination for convenience clause. In that case, it should clearly state we will compensate Stewart for its labor and material costs," I said.

"Aren't they in breach of contract? Wouldn't this entitle us to withhold payment and claim our damages?" John said.

"Yes, it would," I said, nodding. "But when it comes to termination for convenience, we will need to pay them for everything due through the termination date. Let's also consider this point. When a subcontract is terminated (for whatever reason), there may be production equipment, rental equipment, labor hired through employment agencies, and other contracts and subcontracts that must be cancelled or paid. If you terminate a subcontractor for convenience, are they entitled to those costs? Yes, more than likely. Are they entitled to recover lost profits from the incomplete work? Our termination for convenience clause states we will not pay for work not completed or any lost or anticipated profits or overhead on the uncompleted work. It's assumed the profits and overhead would be paid on completed work," I said.

"The clause is silent about the actual and direct costs (demobilization cost) that may result from the termination. The clause should address how you will pay them for (1) their losses (including loss of profit and overhead), (2) the goods and materials ordered, and (3) reasonable demobilization costs. It would be best to add adequate compensation to ensure the clause is not held unenforceable for lack of consideration. So, even if your termination for convenience clause says they are not entitled, they will probably get it. Why? Most things like this usually go into negotiations and settlements. You should consider including additional payment for some of the loss of profit your subcontractor would have received if it completed the project," I said.

"Another crucial point is the warranty. Let's assume we terminated Stewart's subcontract for convenience, but several months later, we found defects in their work or the materials they supplied. Can we call them and ask them to do the repairs? At their costs? Probably not," I said.

"Why is that? We paid them for the work," John said.

"One of the things you should remember is that, in many jurisdictions, once you terminate a subcontractor for convenience and later discover defects in their work, you may be prevented from recovering the costs incurred in repairing the deficient work. Suppose this is reality, and you intend to terminate a subcontractor for convenience. In that case, you should inspect their work thoroughly for possible deficiencies, provide them with the proper notice, and allow them time to cure the defects before terminating their subcontract and offsetting any repair costs you may incur. If you terminate your subcontractor for default, it will give you the right to recover such costs," I said.

"We need to schedule a meeting with the executive team," I said.

"Do you want me to schedule the meeting?" John asked.

"Yes, let's try to meet with them today," I said.

We left the coffee shop and headed to the office. John scheduled the meeting with the executive team in the large conference room. We went in together and sat down. John gave the executive team a quick overview of the project's status and our options to get the project back on schedule. The team heard the facts and asked me if I was comfortable with terminating Stewart's subcontract.

"Based on my experiences in similar situations, I'm hesitant to agree that this is our best option. It's not that we aren't justified, but once litigation attorneys get involved, things escalate pretty quickly, and we move away from 'we are going to fight this because we are right' and shifts to 'what is a good settlement amount?'" I said.

Jim, our CEO, rocked back and forth in his chair and said, "John, do you believe terminating them is our best option?"

John answered quickly, "I do. I won't be able to get the project back on schedule unless I bring in another subcontractor. It looks like I may be able to limit the liquidated damages if the new subcontractor is on-site next week."

"Okay, let's send the termination letter and get the project back on track," Jim said.

Jim and the executive team members stood up and left the conference room. I spun in my chair and leaned back, looking at John.

"John, there are a few things we need to do. We need to make sure it's sent by certified mail. Once you have a clear understanding of the remaining scope and defects, we need to send Stewart an additional letter outlining all delays and damages. We can send an initial letter and update it periodically throughout the remainder of the project," I said.

"I hope to have the replacement subcontractor on-site today, taking inventory and developing their schedule," John said.

"Once the replacement subcontractor is on-site, you should carefully monitor their work and request detailed documentation of any delays, defective work, and other problems they may encounter. I would prefer they keep detailed records, including how much work the terminated subcontractor completed, work remaining to be completed, and all defects discovered and corrected. These things should be on separate work tickets, describing the defects. Please ask them to include photographs," I said.

I took a moment to consider all the ramifications of this action.

"It's a lot of work, but I would require them to take pictures of every water meter and meter box. The pictures may be worth more than you imagine if we get into litigation with Stewart," I said.

"I have a few forms we can use. When I have a chance to meet with them today, I will require them to complete a separate work ticket for each defective installation. I may have to provide them with a camera and figure out a way to upload all those photographs into the project's file. We have a list of the addresses, and I had Stewart indicate the meter's serial numbers and relate them together. I'll get the latest list of water meters the town has been getting calls about and work off that list first," John said.

"Okay, it sounds like you have a plan. How are you managing this with the town? Is our relationship still good?" I asked. "Since we are ultimately responsible for Stewart's failures, we need to get out in front of this and show them we are taking this seriously."

"I'm already ahead of you. I asked the town manager for the time each week to meet with him and discuss the installations and schedules," John said.

Later that day, I called John and asked him to stop by my office. As John walked into my office, I handed him a couple of pieces of paper.

"John, here is the termination notice." (Attachment 10)

As John read the letter, his body language shifted from relaxed to mission-driven.

"John, if there is a difference in completion time between Stewart and the replacement subcontractor, we need to determine how much this delay may cost in terms of additional expenses and other damages, including liquidated damages. Do we have a performance bond in place? If we do, we need to notify Stewart's surety of the specific defaults and provide them with an opportunity to cure them," I said.

That evening, John sent the default notice letter, and the time passed with no response from Stewart. After the required cure period had passed, we sent the notice of termination. Stewart did call after they received that letter, wanting to make a deal, and promised to remobilize if we worked with them. John stood firm and asked them to send him an inventory of any equipment or materials they had in their possession and bring it to the project site.

"Mark, I tried to work with you and gave you several opportunities to continue your work, but you picked up your tools and left. Once we finish the project, if there are additional costs for us to complete the work, I'll send you the invoice," John said.

John closed out the project and did have cost overruns, but the subcontractor he hired stepped up and completed the project before the substantial completion date. The executive leadership team later decided not to pursue the damages against Stewart.

### BEST PRACTICES

A notice of default and a notice of termination should be tied together (i.e., where a warning notice of default is to be issued, followed by a termination notice) to ensure the notices are connected with both content and time.

## Commentary

I tell everyone that terminating a subcontractor should never be impulsive or done out of spite. This action should only be taken with clear justification and sufficient supporting documentation showing that you did everything reasonably possible to get your subcontractor to perform. However, regarding safety violations, the termination decision is different, and aggressive action should be taken.

## Summary

Prequalifying subcontractors is important for ensuring the success of your projects, but the process can be difficult for most contractors. Key areas of scrutiny include a subcontractor's financial data, such as annual contract volume, sales, and net worth, safety management history, Occupational Safety and Health Administration data, insurance coverage, and work history. Vetting subcontractors ensures that the subcontractor is a well-run business and has a proven performance record. This helps to ensure that your projects will be completed on time and on budget with the highest quality.

## ATTACHMENT SIX

SENT BY E-MAIL AND CERTIFIED MAIL

>March 16, 2022
>My Company, Inc.
>157 Evens Street
>Morehead City, NC, 28557
>
>Mark Stewart & Son's Mechanical Contracting Company
>Attention: Mark Stewart, Owner
>111 Atlantic Circle
>Atlantic Beach, NC 28512
>
>SUBJECT: NOTICE OF SCHEDULE DELAYS AND RESERVATION OF RIGHTS
>
>Dear Mr. Stewart:
>
>This letter serves as a follow-up to our telephone conversation and a notice of schedule delays. As you are aware, My Company, Inc. ("My Company") and Mark Stewart & Son's Mechanical Contracting Company ("Stewart") entered enter

an agreement dated February 16, 2022 (the "Subcontract") for the removal and installation of 4,354 water meters for the Crystal Shores Water Meter Project (the "Project"). Capitalized terms used herein without definition shall have the meanings assigned to them in the Subcontract.

On March 15, 2022, Stewart provided My Company with daily site reports indicating that they could only remove and install half of the water meters on a weekly basis. Under the Subcontract's terms, Stewart must complete its Work within 252 business days from Subcontract execution. This schedule requires Stewart to install 172 water meters per week. My Company estimated the average time to remove one water meter and reinstall a new one was 30 minutes. Furthermore, My Company estimated it would take three crews of four people to install 24 water meters daily. Currently, Stewart has only mobilized one crew to perform the Work. Since its crew started Work, it has removed and installed 192 meters. As of this letter, there is a deficiency in the removal and installation of 384 water meters.

My Company requires a corrective action plan outlining the actions Stewart will take to recover from the delays.

Section 29. (Assurances) provides in pertinent part:

If at any point Contractor reasonably determines that Subcontractor is falling short of its obligations under this Subcontract, Contractor may require Subcontractor to submit a corrective action plan within three (3) business days, outlining the steps that will be taken to rectify the issue. Contractor may request changes to the corrective action plan based on their reasonable judgment of whether the corrective action plan will effectively correct the deficiency. Subcontractor must promptly and earnestly implement the corrective action plan and demonstrate to Contractor that the plan has successfully resolved the problem. If Subcontractor fails to implement the corrective action plan, it may result in termination of the Subcontract by Contractor.

Please submit a corrective action plan by March 21, 2025, outlining the steps Stewart will take to recover from the delays.

My Company reserves all rights under contract and applicable law to protect its legal and commercial interests.

If you have any questions or wish to discuss these matters further and work towards a mutually acceptable resolution, don't hesitate to get in touch with me at (555) 999-1111 or e-mail me at johnhardy@mycompany.com.

Regards,

John Hardy, PMP<br>
Project Manager<br>
My Company, Inc.

## ATTACHMENT EIGHT
SENT BY E-MAIL

March 16, 2022
My Company, Inc.
157 Evens Street
Morehead City, NC, 28557

Mark Stewart & Son's Mechanical Contracting Company
Attention: Mark Stewart, Owner
111 Atlantic Circle
Atlantic Beach, NC 28512

SUBJECT: RESPONSE TO SUBCONTRACTOR'S CHANGE ORDER REQUEST

Dear Mr. Stewart:

This letter is in response to your change order request. As you are aware, My Company, Inc. ("My Company") and Mark Stewart & Son's Mechanical Contracting Company ("Stewart") entered enter an agreement dated February 16, 2022 (the "Subcontract") for the removal and installation of 4,354 water meters for the Crystal Shores Water Meter Project (the "Project"). Capitalized terms used herein without definition shall have the meanings assigned to them in the Subcontract.

My Company has reviewed your change order request and determined that the line items you identified as extra are within your scope of work. Section 1 provides in pertinent part:

1. Scope of Work. Subcontractor shall exercise reasonable skill and judgment in the performance of the Work and shall provide all necessary equipment, material, tools, labor, and supervision ("Work") that are required to replace the existing water meters with new water meters. Specifically, Subcontractor's Work shall consist of but is not limited to, removing the existing water meters, installing new water meters (provided by Contractor), and repairing, replacing, or modifying the existing meter boxes and lids. Subcon-

tractor shall complete the Work within 252 business days after the execution of this Subcontract ("<u>Project Schedule</u>"). In addition to the foregoing, it is further understood and agreed that Subcontractor shall furnish all items completely, including all costs for labor, equipment, and materials, regardless of whether or not they are included in the Contract Documents. Drawings and detailed plans are provided for reference only and are not to be considered all-inclusive of the Contract Documents for the particular items referenced.

Before submitting your bid, you were allowed to inspect a random selection of water meters and agreed that you understood your scope of work. The scope of work is part of your signed subcontract.

Furthermore, Stewart failed to follow the procedures and requirements outlined in Section 14 (Notices) and Section 10 (Changes).

Section 14 provided in pertinent part:

Notices of changes, deficiencies, delays, claims, or disputes shall be in writing and delivered within three (3) business days of occurrence or discovery of same and shall furnish complete information to the extent available.

Section 10 provided in pertinent part:

If either Party wishes to change the scope of Work, it shall submit details of the requested change to the other Party in writing. Promptly after receipt of any proposed change, the Parties shall negotiate and agree on the terms of such change.

Contractor shall not be liable for the cost of any extra work or any substitutions, changes, additions, omissions, or deviations from the scope of Work except under a Change Order or written Directive.

The Town of Crystal Shores has notified My Company of defects in 35 water meters. Please provide your plan to address the defects. As of today, the 35 residents do not have running water. My Company expects to receive a corrective action plan within three (3) business days outlining how Stewart will regain the project schedule and correct the defective Work.

In closing, upon review of Stewart's change order request, My Company has determined that the work Stewart is claiming as extra is within their scope of Work. Moreover, Stewart failed to provide the supporting documents to substantiate its request and for My Company to evaluate it effectively. Finally, Stewart failed to provide proper notice before performing the work that was considered extra.

My Company reserves all rights under the contract and applicable law to protect its legal and commercial interests.

If you have any questions or wish to discuss these matters further and work towards a mutually acceptable resolution, don't hesitate to get in touch with me at (555) 999-1111 or e-mail me at johnhardy@mycompany.com.

Regards,

John Hardy, PMP  
Project Manager  
My Company, Inc.

# ATTACHMENT NINE

SENT BY E-MAIL AND CERTIFIED MAIL

March 16, 2022
My Company, Inc.
157 Evens Street
Morehead City, NC, 28557

Mark Stewart & Son's Mechanical Contracting Company
Attention: Mark Stewart, Owner
111 Atlantic Circle
Atlantic Beach, NC 28512

SUBJECT: NOTICE OF DEFAULT

Dear Mr. Stewart:

This letter serves as a formal notice of default. As you are aware, My Company, Inc. ("My Company") and Mark Stewart & Son's Mechanical Contracting Company ("Stewart") entered enter an agreement dated February 16, 2022 (the "Subcontract") for the removal and installation of 4,354 water meters for the Crystal Shores Water Meter Project (the "Project"). Capitalized terms used herein without definition shall have the meanings assigned to them in the Subcontract.

As you are aware, the Project has been delayed due to Stewart's failure to staff the Project adequately. These delays, coupled with Stewart's defective Work and refusal to mobilize and complete its Work, have created significant risks to My Company.

Section 1 (Scope of Work) provides substantially in pertinent part:

Subcontractor shall remove the existing water meters, install new ones, and repair, replace, or modify the existing meter boxes and lids. Subcontractor shall complete the Work within 252 business days after the execution of this Subcontract ("<u>Project Schedule</u>").

Stewart threatened to remove its crews from the Project site and would not remobilize until its change order request was approved. Stewart has failed to provide proper notices (as required under the Subcontract terms), abandoned its Work, and removed its crews and tools from the Project site.

Section 9 (Termination for Default) provides substantially in pertinent part:

Subcontractor, by its conduct, shall be in default if it (i) abandons the Work, (ii) violates any of the conditions of the Subcontract; (iii) acts in bad faith; or (iv) fails to complete the Work within the Project Schedule.

While My Company would prefer to continue to work with Stewart and resolve any disputes amicably, given My Company's contractual obligations to the Town of Crystal Shores, My Company cannot simply afford to sit idly by without a clear plan and timeline to complete the Project. As a result, My Company hereby demands that Stewart provide, within three (3) business days, the following: (1) a corrective action plan; and (2) a realistic timeline for the completion of the Project. Stewart must address these serious issues promptly, or

My Company will be forced to take further action to protect its interests.

My Company reserves all rights under the contract and applicable law to protect its legal and commercial interests.

If you have any questions or wish to discuss these matters further and work towards a mutually acceptable resolution, don't hesitate to get in touch with me at (555) 999-1111 or e-mail me at johnhardy@mycompany.com.

Regards,

John Hardy, PMP
Project Manager
My Company, Inc.

## ATTACHMENT TEN

SENT BY E-MAIL AND CERTIFIED MAIL

March 16, 2022
My Company, Inc.
157 Evens Street
Morehead City, NC, 28557

Mark Stewart & Son's Mechanical Contracting Company
Attention: Mark Stewart, Owner
111 Atlantic Circle
Atlantic Beach, NC 28512

SUBJECT: NOTICE OF TERMINATION

Dear Mr. Stewart:

This letter serves as a formal notice of termination. As you are aware, My Company, Inc. ("My Company") and Mark Stewart & Son's Mechanical Contracting Company ("Stewart") entered enter an agreement dated February 16, 2022 (the "Subcontract") for the removal and installation of 4,354 water meters for the Crystal Shores Water Meter Project (the "Project"). Capitalized terms used herein without definition shall have the meanings assigned to them in the Subcontract.

Based on Stewart's (1) abandonment of the Work site, (2) refusal to remobilize its crews and perform its Work (Exhibit A – Scope of Work), (3) failure to provide the requested corrective action plan, and (4) failure to correct defective Work, My Company has no other recourse except to terminate Stewart's Subcontract for default.

My Company is currently evaluating its rights and remedies under the terms of the Subcontract and will set off any costs, damages, expenses, or charges incurred or paid by My Company in connection with or arising out of such termination amounts owed or damages incurred.

Section 83 (Set-off) provides in pertinent part:

If Subcontractor defaults on any of its obligations under this Subcontract, Contractor has the right to deduct or adjust any payments under any subcontracts with Subcontractor or any of its affiliates without further notice or demand. Such action will not be considered a violation or excuse for non-performance.

In the event that the monies withheld are not sufficient to cover those costs (above), My Company will invoice Stewart, and Stewart shall pay those costs within seven (7) days (Sections 9.3-4).

Stewart shall: (a) promptly discontinue all services to the extent directed; (b) take reasonable precautions to protect the Work that is currently in process; and (c) deliver or otherwise make available to My Company all data, drawings, calculations, reports and all other information and materials which have been accumulated or developed by Stewart in performing this Subcontract, whether completed or in progress. My Company shall be entitled to take and use any materials, equipment, supplies, or tools furnished by or belonging to Stewart at the Project Site (Sections 9.3-4).

Please be advised that nothing contained herein shall constitute a waiver of My Company's rights or remedies, all of which are hereby expressly reserved.

If you have any questions or wish to discuss these matters further and work towards a mutually acceptable resolution, don't hesitate to get in touch with me at (555) 999-1111 or e-mail me at johnhardy@mycompany.com.

Regards,

John Hardy, PMP
Project Manager
My Company, Inc..

# Conclusion

Project-specific subcontract management is complex. It requires strategic planning, careful subcontractor selection, and open communication. Every step, from choosing the right subcontractor to overseeing their work, is vital to the project's success. By working collaboratively, communicating openly, and managing risks, you can build strong partnerships with your subcontractors. Remember, successful subcontract management is about more than just assigning tasks. It's about creating a shared vision and empowering your subcontractors to achieve success together.

In the next chapter, we'll explore the world of bonds and insurance, understanding their complexities and how they help reduce risks for successful project outcomes. Bonds and insurance act as a safety net, protecting everyone involved from financial loss and ensuring the project is completed. They build trust, encourage responsibility, and guarantee that the project will be finished even if unexpected problems arise.

# 9

# BONDS AND INSURANCE

In this chapter, we'll explore the intricate realm of construction, where the role of construction bonds becomes indispensable. These bonds serve as a critical layer of security, knitting together a safety net that encompasses financial assurances and trust between the key players: the project owner, the contractor, and the bond issuer. As contractual linchpins, these bonds guarantee not only financial solvency but also stringent adherence to project specifications, forming a three-party agreement that underlines every stage of the construction process. In this section, we will delve into the various types of construction bonds—bid bonds, performance bonds, payment bonds, and maintenance bonds—and examine their pivotal role in reducing risks, thereby smoothing the path towards successful project completion. Each type of bond plays a strategic role, from ensuring that only serious contenders enter bids to guaranteeing the workforce is paid, thus collectively creating a more reliable, efficient, and fair construction environment.

## Safeguarding Project Success

In the complex world of construction, where risks are abundant, bonds play a pivotal role in ensuring project completion, mitigating financial risks, and promoting trust among stakeholders. Acting as a form of contractual insurance, construction bonds create a three-way agreement between the project owner (obligee), the contractor (principal), and the surety (bond issuer), guaranteeing financial security and contractual performance. Let's explore the major types of construction bonds and how they contribute to reducing project risks:

## Bid Bonds: Ensuring Serious Contenders

At the bidding stage, a bid bond provides a financial assurance that the contractor's proposal is made in good faith and that, if selected, they will enter into the contract at the bid price. It also guarantees the contractor will secure the additional performance and payment bonds required for the project. This protects the owner from financial loss if a winning bidder backs out, encouraging a pool of serious and financially stable contractors.

## Performance Bonds: Guaranteeing Completion

Perhaps the most crucial bond, a performance bond acts as a safety net for project owners, guaranteeing that the contractor will complete the work as per the contract terms and specifications. If the contractor defaults, the surety will step in to cover the costs of completing the project or compensate the owner for financial losses. This protects against non-performance due to insolvency, mismanagement, or failure to comply with project standards, ensuring that project timelines and budgets are maintained.

## Payment Bonds: Protecting the Workforce

Payment bonds guarantee that all subcontractors, laborers, and material suppliers will be paid for their work. This protects these parties from non-payment, which can lead to project delays, mechanic's liens, or legal action. Payment bonds are often required alongside performance bonds, ensuring all parties involved in construction are compensated, even if the contractor faces financial difficulties. This is particularly vital in public projects where mechanic's liens cannot be placed against public property.

## Maintenance Bonds: Assuring Post-Completion Quality

Maintenance bonds, also known as warranty bonds, guarantee that the contractor will adhere to maintenance and quality standards for a specified period after the project is completed. This protects the owner from defects caused by poor workmanship or materials during that period. It ensures any necessary repairs or adjustments won't incur additional costs for the owner, mitigating the risk of unforeseen expenses after project handover.

## How Construction Bonds Reduce Risk

- Enhanced Reliability and Quality: Bonds prequalify contractors based on their financial and performance history, ensuring only capable and experienced parties are involved, leading to better quality work.
- Financial Security and Risk Mitigation: Bonds act as a financial safety net, covering losses from non-completion, non-payment, and post-completion defects, reducing financial risks for owners and investors.
- Dispute Prevention: Clear obligations and assurances provided by bonds minimize disagreements among parties, fostering smoother project execution.
- Facilitated Project Financing: Many lenders require bonds as a condition for financing construction projects, demonstrating reduced risk and enhancing project viability.

In summary, construction bonds are indispensable tools for managing risk in the construction industry. They safeguard project owners, ensure fairness and timely payment for workers and suppliers, and contribute to more successful project outcomes overall.

## Insurance for Construction and Engineering Firms

In the construction and engineering sectors, managing risks through comprehensive insurance coverage is essential. This protection extends beyond the conventional policies for on-site activities to specialized insurance types like aircraft and marine insurance, especially pertinent for firms engaged in projects that involve aerial or marine operations. Here's a deeper look into the various types of insurance vital for construction and engineering firms, including the integration of aircraft and marine insurance and the significance of procuring and verifying certificates of insurance (COI).

## Types of Insurance for Construction and Engineering Firms

1. General Liability Insurance: This foundational insurance covers bodily injuries, property damage, and advertising injuries. It's essential as it protects firms from the common hazards encountered on worksites, such as third-party injuries or property damage due to construction activities.

2. Professional Liability Insurance (Errors & Omissions): For engineering firms, this insurance covers claims of negligence or inadequate work, such as design flaws or construction errors that lead to financial losses or physical damage.

3. Workers' Compensation Insurance: Mandatory in most regions, this insurance covers medical costs, death benefits, and lost wages for employees injured on the job, which is crucial given the high-risk nature of the construction and engineering industries.

4. Commercial Auto Insurance: This covers damages and liability costs from accidents involving company vehicles, essential for firms that transport materials, equipment, or personnel.

5. Builders Risk Insurance: Specific to the construction phase, this insurance covers buildings under construction against damage or loss from events like fire, theft, or natural disasters.

6. Umbrella Insurance: Providing extra coverage beyond the limits of other liability policies, umbrella insurance is crucial for large-scale or high-risk projects where typical policy limits may be insufficient.

7. **Environmental Liability Insurance:** This covers costs related to environmental damage, such as pollution cleanup and hazardous materials management, critical for projects with potential environmental impacts.

8. **Aircraft Insurance:** For construction and engineering firms that utilize aircraft, such as drones for aerial surveying or helicopters for transporting materials to inaccessible areas, aircraft insurance is crucial. It covers the aircraft and liability for any damage or injuries caused by aerial operations. This type of insurance ensures that firms can safely and effectively integrate aerial technologies into their projects without undue financial risk.

9. **Marine Insurance:** Firms involved in marine construction, such as bridges, ports, or offshore facilities, require marine insurance. This includes losses or damages caused by marine operations, such as the transport of goods and equipment over water. Marine insurance mitigates the risks associated with working in challenging and often unpredictable marine environments.

## Owner's Insurance Policy (OIP)

The Owner's Insurance Policy (OIP) stands out as a critical tool designed specifically for project owners to manage risks associated with large-scale construction projects. This policy supplements the standard insurance coverage held by contractors and provides an additional layer of protection tailored to the unique needs and concerns of the project owner. Here, we expand on the array of insurance options, integrating the Owner's Insurance Policy and explaining its functionality along with the significance of obtaining and verifying certificates of insurance (COI).

The Owner's Insurance Policy is a tailored insurance solution designed to cover the specific risks faced by the owner of a construction project. Unlike the policies held by contractors, the OIP provides direct coverage to the owner for a broad range of potential risks, including project delays, financial losses due to contractor default, and additional costs incurred from unforeseen project extensions.

## How the Owner's Insurance Policy Works:

- Custom Coverage: The OIP is highly customizable according to the project's scope and potential risks. It can include aspects of liability, property damage, and even business interruption insurance.

- Direct Claim Handling: In the event of a claim, the owner can directly engage with the insurer without depending on the contractor's policy. This can be crucial in situations where the contractor's insurance fails to fully cover a loss or when disputes arise about liability.

- Supplemental Protection: Often, the OIP acts as a supplement to the contractor's provided coverage, filling in gaps and providing additional protection where contractor policies may fall short, such as in complex claims related to design flaws attributed to the owner's directives.

## Importance of Obtaining Insurance

A Certificate of Insurance (COI) is a document summarizing the insurance policies held by a firm. Verifying these certificates is critical for several reasons:

1. Proof of Insurance: Clients and partners often require a COI to ensure that a firm has sufficient insurance coverage to handle potential project risks.

2. Risk Management: Checking the COI of subcontractors and partners confirms that they are properly insured, minimizing the risk of liability for accidents or negligence occurring under their responsibility.

3. Compliance and Legal Assurance: Many jurisdictions require specific types of insurance for construction and engineering operations. A COI serves as proof of compliance with these legal mandates.

4. Building Trust: Providing a COI to clients and stakeholders builds trust, showing that the firm is responsible and prepared to professionally handle complications.
5. Contractual Requirements: Contracts typically specify certain types and amounts of insurance. A COI verifies that these insurance obligations are fulfilled before work commences.

In summary, understanding the various insurance types, including specialized policies like aircraft and marine insurance, and the critical role of COIs can greatly influence a firm's operational stability and growth in the construction and engineering industries. This comprehensive approach to insurance not only safeguards financial interests but also fosters reliability and compliance in these high-risk fields.

## Verifying a Certificate of Insurance

Verifying a Certificate of Insurance (COI) is a crucial step in managing risk for any business involved in partnerships, particularly in fields like construction, engineering, or any industry where subcontracting is common. A COI is a document issued by an insurance company or broker that confirms a policy is in effect and provides details about the coverage. It ensures all parties in a project are adequately insured, which is critical for mitigating risk and avoiding potential financial liabilities.

## Understanding a Certificate of Insurance

Before delving into the verification process, it's important to understand what a COI contains. Typically, a COI will list:

- The policyholder's name and contact information.
- The types of coverage (e.g., general liability, workers' compensation, professional liability).
- Effective dates of the policy.
- Policy limits.

- The insurance company's name.
- Additional insureds, if applicable.
- Steps to Verify a Certificate of Insurance

*Process for Verifying COI*

1. Request the COI Directly: Always request the COI directly from the party you are doing business with. To allow sufficient time for verification, ensure it is received well before the work or contract signing. Avoid accepting COIs from third parties unless they come from reputable brokers or agents.

2. Check the Insurer's Details: Verify that the listed insurance company is genuine and licensed to operate in the jurisdiction where the project is located. This can generally be done through online searches on state insurance department websites, which provide lists of licensed insurers.

3. Examine Coverage Types and Limits: Carefully review the types and limits of the coverage provided. Ensure that they meet the minimum requirements specified in your contract. Pay special attention to whether the coverage is aggregate or per occurrence and confirm that it aligns with what's required for the scope of the project or partnership.

4. Validate Policy Dates: Check that the policy is active and covers the relevant period, especially the dates during which the work will be performed. This is crucial, as any work done outside of these dates may not be covered by the insurance.

5. Confirm Additional Insureds: If your agreement requires that your company be added as an additional insured, verify that this is reflected on the COI. Being listed as an additional insured extends certain coverages to you, providing protection under the policyholder's insurance policy.

6. Authenticate the Document: For high-risk contracts, it may be necessary to authenticate the COI further by contacting the insurance broker or

company listed on the document. This step can help to ensure that the COI is not fraudulent and that the broker or insurer has issued the document.

7. Regular Updates and Renewals: Since insurance policies are subject to expiration and renewal, it is important to set reminders to request updated COIs periodically. This is especially vital for long-term contracts or ongoing business relationships.

8. Document Your Verification Process: Keep a log or database of your verification process, including who verified the COI, the date of verification, and any pertinent notes. This documentation can be crucial in cases of disputes or if a claim arises.

### *Why Verification Matters*

The process of verifying a COI protects your business from potential uninsured losses and contractual breaches. It helps ensure that all parties involved adhere to the agreed-upon risk management strategies, thereby maintaining the integrity and financial stability of your operations. Furthermore, diligent verification of COIs can help build stronger business relationships by demonstrating professionalism and attention to detail, crucial for long-term success in industries where risk management is paramount.

## The Growing Challenge of Fraudulent COIs

The prevalence of fraudulent or inaccurate Certificates of Insurance poses a significant risk in the construction industry, highlighting the critical need for thorough verification and robust risk management protocols. The widespread nature of this issue underscores the potential financial implications for the construction sector, emphasizing the importance of due diligence in ensuring the validity and accuracy of insurance documentation.

## Identifying Fraudulent COIs: Key Indicators

Recognizing the signs of a counterfeit COI is essential for protecting your business from potential liabilities. Here are crucial indicators to watch for:

1. Questionable Insurance Company Credentials: Verify the authenticity of the insurance provider by checking their official website or directly contacting them.
2. Inconsistencies in Policy Details: Look for discrepancies in policy numbers, coverage specifics, or effective dates, as these may signal tampering.
3. Absence or Alteration of Endorsements: Ensure all required endorsements are intact and unaltered.
4. Document Quality: Be wary of poor-quality documents; blurred or pixelated COIs can be red flags for fraudulent activities. Always request a high-resolution copy if the document's quality is questionable.

### BEST PRACTICES

Implementing a comprehensive approach to COI management is critical for mitigating the risks associated with fraudulent certificates. Effective strategies include:

1. Rigorous Contractor Vetting: Conduct thorough background checks on all contractors and subcontractors. Employing prequalification software can facilitate this process, enhancing efficiency and reliability.
2. Centralized COI Tracking: Develop a centralized system for managing and verifying all COIs, which helps maintain consistency and traceability.
3. Staff Training: Equip your team with the knowledge to identify fake COIs and encourage regular interactions with insurance providers to confirm details.

4. **Digital COI Solutions:** Consider adopting digital COI management tools that automate the verification process, reducing the likelihood of human error and increasing the speed of validation.

## Insight Story: Bridge Over Troubled Waters

The sun blazed down on the massive construction site of the new bridge over the Intracoastal Waterway, its heat serving as a constant reminder to everyone working there. Despite the noise of heavy machinery and the shouts of workers, John kept a watchful eye on the operation. But today, something was off.

The problem was a piece of custom-made lifting equipment from Uplift Engineering, a minority-owned business that the client had been excited to hire. Zack, the young and energetic owner of Uplift, had made a good impression with his qualifications and confident pitch.

However, when the equipment was put to use, it didn't perform as expected. The hydraulics were slow, and the crane arm didn't seem sturdy, leading to a few close calls that had everyone on edge.

John decided to talk to Zack. "Zack, we need to chat about the lifting equipment. It's not working right, and the guys are getting worried."

Zack got defensive. "John, I promise you, our equipment is the best. We've done tons of projects with no problems. I trust our work."

John understood Zack's pride but suggested, "I get that, Zack, but let's have an independent company check it out, just to be sure. It's normal for a big project like this."

Zack wasn't thrilled but agreed.

The assessment was bad news. The report pointed out serious design flaws and cheap materials, a major safety risk they couldn't ignore.

My phone rang. John's voice was urgent. "We need to talk. Got a minute?"

"Sure. What's up?"

John got straight to the point. "The equipment is messed up. We're lucky no one's been hurt."

"What about the performance and warranty bonds?"

John's answer was grim. "There aren't any. Uplift didn't get them."

They talked about insurance. Uplift's Certificate of Insurance (COI) looked fishy. The details didn't match up, and the contact info was vague. Turns out, the insurance was fake.

John confronted Zack in his office. "Zack, the equipment you gave us is faulty and dangerous. We've shut it down."

Zack's confidence was gone. "John, I can fix this, please."

John was firm. "It's beyond fixing. We also found out your insurance is bogus. You put the project and everyone's safety at risk."

Zack, defeated, admitted he messed up, blaming financial problems—a weak excuse considering the potential disaster.

"There will be legal consequences for this, Zack. Expect to hear from our lawyers, and we'll likely terminate your contract."

As they left, the threat of legal trouble hung in the air, but John was determined. He had a responsibility to his team and the project. Despite the setback, the bridge would be built, not just on time but safely, no matter what one contractor did.

## Drawbacks and Limitations of Bonds and Insurance

While bonds and insurance offer crucial protection in the construction industry, they also come with certain drawbacks and limitations. The cost of obtaining bonds and insurance premiums can be substantial, particularly for smaller firms or those with limited financial resources. The claims process itself can be complex and time-consuming, potentially leading to delays in project completion or disputes between parties. Additionally, insurance policies often contain exclusions or limitations that may leave certain risks uncovered, requiring careful scrutiny of policy terms and conditions.

In the case of bonds, the surety may require collateral or other financial guarantees, which can tie up a company's assets and limit their financial flexibility. Furthermore, obtaining bonds can be challenging for firms with less-than-perfect credit or performance histories. Therefore, while bonds and insurance are invaluable tools for risk management, it's crucial to weigh their costs, limitations, and potential complexities against the benefits they offer.

## Conclusion

In this chapter, we explored bonds and insurance. They emerge as the unsung heroes, safeguarding projects from unforeseen risks and fostering trust among stakeholders. From the initial bid to the final handover, these financial instruments provide a safety net, ensuring project completion, protecting workers and suppliers, and mitigating potential losses. By understanding the diverse types of bonds and insurance policies available and diligently verifying certificates of insurance, you can navigate the complexities of these industries with confidence and ensure the success of your projects. Remember, in the world of construction and engineering, where risks are abundant, bonds and insurance are not just options; they are essential tools for building a secure and prosperous future.

In the next chapter, we'll examine the profound changes in the world of contracts as traditional models, often characterized by rigidity and adversarial dynamics, give way to innovative approaches that prioritize adaptability, collaboration, and mutual value creation. This evolution is driven by the increasing complexity and dynamism of today's business environment, where conventional contracts often prove inadequate for fostering successful, enduring partnerships.

# 10

# THE NEW LANDSCAPE OF CONTRACTS

In this chapter, we delve into the evolution from traditional transaction-focused contracts to relational contracting. This approach emphasizes trust, open communication, and shared goals, recognizing that successful collaborations are built on mutual understanding, respect, and a proactive approach to conflict resolution. It represents a significant shift from merely defining obligations to fostering partnerships where both parties are equally invested in each other's success.

Traditional contracts, often rigid and prone to conflict, are being reevaluated in favor of models that promote flexibility, open communication, and shared objectives. This shift reflects a fundamental rethinking of business interactions, acknowledging that effective collaboration goes beyond legal obligations. It necessitates trust, shared values, and a collective commitment to achieving mutual success.

Recognizing the need for a structured approach to relational contracting, researchers at the University of Tennessee developed the "Vested" methodology. This approach establishes a "what's in it for we" partnership mentality, where both parties have a personal stake in each other's success[18]. Vested contracts are legally enforceable and incorporate traditional contract elements alongside relationship-building components like a shared vision, guiding principles, and robust governance structures to ensure ongoing alignment.

Innovative contracting models, including relational, outcome-based, agile, value-based, and collaborative contracting, as well as the Vested methodology, are emerging to meet the evolving needs of modern businesses. These models highlight the importance of building strong relationships, focusing on strategic outcomes rather than prescriptive tasks, embracing iterative development and continuous feedback, aligning incentives with tangible value delivery, and fostering a shared sense of ownership and accountability.

This transformation in contracting practices is part of a broader movement towards recognizing the importance of human connection and shared purpose in business relationships. By moving from adversarial to cooperative, value-driven frameworks, organizations can unlock new opportunities for innovation, growth, and mutual prosperity. The future of contracting lies in flexible, adaptive structures like Vested agreements, which promote trust, collaboration, and the co-creation of value, ultimately leading to a more resilient and interconnected business environment.

## Key Principles of Relational Contracting

1. Trust and Mutual Respect: The foundation of relational contracts is built on trust and respect, enabling open communication, transparent information sharing, and a collaborative approach to challenges.

---

[18] D. Frydlinger, O. Hart, and K. Vitasek, "A New Approach to Contracts: How to Build Better Long-Term Strategic Partnerships," *Harvard Business Review* 97, no. 5 (2019), https://link.gale.com/apps/doc/A599089506/AONE?u=anon~21a05974&sid=googleScholar&xid=189fc576.

2. Shared Goals and Vision: Both parties align on overarching objectives, fostering a sense of collective responsibility and commitment to achieving desired outcomes.
3. Open Communication and Collaboration: Regular dialogue and proactive collaboration are vital for maintaining strong relationships and addressing issues early. This includes regular meetings, open feedback channels, and adaptability.
4. Flexibility and Adaptability: Relational contracts acknowledge that circumstances can change, including provisions for flexibility and renegotiation, ensuring the contract remains relevant even as the environment evolves.
5. Long-Term Focus: These contracts are designed for enduring collaborations, encouraging investment in the relationship and a shared commitment to mutual success over time.

## The Vested Methodology

The Vested methodology formalizes relational contracting by creating legally enforceable agreements that incorporate traditional contract components alongside relationship-building elements. The result is a "what's in it for we" partnership mentality, where both parties are equally invested in each other's success.

## Innovative Contracting Models

While relational contracting lays a strong foundation for collaborative business relationships, the evolving business landscape demands even more innovative and adaptable approaches. Several other contracting models have emerged:

1. Outcome-Based Contracting: Focuses on achieving desired outcomes rather than specific tasks, allowing for greater flexibility and encouraging innovation, risk-sharing, and value delivery.

2. Agile Contracting: Inspired by agile software development, this approach prioritizes iterative development, continuous feedback, and adaptability to changing circumstances, making it well-suited for complex environments.

3. Value-Based Contracting: Aligns incentives with the delivery of value to the end customer, fostering continuous improvement, innovation, and a customer-centric focus.

4. Collaborative Contracting: Involves all stakeholders from inception to completion, cultivating shared ownership and responsibility, leading to more innovative solutions and stronger relationships.

## Benefits and Challenges of Innovative Contracting

Innovative contracting offers numerous benefits, including improved project outcomes, increased efficiency, heightened innovation, and stronger inter-party relationships. However, it also presents challenges, such as the need for trust and collaboration, the complexity of contract design and management, and the potential for disputes.

## Embracing a New Era of Contracting

As businesses navigate an increasingly complex and dynamic landscape, innovative contracting models will play a crucial role in fostering collaboration, driving innovation, and delivering value. By embracing these forward-thinking approaches, organizations can unlock new opportunities for growth, competitiveness, and long-term success. These evolving models represent not just a shift in how business is conducted but also a roadmap for the future of partnerships across various industries.

# Insight Story: The Collaborative Build

One morning in John's construction site trailer, John sat across from Phillip, the owner of the company. Blueprints and contracts were spread out on the table before them.

John, leaning forward and tapping a blueprint, said, "Phillip, I've been thinking about how we approach subcontracting for this new project. We've had issues before with misalignment, delays, and even disputes over scope. I think we need a different strategy this time—one that ensures everyone is fully invested in the success of the project, including our subcontractors."

Phillip nodded thoughtfully and replied, "I agree, John. The last project had its fair share of challenges. What do you have in mind? Are you suggesting we shift away from our traditional contract model?"

"Exactly," John said. "I've been reading up on relational contracting. The idea is to tie each other's success directly to the success of the project. It's more about partnership than just fulfilling obligations. I want to propose this approach to the subcontractor we hire for the electrical work on this project."

Phillip raised an eyebrow and inquired, "That's interesting. So, instead of just setting milestones and deliverables, we're looking at aligning our goals with theirs, making them just as accountable for the project's overall success as we are?"

John smiled and confirmed, "Precisely. The key is to establish a shared vision from the start. We'll make it clear that their success is our success—and vice versa. It's not just about getting the work done; it's about how well the project performs as a whole. We could set up incentives based on quality, timeliness, and even client satisfaction. If they exceed expectations, they benefit more, but if they fall short, we all feel the impact."

Phillip leaned back, considering, and then said, "I like the sound of that. It feels like a win-win. But how do we ensure they're on board with this idea?

Contractors are used to traditional models where their focus is just on their piece of the pie."

John confidently replied, "That's where our approach to the conversation will matter. I've already reached out to Brian over at Elite Electrical. He's a sharp guy, and I think he'll see the value in this. If we present this as a partnership opportunity rather than just another contract, I think he'll be receptive."

Phillip smiled and said, "You've always been good at reading people, John. If anyone can get them on board, it's you. How do you plan to present this?"

John flipped through his notes and explained, "I've drafted an outline. First, I'll start by emphasizing the complexity and scale of the project. Then, I'll pivot to the mutual benefits of this approach—how it can reduce risks for everyone involved and potentially increase profitability. I'll make it clear that we're looking for a long-term relationship, not just a one-off job."

Phillip nodded and asked, "And if they push back?"

John thoughtfully responded, "We'll need to be flexible. The goal is to find common ground. If they have concerns, we address them collaboratively. We could even bring in examples of other companies that have successfully implemented this model—show them it's not just theoretical."

Phillip leaned forward, placing his hands on the table, and said, "Alright, John. You have my full support. Go ahead and set up the meeting with Brian. I'll be there to back you up if needed, but I trust you to lead the discussion."

John smiled and said, "Thanks, Phillip. I'll get in touch with Brian and set something up for tomorrow. I have a good feeling about this. If we can pull this off, it could be a game-changer for how we manage all our subcontractor relationships moving forward."

Phillip stood up, offered his hand, and said, "Let's make it happen, John. If this works out, it could redefine how we do business and set us apart from our competitors."

John shook Phillip's hand and replied, "Absolutely. I'll keep you updated."

The next day, in a small, cozy conference room at Elite Electrical's office. John and Brian, the subcontractor, sit across from each other, both looking over the proposed contract (see below).

Brian furrowed his brow slightly and said, "John, I appreciate the innovative approach here, but I have to admit, this is a bit different from what we're used to. The contract looks totally different. You're suggesting we're not just responsible for our part, but for the entire project's success?"

John leaned forward, earnestly, and replied, "That's the core of it, Brian. This contract is just the shell, and we can work out the details. We want to shift the dynamic from a traditional client-contractor relationship to a true partnership. If the project succeeds, we will all prosper. There's a shared incentive structure tied to overall performance—on-time completion, budget adherence, client satisfaction. It's about aligning our interests for mutual benefit."

Brian nodded slowly and said, "I see. So, it's not just about us getting in, doing our part, and getting out. It's about being invested in the bigger picture."

John agreed, "Exactly. We believe this approach fosters a more collaborative environment. If challenges arise, we tackle them together. There's open communication, regular check-ins, and the flexibility to adapt as needed. It's about building something great, collectively."

Brian paused thoughtfully and then said, "This is certainly intriguing. I've seen too many projects where subcontractors are left out of the loop or blamed when things go south, even if it wasn't their fault. This . . . this feels different."

John smiled and said, "That's the intention, Brian. We're not just hiring you for a job; we're inviting you to be an integral part of the project's success story."

Brian leaned back, a hint of a smile on his face, and replied, "Alright, John. You've piqued my interest. Let me discuss this with my team, but I'm definitely open to the idea. If this works out, it could change the way we do business too."

John extended his hand and said, "That's all I ask, Brian. Let's build something great together."

John stepped out of the office, a smile on his face as he dialed Phillip's number.

"Phillip, we're all set," John said on the phone. "Brian's on board. Looks like we're about to set a new standard for how we do business."

Phillip's voice, smiling, came over the phone, "Well done, John. Let's show everyone what true collaboration looks like."

John hung up, looking forward with determination. "Here's to the future," he said to himself.

## Collaborative Agreement

*Parties:*

[Name of Construction Company], represented by [Name of Project Manager]

[Name of Subcontractor Company], represented by [Name of Subcontractor Representative]

Project: [Project Name and Brief Description]

*Purpose of Agreement:*

This agreement outlines a collaborative approach to the successful completion of the [Project Name] project. Both parties recognize the value of shared responsibility and mutual benefit, fostering a true partnership beyond a traditional client-contractor relationship.

*Key Principles:*

1. Shared Vision: Both parties are committed to the project's overall success, aligning their goals and working collaboratively to achieve them.
2. Open Communication: Regular and transparent communication will be maintained to ensure everyone is informed, issues are addressed promptly, and the project stays on track.

3. Flexibility and Adaptation: Both parties acknowledge that unforeseen challenges may arise, requiring flexibility and a willingness to adapt plans as needed.
4. Mutual Benefit: Incentives are structured to reward exceptional performance, recognizing the contributions of both parties to the project's overall success.

## *Specifics:*

1. Scope of Work: [Clearly define the specific tasks and responsibilities of the subcontractor.]
2. Performance Metrics: [Outline the key metrics that will be used to evaluate project success, such as timelines, budget adherence, quality standards, and client satisfaction.]
3. Incentive Structure: [Describe the financial or other incentives that will be awarded for exceeding expectations.]
4. Communication Protocols: [Establish regular meeting schedules, reporting procedures, and preferred communication methods.]
5. Dispute Resolution: [Outline a clear process for addressing any disagreements or conflicts that may arise during the project.]
6. Term: [Specify the start and end dates of the agreement.]
7. Termination: [Describe the conditions under which either party can terminate the agreement.]

## *Signatures:*

[Signature of Construction Company Representative]

[Signature of Subcontractor Representative]

Date:

## Conclusion

In this chapter, we've witnessed the dawn of a new era in contracting, where traditional models are being challenged and redefined. The rise of relational contracting, outcome-based agreements, and collaborative approaches signals a shift towards partnerships built on trust, shared goals, and mutual success. The Vested methodology, with its emphasis on a "what's in it for we" mentality, exemplifies this transformative approach, offering a framework for legally enforceable agreements that prioritize collaboration and value creation. As the business landscape continues to evolve, embracing these innovative contracting models will be crucial for fostering long-term success, driving innovation, and navigating the complexities of the modern marketplace. The future of contracting lies in adaptability, flexibility, and a shared commitment to achieving collective goals.

In the dynamic realm of project management, where challenges abound and uncertainties persist, leadership emerges as the guiding light, illuminating the path to success. The traditional focus on technical expertise and process adherence is now complemented by a profound recognition of the human element. The ability to inspire, motivate, and unite teams around a shared vision has become a defining characteristic of exceptional project managers. In the next chapter, we will embark on a journey through the multifaceted landscape of project leadership, exploring the various styles, strategies, and skills that empower project managers to navigate complexities, overcome obstacles, and achieve remarkable outcomes.

# 11
# LEADING THE WAY IN PROJECT MANAGEMENT

This chapter, presented as bonus material and a introduction to concepts explored in an upcoming book, provides a glimpse into the evolving world of project management. We'll uncover a pivotal shift in emphasis from traditional concerns like timelines and budgets to the critical human elements that drive project success. Discover how soft skills like communication, collaboration, motivation, and emotional intelligence are often the deciding factors in any endeavor, regardless of meticulous planning.

Through real-world examples of both successful and failed projects, we'll illustrate how leadership plays a pivotal role in shaping project outcomes. We'll also introduce five key leadership styles—transactional, servant, transformational, laissez-faire, and situational—highlighting their strengths, weaknesses, and applicability in different contexts.

By the end of this chapter, you'll gain a deeper understanding of the multifaceted nature of leadership styles in project management and be equipped to identify the most effective approach for your unique team and project needs.

## The New Paradigm in Project Management: The Rise of Leadership

In the ever-evolving landscape of project management, a new paradigm is emerging, one that transcends the traditional reliance on timelines and budgets. Recent research has revealed a surprising truth: the human factor, encompassing elements like communication, collaboration, motivation, and emotional intelligence, is often the linchpin of project success or failure[19]. This means that even the most meticulously planned project can be derailed by a dysfunctional team, a disengaged leader, or a toxic workplace culture[20]. Conversely, a passionate and cohesive team, led by a skilled and inspiring leader, can overcome unexpected challenges and achieve remarkable results[21].

This realization has made leadership a crucial factor in project management[22]. The ability to build trust, foster collaboration, and motivate individuals towards a shared vision is now considered a core competency for successful project managers[23]. Project managers must also be adept at navigating the complex dynamics of human interaction. This involves understanding different leadership styles, such as the transactional leader who focuses on rewards and punishments, the servant leader who prioritizes the needs of their team, and

---

19 Thuy Thanh Thi Doan, Linh Cam Tran Nguyen, and Thanh Dan Ngoc Nguyen, "Emotional Intelligence and Project Success: The Roles of Transformational Leadership and Organizational Commitment," *The Journal of Asian Finance, Economics and Business* 7, no. 3 (2020), https://doi.org/10.13106/jafeb.2020.vol7.no3.223.
20 Olga Fokina et al., "The Conceptual Role of Leadership in Project Management," *E3S Web of Conferences* 458 (2023), https://doi.org/10.1051/e3sconf/202345804020.
21 H. Lei, L. Leaungkhamma, and P. B. Le, "How Transformational Leadership Facilitates Innovation Capability: The Mediating Role of Employees' Psychological Capital," *Leadership and Organization Development Journal* 41(4) (2020), https://doi.org/10.1108/LODJ-06-2019-0245.
22 Shayan, Pyung Kim, and Tam, "Critical Success Factor."
23 Shazia Nauman et al., "Enhancing the Impact of Transformational Leadership and Team-Building on Project Success: The Moderating Role of Empowerment Climate," *International Journal of Managing Projects in Business* 15, no. 2 (2021), https://doi.org/10.1108/ijmpb-02-2021-0031.

the transformational leader who inspires and empowers others to reach their full potential.

Are you ready to unlock the full potential of your team and achieve extraordinary results? This chapter will equip you with the knowledge and skills to navigate the complexities of project leadership and build a high-performing team. Discover proven strategies, real-world case studies, and actionable insights that will transform how you lead and inspire your team to success. It's time to unleash your leadership potential. Let's get started.

## The Human Factor: A Game Changer

Imagine two contrasting projects. In the first, every detail is meticulously planned, yet the team is riddled with conflict and discouragement. The second project's plan might have a few rough edges, but the team is buzzing with energy, collaboration, and a shared sense of purpose. Which project is more likely to achieve its goals?

Research consistently reveals a surprising truth: the project with the passionate, unified team often outperforms the one with the perfect plan[24]. It turns out that human factors like trust, open communication, and a motivating work environment can make or break a project, even when the technical aspects are flawlessly executed[25]. Overlooking these elements can lead to costly delays, increased errors, and even complete project failure[26].

---

24 Inge E. M. Hendrikx et al., "Is Team Resilience More Than the Sum of Its Parts? a Quantitative Study on Emergency Healthcare Teams During the Covid-19 Pandemic," *International Journal of Environmental Research and Public Health* 19, no. 12 (2022), https://doi.org/10.3390/ijerph19126968.

25 Muhammad Zeeshan Fareed, Qin Su, and Muhammad Umer Aslam, "Transformational Leadership and Project Success: The Mediating Role of Psychological Empowerment," *SAGE Open* 13, no. 1 (2023), https://doi.org/10.1177/21582440231154796.

26 Maryam Elmezain, Wan Hamidon Wan Baduruzzaman, and Muhamad Azry Khoiry, "The Impact of Project Manager's Skills and Age on Project Success," *Brazilian Journal of Operations and Production Management* 18, no. 4 (2021), https://doi.org/10.14488/bjopm.2021.017.

This profound insight has shifted the focus of project management towards leadership. Effective leaders who can cultivate strong team dynamics and foster a positive atmosphere are increasingly recognized as the key to a project's success[27]. Different leadership styles, such as transformational leadership, which inspires and motivates through a shared vision, or servant leadership, which prioritizes the needs of the team, can significantly impact team motivation and performance.

Consider the example of the Manhattan Project, where a team of brilliant scientists, engineers, and military personnel, driven by a shared sense of urgency and purpose, successfully developed the atomic bomb in a remarkably short time frame[28]. This extraordinary feat was achieved not only through technical expertise but also through strong leadership and a collaborative spirit that overcame numerous challenges.

In stark contrast, countless projects have floundered due to a lack of strong leadership or the presence of a toxic work environment. These failures often manifest as missed deadlines, budget overruns, and ultimately, a project that falls far short of its potential. Consider these cautionary examples:

- Berlin Brandenburg Airport (BER)[29]: Initially slated to open in 2011, this project became synonymous with mismanagement. A revolving door of project managers, coupled with poor communication and allegations of corruption, resulted in a nine-year delay and billions of euros in excess costs.

---

27 Fareed, Su, and Aslam, "Transformational Leadership."
28 Alex Wellerstein, "The History and Science of the Manhattan Project," *American Journal of Physics* 82, no. 9 (2014), https://doi.org/10.1119/1.4871815.
29 J. Geraldi and V. Stingl, "From Visions of Grandeur to Grand Failure: Alternative Schools of Descriptive Decision Theories to Explain the Berlin Brandenburg," *EURAM - European Academy of Management* 16 (2016), https://www.researchgate.net/publication/313764520_From_Visions_of_Grandeur_to_Grand_Failure_Alternative_schools_of_descriptive_decision_theories_to_explain_the_Berlin_Brandenburg_Airport_fiasco.

- Denver International Airport Baggage Handling System[30]: Ambition outpaced reality in this 1990s project. The technologically complex automated system was plagued by poor planning and stakeholder conflict. Ultimately, the system was scrapped, replaced by a conventional conveyor belt system, and resulted in significant financial losses.
- Boston's Big Dig[31]: This ambitious undertaking to bury a major highway underground was marred by cost overruns, delays, design flaws, and even a tragic fatality. A lack of clear vision, inadequate risk management, and inter-agency conflict all contributed to this project's troubled legacy.
- California High-Speed Rail Project[32]: This project, intended to revolutionize transportation in California, has been hampered by ballooning costs, ongoing delays, and political obstacles. A lack of clear direction, scope creep, and funding challenges have cast a shadow over the project's future viability.
- London's Millennium Dome[33]: Conceived as a grand celebration of the new millennium, this project fell flat due to its exorbitant cost, lack of focus, and disappointing attendance. Unrealistic expectations, financial mismanagement, and a failure to engage the public were key factors in its underwhelming performance.

These examples serve as glaring reminders that even the most meticulously planned projects can be derailed by poor leadership and a dysfunctional work

---

30 Stasys Lukaitis and Jacod Cybulski, "The Denver International Airport Baggage Handling System," in *Information Systems Foundations: Constructing and Criticising* (n.p.: ANU Press, 2019), https://doi.org/10.22459/isf.06.2005.06.
31 Virginia Greiman, *The Big Dig: Learning from a Mega Project* (n.p.: APPEL Knowledge Services, NASA, 15 July 2010), Case Study, https://appel.nasa.gov/2010/07/15/the-big-dig-learning-from-a-mega-project/.
32 B Rajesh Kumar, "Case 7: California High Speed Rail Project," in *Management for Professionals* (n.p.: Springer International Publishing, 2022), https://doi.org/10.1007/978-3-030-96725-3_11.
33 "Case Study: The Millennium Dome — Marvel or Disaster?," *Tourism and Hospitality Research* 2, no. 2 (2000), https://doi.org/10.1177/146735840000200206.

environment. The consequences are not only financial, but they also undermine trust and confidence in the company and project team.

## Leadership Styles: A Multifaceted Landscape

Modern project managers have evolved beyond simply overseeing tasks and timelines. They are now leaders, navigating the complex web of human dynamics. This requires a deep understanding of various leadership styles and the ability to wield them strategically to inspire, motivate, and unite teams around common goals.

To help you understand how to harness the power of leadership, this chapter will provide a brief overview of various leadership styles, setting the stage for a more in-depth exploration. We will then explore these essential leadership styles in greater depth in the following chapters, equipping you with the tools to adapt your approach and elevate your project leadership.

**Transactional Leadership**: Grounded in the principles of operant conditioning, this style leverages rewards and punishments to reinforce desired behaviors and correct deviations[34]. It draws inspiration from the works of theorists like B.F. Skinner and his concept of reinforcement.

- Strengths: This style provides clear expectations and rewards, promoting efficiency and productivity in well-defined tasks and stable environments. It can be particularly effective when dealing with large teams or projects with tight deadlines.

- Weaknesses: It can stifle creativity and innovation as it focuses on compliance rather than inspiring initiative. Team members may feel undervalued or unchallenged, leading to decreased morale and engagement.

---

34 Galit Klein, "Transformational and Transactional Leadership, Organizational Support and Environmental Competition Intensity as Antecedents of Intrapreneurial Behaviors," *European Research on Management and Business Economics* 29, no. 2 (2023), https://doi.org/10.1016/j.iedeen.2023.100215.

- Applicability: Transactional leadership is best suited for projects with clear goals, well-established procedures, and team members who respond well to structured environments and external rewards.

**Servant Leadership**: This style is rooted in the philosophy of serving others first, as articulated by Robert Greenleaf. It emphasizes empathy, humility, and a focus on the growth and well-being of team members[35].

- Strengths: This style fosters trust, collaboration, and a strong sense of community within the team. It empowers team members, encourages their development, and promotes a positive work environment. This can lead to increased motivation, innovation, and job satisfaction.
- Weaknesses: Servant leaders may struggle to make tough decisions or enforce discipline when necessary. Their emphasis on consensus building may slow down decision-making processes.
- Applicability: Servant leadership is ideal for projects that require high levels of collaboration, creativity, and adaptability. It is particularly effective with teams composed of experienced and self-motivated individuals.

**Transformational Leadership**: This style builds upon the concept of charisma and idealized influence, as proposed by James MacGregor Burns and further developed by Bernard Bass. It focuses on inspiring and motivating followers to transcend their self-interest for the good of the team or organization[36].

- Strengths: This style inspires and motivates team members to exceed expectations by fostering a shared vision and empowering individuals to reach their full potential. It encourages creativity, innovation, and a

---

35 Adnan Mahmod M. Rashid and Shiva Ilkhanizadeh, "The Effect of Servant Leadership on Job Outcomes: The Mediating Role of Trust in Coworkers," *Frontiers in Communication* 7 (2022), https://doi.org/10.3389/fcomm.2022.928066.
36 Connie Deng et al., "Transformational Leadership Effectiveness: An Evidence-Based Primer," *Human Resource Development International* 26, no. 5 (2022), https://doi.org/10.1080/13678868.2022.2135938.

strong sense of purpose, leading to high levels of engagement and exceptional performance.

- Weaknesses: Transformational leadership can be demanding and requires strong communication and interpersonal skills. It may not be suitable for teams that prefer a more structured and directive approach.

- Applicability: This style is most effective in dynamic and complex projects that demand creativity, innovation, and adaptability. It is particularly well-suited for teams that are open to change and willing to embrace new challenges.

**Laissez-Faire Leadership**: This style stems from a belief in individual autonomy and self-direction. It is influenced by the ideas of libertarian thinkers who advocate for minimal intervention and maximum freedom for individuals to make their own choices[37].

- Strengths: This "hands-off" approach allows team members to exercise autonomy and make independent decisions, which can foster creativity and innovation. It can be highly motivating for highly skilled and self-directed individuals.

- Weaknesses: Laissez-faire leadership can lead to a lack of direction, coordination, and accountability. It may not be suitable for less experienced teams or projects that require close supervision and guidance.

- Applicability: This style is most appropriate for teams composed of highly skilled, experienced, and self-motivated individuals working on projects that require minimal supervision and allow for a high degree of autonomy.

---

37 Clément Desgourdes et al., "Decoding Laissez-Faire Leadership: An In-Depth Study on Its Influence Over Employee Autonomy and Well-Being at Work," *International Entrepreneurship and Management Journal* (2023), https://doi.org/10.1007/s11365-023-00927-5.

**Situational Leadership**: Developed by Paul Hersey and Ken Blanchard, this theory suggests that the most effective leadership style depends on the maturity and competence of the team members. Leaders must adapt their style to match the developmental needs of their followers[38].

- Strengths: This adaptable approach allows leaders to tailor their style to the specific needs of the team and project. It takes into account team members' maturity and competence, adjusting the level of direction and support accordingly.
- Weaknesses: Situational leadership requires a high degree of self-awareness and flexibility from the leader. It can be challenging to assess the readiness level of team members accurately.
- Applicability: Situational leadership is a versatile approach that can be effective in a wide range of contexts. It is particularly well-suited for projects with diverse teams or those that undergo significant changes throughout their lifecycle.

The dynamic landscape of project leadership offers a diverse array of styles, each with distinct strengths and potential drawbacks. Selecting the optimal approach involves careful consideration of project needs, team composition, and organizational culture. By delving deeper into these leadership styles, you can cultivate a versatile toolkit, empowering you to adapt your approach and inspire your team towards unparalleled success.

## Beyond Theory: Leadership Styles in Action

To bridge theory and practice, let's explore some scenarios that illuminate how different leadership styles can be adapted to unique project challenges. These examples will provide a solid foundation for our deeper dive into specific leadership approaches in the following chapters.

---

38 Sahala Benny Pasaribu et al., "The Role of Situational Leadership on Job Satisfaction, Organizational Citizenship Behavior (Ocb), and Employee Performance," *Frontiers in Psychology* 13 (2022), https://doi.org/10.3389/fpsyg.2022.896539.

1. **Tech Startup: Navigating Uncharted Territory**

   In a fast-paced tech startup, where innovation is paramount and the team consists of highly skilled, self-motivated individuals, a laissez-faire or transformational leadership style might be most effective. These styles foster autonomy, creativity, and a shared vision, essential ingredients for success in such a dynamic environment. However, as the startup grows and processes become more established, a shift towards a situational leadership approach might be necessary to provide structure and guidance to newer team members.

2. **Emergency Response Team: Swift Action Under Pressure**

   In crisis situations, such as a natural disaster or a major accident, a transactional leadership style can be highly effective. Clear directives, decisive action, and a focus on immediate results are essential when lives are at stake. However, once the crisis subsides and the team transitions into recovery mode, a servant leadership approach might be more appropriate to rebuild morale, foster collaboration, and support the team's well-being.

3. **Non-Profit Organization: Motivating Volunteers**

   In non-profit organizations where volunteers often drive the work, transformational or servant leadership styles can be particularly effective. Inspiring a shared vision, empowering individuals, and creating a sense of community are crucial for motivating and retaining volunteers who are driven by intrinsic rewards rather than financial compensation.

4. **Large Corporation: Maintaining Stability and Efficiency**

   In large corporations with well-established hierarchies and standardized processes, a transactional leadership style might be the norm. However, in departments that require innovation and adaptability, such as research and development or marketing, a transformational or situational leadership approach might be more appropriate to foster creativity and encourage risk-taking.

These examples illustrate the importance of a project manager's ability to adapt their leadership style to the unique demands of each project and team. However, as these examples demonstrate, there's no single "right" way to lead. The most effective project managers understand that their leadership style must be as dynamic as the projects they oversee. In the next section, we will explore the factors that influence this critical decision and discuss how to develop the flexibility to adapt your leadership style as needed

## The Quest for the "Right" Leadership Style

With such a diverse array of leadership styles, the question naturally arises: which one is the "right" one? The reality is that there is no single, universally applicable leadership style. Effective leaders understand that successful project management isn't about finding a one-size-fits-all solution, but rather about cultivating adaptability and flexibility. The optimal leadership style will vary depending on several key factors:

- **Project Nature**: A routine project with clear objectives and deadlines might thrive under a transactional style, where structure and rewards ensure efficient task completion. Conversely, complex projects demanding innovation and calculated risk-taking often benefit from a transformational style that fosters creativity and a shared vision.

- **Team Characteristics**: A team of highly skilled and experienced professionals may flourish with the autonomy granted by a laissez-faire approach. However, less experienced or less confident teams often require the clear guidance and support of a more directive style, such as transactional or situational leadership.

- **Organizational Culture**: A hierarchical, top-down culture may be more receptive to a transactional leadership style, while a more collaborative and innovative culture might be better suited to a transformational or servant leadership approach.

Understanding these factors is crucial, as the wrong leadership style can stifle team potential and hinder project success. For instance, adopting a laissez-faire approach with a team lacking experience could lead to confusion and disarray. Similarly, imposing a transactional style on a highly creative team might suppress innovation and diminish morale.

Ultimately, the most successful project managers are those who can adapt their leadership style to the specific context of their project and team. This requires a deep understanding of different leadership styles and the ability to assess the unique needs of each situation, ultimately choosing the approach that is most likely to yield positive outcomes. The ability to flex and adapt their leadership style is a hallmark of exceptional project managers, enabling them to navigate diverse challenges and unlock the full potential of their teams.

## The Journey Continues: Your Leadership Evolution

As we conclude this chapter, you now possess a deeper understanding of the multifaceted nature of leadership in project management. This knowledge is not just theoretical—it's the foundation upon which you'll build your own leadership journey. Remember, adaptability is key. The most effective project leaders are those who can flex their style to meet the unique challenges of each project and inspire the diverse individuals on their teams.

## Conclusion

As we conclude this exploration of the human element in project leadership, it's clear that successful project management is as much about leading people as it is about managing tasks. We've explored how leadership styles, communication, collaboration, motivation, and emotional intelligence can profoundly impact project outcomes.

From fostering a positive organizational culture to navigating complex team dynamics, we've established the pivotal role of project leaders in shaping a project's trajectory. By embracing the adaptability and flexibility required to tailor your leadership approach to each unique project and team, you unlock the potential for innovation, high performance, and remarkable success. As you embark on your next project, remember that the power to transform your team and achieve extraordinary results lies in your hands. Embrace the principles of effective leadership and watch your projects soar.

# FINAL THOUGHTS

As we conclude "The Practical Guide to Contracts & Other Essential Knowledge 2nd Edition," it is essential to reflect on the critical role that contracts play in the success of any project or business endeavor. Throughout this guidebook, we have explored the fundamental principles of contract management, from the basics of contract formation to the intricacies of drafting clear and enforceable agreements.

Contracts are not merely legal documents; they are strategic tools that help define relationships, allocate risks, and ensure that all parties involved understand their rights and obligations. Whether you are an executive, a project manager, or a business owner, having a solid grasp of contract law and its practical applications is indispensable.

We began by demystifying the concept of contracts, emphasizing their importance in formalizing agreements and managing potential risks. We then delved into the anatomy of contracts, breaking down each component to highlight how every detail—from preambles and recitals to specific terms and conditions—contributes to the overall enforceability and success of the agreement.

This guide also stressed the importance of precision in contract drafting. By avoiding ambiguity and ensuring that all terms are clearly defined, you can minimize the likelihood of disputes and protect your interests. We also underscored the value of creating project-specific contracts rather than relying on recycled documents, which may contain outdated or irrelevant provisions. Moreover, we explored modern contracting approaches, such as relational contracting and innovative models, which reflect the evolving nature of business relationships in today's world. These approaches emphasize collaboration, trust, and mutual benefit, setting the stage for more sustainable and successful partnerships.

In essence, mastering the art of contract management is about more than just understanding legal jargon; it is about strategically using contracts to guide projects to successful outcomes. By applying the knowledge and insights from this guide, you can navigate the complexities of contract management with confidence, ensuring that your projects are completed on time, within budget, and without unnecessary legal complications.

Remember, the key to successful contract management lies in preparation, clear communication, and a thorough understanding of the principles discussed in this book. As you continue to refine your skills and expand your knowledge, you will find that contracts can be powerful tools for achieving your professional goals. Thank you for taking the time to engage with this guidebook. May the principles and practices outlined here serve as a valuable resource in your journey to becoming a more effective and knowledgeable contract manager.

# ADDITIONAL RESEARCH

Fong, K. (2014). *Contract Management and Administration for Contract and Project Management Professionals: A Comprehensive Guide to Contracts, the Contracting Process, and to Managing and Administering Contracts.* J. Ross Publishing.

Van der Puil, J., & Van Weele, A. (2014). *International Contracting: Contract Management in Complex Construction Projects* (2nd ed.). Wiley-Blackwell.

Levin, P. (2019). *Construction Contract Claims, Changes & Dispute Resolution* (4th ed.). American Society of Civil Engineers.

Bunni, N. G. (2017). *The FIDIC Contracts: Law and Practice* (2nd ed.). Informa Law from Routledge.

Ware, G. (2016). *Managing Subcontracts: Subcontract Management for the 21st Century.* Routledge.

# GLOSSARY

**Acceptance**: The acknowledgment that the delivered goods or services meet the contract's requirements. Acceptance can be explicit or implied and is crucial in determining contract completion.

**Actual Breach**: Happens when one party fails to perform their contractual duties on the date specified in the contract or performs them improperly. This breach can lead to a lawsuit for damages or specific performance (forcing the breaching party to fulfill their obligations). If a contractor fails to deliver the agreed-upon service by the specified deadline, this is an example of an actual breach.

**Actual Damages**: Also known as "compensatory damages," these are awarded to cover the loss or injury directly resulting from a breach of contract. The goal is to restore the injured party to the position they would have been in had the breach not occurred.

**Aircraft Insurance**: Insurance that covers aircraft and liability for any damage or injuries caused by aerial operations, essential for firms that utilize aircraft such as drones or helicopters for construction projects.

**Anticipatory Breach** (Anticipatory Repudiation): Occurs when one party indicates, before the time for performance, that they will not fulfill their contractual obligations. This breach allows the non-breaching party to treat the contract as breached immediately and seek remedies, even before the breach actually occurs. For instance, if a supplier informs you in advance that they won't be able to deliver the goods on time, you can take action before the due date.

**Arbitration Clause**: A contract clause that requires the parties to resolve their disputes through arbitration rather than court litigation. Arbitration is typically binding and conducted by a neutral third-party arbitrator.

**Bid Bonds:** bonds that provide financial assurance that the contractor's proposal is made in good faith. If the contractor is awarded the contract, they will enter into it at the bid price and secure the necessary performance and payment bonds.

**Breach of Contract**: The failure to perform any term of a contract, written or oral, without a legitimate legal excuse. A breach can include failure to complete a job, failure to pay on time, failure to deliver goods or services as promised, or any deviation from the agreed-upon terms.

**Builders Risk Insurance**: Specific to the construction phase, this insurance covers buildings under construction against damage or loss from events like fire, theft, or natural disasters.

**Change Directive**: A written instruction issued by the owner directing a change in the work that the contractor is obligated to perform. The contractor must carry out the work as directed, even if there is disagreement about the change's impact on cost or schedule, with adjustments to be negotiated later.

**Change Order**: A formal document that alters the original terms of a contract, typically involving changes to the scope of work, cost, or timeline. Change orders must be agreed upon by both parties and are necessary for any work or changes beyond the original contract terms.

**Commercial Auto Insurance**: Covers damages and liability costs from accidents involving company vehicles, essential for firms that transport materials, equipment, or personnel.

**Communication Plan**: A section of the project management plan that establishes communication channels, frequencies, and formats for sharing information with stakeholders. It ensures transparency, collaboration, and timely decision-making.

**Compensatory Damages**: These are intended to compensate the injured party for the actual loss suffered due to the breach of contract. They include both direct and consequential damages, covering financial losses directly and indirectly caused by the breach.

**Condition Precedent**: A contractual provision that must be met before a party's obligation under the contract becomes effective. For example, payment obligations might only arise once goods are delivered.

**Condition Subsequent**: A condition that, if it occurs, will terminate a party's obligation under the contract. For example, failure to meet a deadline could result in the termination of the agreement.

**Consequential Damages**: Also known as "special damages," these cover indirect and foreseeable losses that result from the breach of contract. They arise from specific circumstances that the breaching party knew or should have known at the time of the contract.

**Consideration**: The value exchanged between parties in a contract, which can be in the form of money, goods, services, or a promise to act or refrain from acting in a certain way. Consideration is essential for a contract to be legally enforceable.

**Contract Documents**: This is a term used to collectively describe all documents that form the foundation of a contract. This can include the agreement itself, schedules, solicitation documents, requests for proposals, general and special conditions, plans, drawings, specifications, addenda, modifications, pricing schedules, various forms (like change orders and lien waivers), and sometimes even the prime contract if applicable.

**Definitions**: Specific terms within a contract that are given a particular meaning. These terms are usually capitalized throughout the document to maintain clarity and avoid ambiguity.

**Direct Damages**: These refer to damages that flow directly and immediately from the breach of contract. They are the natural result of the breach and are typically easier to calculate than consequential damages.

**Dispute Resolution Clause**: A section of a contract that outlines the process by which any disputes between the parties will be handled, such as mediation, arbitration, or litigation.

**Environmental Liability Insurance**: Covers costs related to environmental damage, such as pollution cleanup and hazardous materials management, critical for projects with potential environmental impacts.

**Express Authority**: The authority explicitly granted to an individual, either in writing (e.g., a contract or job description) or verbally by their employer. It is clear and specific, leaving no room for interpretation.

**Final Completion**: The stage in the construction process where all work has been finished in accordance with the contract documents and the project has been fully inspected and accepted by the owner. This includes completing any outstanding punch list items and delivering all required documentation. Final completion marks the end of the contractor's obligations under the contract.

**Force Majeure**: A clause that frees parties from liability or obligation when an extraordinary event or circumstance beyond their control, such as natural disasters or war, prevents one or both parties from fulfilling their obligations under the contract.

**General Contract (Prime Contract)**: The primary agreement between the owner and the contractor, outlining the overall terms and conditions, scope of work, responsibilities, and obligations of the parties involved in a construction project. The general contract is the central document that governs the relationship between the owner and the contractor.

**General Contractor**: The main contractor responsible for the day-to-day oversight of a construction site, management of vendors and trades, and communication of information to all parties involved throughout the course of a building project. The general contractor is typically hired by the owner and is responsible for overall project coordination.

**General Liability Insurance**: This foundational insurance covers bodily injuries, property damage, and advertising injuries. It protects firms from common hazards encountered on worksites.

**Governing Law**: A clause specifying which jurisdiction's laws will be applied to interpret and enforce the contract. This is particularly important in contracts involving parties from different states or countries.

**Implied Authority**: Authority that is not explicitly stated but is inferred from a person's position or actions. For example, a project manager might have implied authority to approve minor changes within a certain budget, even if the contract doesn't explicitly state it.

**Indemnification**: An agreement within a contract where one party agrees to compensate the other for certain costs and damages that might arise out of the contract. Indemnification clauses are crucial for risk management.

- **Narrow Indemnification**: This type of indemnification restricts the indemnitor's responsibility to losses or damages directly caused by their own negligence or willful misconduct, with no obligation to indemnify for acts or omissions beyond their direct control or responsibility.

- **Intermediate Indemnification**: This indemnification covers liabilities arising from the combined negligence of both the indemnitor and the indemnitee but does not extend to damages caused solely by the indemnitee's negligence.

- **Broad Indemnification**: This indemnification covers all potential liabilities, including those arising from the indemnitee's own negligence or wrongful acts, placing the greatest responsibility on the indemnitor.

**Liquidated Damages**: A pre-determined amount of money that a party agrees to pay if they breach certain terms of the contract. This is often used as a way to estimate potential damages and avoid litigation.

**Lien Waiver**: A lien waiver is a legal document used in the construction industry that a contractor, subcontractor, or supplier signs to acknowledge that they have received payment and waive their right to file a mechanic's lien against the property for the work or materials provided. There are different types of lien waivers, including partial and final waivers:

- **Partial Lien Release**: The general contractor is released from liability for payments made up to a certain point in time.
- **Full Lien Release**: Releases the contractor or owner from all issues, including claims, change orders, and disputes.

**Maintenance Bonds**: Also known as warranty bonds, these guarantee that the contractor will adhere to maintenance and quality standards for a specified period after the project is completed.

**Marine Insurance**: Insurance for firms involved in marine construction, covering losses or damages caused by marine operations such as the transport of goods and equipment over water.

**Material Breach**: A significant violation of the contract that goes to the heart of the agreement and undermines the contract's entire purpose. This type of breach is so substantial that it allows the non-breaching party to terminate the contract and seek damages. For example, if a contractor fails to complete the work as specified, that could constitute a material breach.

**Minor Breach** (Partial or Immaterial Breach): Occurs when one party fails to fulfill a small part of the contract. While the breach does not void the entire agreement, it may still entitle the non-breaching party to seek damages. An example would be delivering goods a day late; this might not fundamentally alter the contract, but it could still cause some inconvenience.

**Nominal Damages**: A small monetary award (often symbolic, such as $1) granted when a breach of contract has occurred, but the non-breaching party has not suffered a significant financial loss as a result. Nominal damages recognize the breach without providing substantial compensation.

**Non-Disclosure Agreement** (NDA): A legally binding contract in which one or more parties agree not to disclose certain confidential information. NDAs are commonly used to protect trade secrets or sensitive information.

**Non-Material Breach**: A minor breach that does not affect the contract's overall performance. This type of breach usually does not entitle the nonbreaching party to terminate the contract, but it may allow them to claim damages. For example, a slight deviation in the quality of materials used could be considered a non-material breach.

**Notice**: A formal communication required by a contract to inform a party of an important event, claim, or action. Notices must typically be in writing, signed by the sender, and delivered via specific methods outlined in the contract, such as registered mail or email followed by a registered letter.

**Notice to Proceed** (NTP): A formal notice issued by the owner to the contractor authorizing the commencement of work on a project. The notice typically marks the official start date of the contract's performance period.

**Owner**: The entity (individual or organization) that commissions and finances the construction project. The owner is responsible for defining the project's requirements and selecting the contractor and is typically the party with whom the contractor enters into the general contract.

**Owner's Insurance Policy** (OIP): A tailored insurance solution designed to cover the specific risks faced by the owner of a construction project. It supplements standard insurance coverage and provides additional protection for the project owner.

**Parol Evidence Rule**: A legal doctrine that prevents parties in a written contract from presenting extrinsic evidence of terms that contradict, modify, or vary the written terms of the contract. Essentially, the rule upholds the integrity of the written agreement as the final and complete expression of the parties' intentions, barring the introduction of prior or contemporaneous agreements that are not included in the document.

**Payment Application**: A payment application is a document submitted by a contractor, subcontractor, or supplier to request payment for the work completed or materials supplied up to a certain date on a construction project. The payment application typically includes details such as the amount due, the work performed, and the percentage of completion. It is an essential part of the construction payment process and often must be submitted regularly (e.g., monthly) in accordance with the contract terms.

**Payment Bonds**: Bonds that guarantee that all subcontractors, laborers, and material suppliers will be paid for their work, protecting these parties from non-payment.

**Performance Bonds**: Bonds that guarantee that the contractor will complete the work as per the contract terms and specifications. If the contractor defaults, the surety will step in to cover the costs of completing the project.

**Prime Contractor**: A contractor who has a direct contractual relationship with the project owner and is responsible for completing the project in accordance with the contract's terms and conditions. The prime contractor may hire subcontractors to perform portions of the work but remains the primary entity responsible to the owner.

**Privity**: Privity refers to the direct relationship between the parties involved in a contract, conferring rights and obligations only to those who are parties to the contract. In other words, only those who are in privity of contract can sue or be sued on the contract's terms.

**Privity of Contract**: A legal concept closely related to privity, which states that a contract cannot confer rights or impose obligations upon any person who is not a party to the contract. This principle enforces the idea that only the individuals or entities directly involved in the contract have the legal standing to enforce or challenge its terms.

**Procurement Management Plan**: This is a section of the project management plan that outlines the procurement process for acquiring goods or services from external vendors. It covers supplier selection, contract negotiation, and performance monitoring.

**Project Budget**: A section of the project management plan that outlines the project's financial plan, including estimated costs, resource allocation, and contingency reserves. It ensures financial viability and enables effective cost control throughout the project lifecycle.

**Project Management Plan**: A comprehensive document that acts as a roadmap, guiding the project team through the intricate phases of execution, ensuring alignment with objectives, and mitigating potential risks. It serves as a single source of truth, providing a reference point for all stakeholders involved. It typically includes sections such as the executive summary, project scope statement, project schedule, project budget, resource management plan, communication plan, risk management plan, quality management plan, procurement management plan, and stakeholder management plan.

**Project Schedule**: A section of the project management plan that details the project timeline, including key milestones, activities, dependencies, and deadlines. It often includes a Gantt chart or other visual representation of the schedule, facilitating progress tracking and resource allocation.

**Project Scope Statement**: A section of the project management plan that delineates the project's boundaries, outlining what is included and what is excluded. It clarifies deliverables, acceptance criteria, and constraints, preventing scope creep and ensuring everyone is on the same page.

**Punitive Damages**: These are awarded to punish the breaching party for particularly egregious or malicious conduct. Punitive damages go beyond compensating the injured party and are intended to deter similar behavior in the future.

**Quality Management Plan**: A section of the project management plan that defines quality standards and processes for ensuring that deliverables meet or exceed expectations. It outlines quality control measures, inspections, and testing procedures.

**Repudiatory Breach:** Occurs when one party's behavior indicates that they will not honor the contract's terms. This breach allows the non-breaching party to terminate the contract and seek damages. An example might be a contractor abandoning a project without completing it, signaling that they do not intend to fulfill their contractual obligations.

**Requirements:** Requirements are the conditions or capabilities that must be met or possessed by a project, product, service, or result in order to satisfy a contract, standard, specification, or other formally imposed document. They describe the essential functions, characteristics, or outcomes needed to meet the project's objectives.

**The Resource Management Plan:** The Resource Management **Plan** is a section of the project management plan that identifies the resources required for the project, including personnel, equipment, materials, and technology. It outlines roles and responsibilities, staffing plans, and resource allocation strategies.

**Retention** (or Retainage): A percentage of the contract price withheld from the contractor until the project is satisfactorily completed. This ensures that the contractor finishes the work according to the contract terms.

**Risk Management Plan**: This is a section of the project management plan that identifies potential risks that could impact the project and outlines strategies for mitigating and responding to them. It includes a risk register, which documents each risk's probability, impact, and mitigation measures.

**Scope of Work**: A detailed description of the work to be performed under the contract, including the responsibilities, tasks, and deliverables. This section is critical for ensuring both parties understand the expectations and requirements.

**Severability**: A severability clause is a provision in a contract that states that if any part of the contract is found to be invalid or unenforceable, the remaining provisions will continue to be in effect. This helps to preserve the integrity of the contract.

**Special Damages**: Special damages are another term for consequential damages; they cover losses that do not flow directly from the breach but occur as a result of special circumstances. They must be clearly proven and directly linked to the breach.

**Specifications**: These are detailed, precise descriptions of the technical requirements and criteria for materials, products, or services to be delivered under a contract. Dimensions, quality standards, performance requirements, and other details necessary for a project's production or execution are often included. Specifications serve as a blueprint for the work to be performed and are used to ensure that the final deliverable meets the required standards.

**Stakeholder Management Plan**: This is a section of the project management plan that identifies project stakeholders and their interests, outlining strategies for engaging and managing their expectations throughout the project.

**Subcontractor**: A third party hired by the primary contractor to perform a specific task as part of a larger project. The subcontractor is bound by the terms of the subcontract and, indirectly, by the terms of the main contract through "flow-down" clauses.

**Subrogation**: The process by which an insurance company, after paying a loss to the insured, seeks to recover the amount of the loss from the responsible third party. This is often applicable in insurance contracts.

**Substantial Completion**: This is the stage in the construction process where the project is sufficiently complete according to the contract documents so that the owner can occupy or use the work for its intended purpose. Substantial completion often triggers the release of retainage, the start of warranties, and the reduction or elimination of liquidated damages for delay.

**Termination for Convenience**: A clause that allows one party to terminate the contract without cause, usually requiring that they compensate the other party for work completed up to the termination date.

**Time is of the Essence**: A clause indicating that deadlines and dates specified in the contract are critical and must be strictly adhered to. Failure to meet deadlines may be considered a breach of contract.

**Umbrella Insurance**: Providing extra coverage beyond the limits of other liability policies, umbrella insurance is crucial for large-scale or high-risk projects where typical policy limits may be insufficient.

**Uniform Commercial Code** (UCC): A comprehensive set of laws governing commercial transactions in the United States. The UCC covers various aspects of commercial law, including sales of goods, leases, negotiable instruments, bank deposits, letters of credit, investment securities, and secured transactions. It is designed to provide a uniform legal framework for businesses across different states.

**Waiver**: The voluntary relinquishment of a known right, claim, or privilege. A waiver in a contract context can refer to a party's decision not to enforce a specific term or condition of the contract.

**Warranty**: A promise within a contract that certain aspects of the contract (e.g., materials, services) will meet specified standards. A breach of warranty could lead to remedies such as repair, replacement, or reimbursement.

**Warranties and Representations**: Statements within a contract that assert certain facts or conditions to be true. Warranties often relate to the quality or performance of goods or services, while representations may pertain to the status or capacity of the parties entering into the contract.

**Work for Hire**: A concept in copyright law indicating that the work created by an employee or contractor within the scope of employment or under certain contract terms belongs to the employer or the person who commissioned the work, rather than the creator.

**Workers' Compensation Insurance**: Mandatory in most regions, this insurance covers medical costs, death benefits, and lost wages for employees injured on the job, which is crucial given the high-risk nature of the construction and engineering industries.

# INDEX

## A

Acceptance 10, 15
 Formal Acknowledgement 10
Acceptance of Products and Services 58
Actual Breach 86
Actual damages 131
Agenda 210
Aircraft Insurance 317
Anticipatory Breach 86
Arbitration 109

## B

Be Cautious of Implied Authority 253
Bid Bonds 314
Boilerplate 25
Breach 86
Broad Form
 Indemnity 133
Builders Risk Insurance 316

## C

Capacity 16
Certificate of Insurance 318
Changed Conditions 101
Change Order Log 253
Choice of Words 52
Commercial Auto Insurance 316
Communication Plan 214
Compensatory damages 132

Competent Parties  31
Compliance and Change Management  73
Conditional Acceptance and Counteroffers  32
Condition Precedent  30
Condition Precedents  16
Conditions  30
Condition Subsequent  30
Confidentiality Checklist  76
Consequential Damages  136
Consideration  16
Contingent Payment Clauses  159
Contract
  What is a Contract?  9
  What is the Purpose of a Contract?  9
Contract Checklist  36
Contract Documents  77
Contract Recitals  27
Contractual Elements  26
Counteroffer  32, 34

# D

Damages Caused by Owner's Delay  10
Damages for Contractor's Delay  10
Decision and Award  269
Default  86
Defend  133
Definitions  27
  Importance of  39
Differing Site Conditions  10, 99
Diligent Effort  107
Direct damages  131
Dispute Resolution  10, 108
Document Everything  254
Drafting Checklist
  Warranty  183

# E

Elephant  12
e-mail  302, 305, 308
Enforceability  34
Enforceable  34

Environmental Liability Insurance 317
Evaluation Criteria
  Subcontractor 268
Executive Summary 213
Express
  Warranty 184
Express Authority 251

**F**

Financial Assessment 269
Flow-Down 22
Force Majeure 10
Full Lien Releases 199

**G**

General damages 131
General Liability Insurance 316

**H**

Headings 28
Hold Harmless 132

**I**

Implied
  Warranty 184
Implied Authority 251
Incidental Damages 137
Indemnification 10
Indemnify 132
Indemnitee 132
Indemnitor 132
Indirect damages 132
Indirect Damages 136
Inspection 10
Intermediate Form
  Indemnity 133
Interpretation Clause 27
Interviews 269
Issue Log 252

## J

Journals  226

## K

Know Your Contract  253

## L

Late Payments by the Owner  10
Legality  16
Legality of Purpose  31
Lessons Learned  243
Limitation of Liability and Cap  11
Liquidated damages  132
Litigation  109

## M

Main Body of the Contract  28
Maintenance Bonds  315
   Warranty  315
Managing Change Orders  252
Marine Insurance  317
Material Breach  86
Mediation  109
Memorandum of Understanding  14
Milestone Criteria  107
Milestones  11, 106
Minor Breach  86

## N

Narrow Form
   Indemnity  133
No Damages for Delay  11
Notice Letter  93
Notice of Default  306
Notice of Schedule Delays  94, 300
Notice of Termination  309
Notice Response Letter  226
Notices  150

## O

Offer 15
Order of Precedence 157
Owner's Insurance Policy 317

## P

Paid if Paid 17, 18
Paid When/If Paid 11
Partial Lien Releases 199
Parties 31
Past behavior 21
Pay-if-Paid 16
Payment Bonds 314
Payment Schedule 107
Pay-when-Paid 16
Performance Bonds 314
Preamble 26
Price Escalation 11
Privity of Contract 22, 31
Procurement Management 214
Professional Liability Insurance 316
Project Budget 214
Project Documentation 202, 210
Project Kickoff Meetings 73
Project Management Plan 213
Project Schedule 214
Project Scope Statement 213
Proof of Insurance 318
Proposal Review 269
Protect Your Interests 254
Punitive Damages 137
Punitive/Exemplary damages 132

## Q

Quality Management 214

## R

RACI 229
RACI matrix 234
Reference Checks 269

Regular Internal Audits 73
Regulatory Monitoring 73
Request for Information 268
Request for Proposal 269
Requirements 41, 48
Resource Management 214
Response to Change Order Request 303
Risk Allocation 9
Risk Assessment 269
Risk Management Plan 214
Risk Register 242, 252

## S

Set-off 166
Silence 20
Site Visits 269
Special/Consequential damages 132
Specification 50
Specifications 41, 44, 48
Stakeholder Management 215
Synopsis 271

## T

Termination 11

## U

Umbrella Insurance 316
Uniform Commercial Code 32
Unliquidated damages 132

## V

Verbal Agreements 13
Verify Express Authority 253

## W

Waiver and Liens 11
Warranty Terms 182
Workers' Compensation Insurance 316

# BIBLIOGRAPHY

Butković, Lana Lovrenčić. "A New Framework for Ranking Critical Success Factors for International Construction Projects." *Organization, Technology and Management in Construction: an International Journal* 13, no. 2 (2021): 2505–20. https://doi.org/10.2478/otmcj-2021-0030.

"Critical Success Factors for Effective Internal Construction Stakeholder Management in Nigeria." *Acta Structilia* 28, no. 1 (2021). https://doi.org/10.18820/24150487/as28i1.1.

Damoah, Isaac Sakyi, Anthony Ayakwah, and Paul Twum. "Assessing Public Sector Road Construction Projects' Critical Success Factors in a Developing Economy: Definitive Stakeholders' Perspective." *Journal of Project Management* 7, no. 1 (2022): 23–34. https://doi.org/10.5267/j.jpm.2021.7.003.

Frydlinger, D., O. Hart, and K. Vitasek. "A New Approach to Contracts: How to Build Better Long-Term Strategic Partnerships." *Harvard Business Review* 97, no. 5 (2019). https://link.gale.com/apps/doc/A599089506/AONE?u=anon~21a05974&sid=googleScholar&xid=189fc576.

Greenberg, Karra, Evgenia Jane Kitaevich, Siddharth Chaudhari, and Anna Kirkland. "Analyzing Contracts: State of the Field, Mixed-Methods Guiding Steps, and an Illustrative Example." *Law and Social Inquiry* 49, no. 1 (2023): 423–50. https://doi.org/10.1017/lsi.2022.82.

Hamad, Rami J.A, Bassam A. Tayeh, and Hamdan A. Al Aisri. "Critical Factors Affecting the Success of Construction Projects in Oman." *Journal of Sustainable Architecture and Civil Engineering* 29, no. 2 (2021): 121–38. https://doi.org/10.5755/j01.sace.29.2.29269.

Hanák, Tomáš, and Eva Vítková. "Causes and Effects of Contract Management Problems: Case Study of Road Construction." *Frontiers in Built Environment* 8 (2022). https://doi.org/10.3389/fbuil.2022.1009944.

Hansen, Seng. "Developing a Model of Construction Contract Management Competency in a Developing Country: Quantitative Approach." *Journal of Legal Affairs and Dispute Resolution in Engineering and Construction* 13, no. 4 (2021). https://doi.org/10.1061/(asce)la.1943-4170.0000504.

Lester, Albert. "Project Management Plan." In *Project Management, Planning and Control*, 67–71. N.p.: Elsevier, 2021. https://doi.org/10.1016/b978-0-12-824339-8.00014-6.

Maylor, Harvey, Joana Geraldi, Alexander Budzier, Neil Turner, and Mark Johnson. "Mind the Gap: Towards Performance Measurement Beyond a Plan-Execute Logic." *International Journal of Project Management* 41, no. 4 (2023): 102467. https://doi.org/10.1016/j.ijproman.2023.102467.

Rani, Hafnidar A., Tamalkhani Syammaun, Fatimah Azzahra, Afizah Ayob, Mohammad Harith Amlus, Zakirullah, and Muhammad Shafly

Aqsha. "Risk Management Planning by Risk Register in Building Construction Project." *IOP Conference Series: Earth and Environmental Science* 1303, no. 1 (2024): 012034. https://doi.org/10.1088/1755-1315/1303/1/012034.

Shalwani, Amirali, and Brian Lines. "Using Issue Logs to Improve Construction Project Performance." *Engineering, Construction and Architectural Management* 29, no. 2 (2021): 896–915. https://doi.org/10.1108/ecam-12-2020-1089.

Shayan, Shadi, Ki Pyung Kim, and Vivian W. Y. Tam. "Critical Success Factor Analysis for Effective Risk Management at the Execution Stage of a Construction Project." *International Journal of Construction Management* 22, no. 3 (2019): 379–86. https://doi.org/10.1080/15623599.2019.1624678.

van Niekerk, Jaques, Jan Wium, and Nico de Koker. "The Value of Data from Construction Project Site Meeting Minutes in Predicting Project Duration." *Built Environment Project and Asset Management* 12, no. 5 (2022): 738–53. https://doi.org/10.1108/bepam-03-2021-0047.

Vidogah, William, and Issaka Ndekugri. "Improving the Management of Claims on Construction Contracts: Consultant's Perspective." *Construction Management and Economics* 16, no. 3 (1998): 363–72. https://doi.org/10.1080/014461998372385.

Zwikael, Ofer, and Jack Meredith. "Evaluating the Success of a Project and the Performance of Its Leaders." *IEEE Transactions on Engineering Management* 68, no. 6 (2021): 1745–57. https://doi.org/10.1109/tem.2019.2925057.

# ABOUT THE AUTHOR

Dr. Dondi M. Day is a seasoned professional with extensive experience in contract and subcontract management, procurement, and project management. He holds a Doctorate in Business Administration, Leadership from Liberty University and credentials from the NCMA and PMI. Dr. Day has a proven track record of successfully negotiating and managing complex agreements, streamlining organizational processes, and mitigating and managing claims and disputes. He has worked with leading Fortune 500 companies, consistently delivering results and exceeding expectations. In addition to his corporate experience, Dr. Day is a passionate educator and author who has taught over 5,000 project management professionals, sharing his expertise and insights.

# LET'S STAY IN TOUCH!

Dear Colleagues and Industry Professionals,

I'm eager to continue our collaboration and explore new opportunities to achieve mutual success. Whether you have questions about my workshops, coaching, are interested in potential partnerships, or simply want to stay in touch, please don't hesitate to reach out. You can contact me via email at dondi.day@emeraldislepublishing.com.

I'm excited to navigate the dynamic landscape of our industry alongside you and contribute to your ongoing success. Let's work together to achieve remarkable milestones and chart new territories.

For those who prefer traditional communication, I'm also available at P.O. Box 5041, Emerald Isle, NC 28594-5041.

Feel free to connect with me on LinkedIn: https://www.linkedin.com/in/dondimday/ or Facebook @ Dondi Day to stay updated on my professional journey.

Please visit my website at islepublishing.com

Best regards,

Dr. Dondi Day

# BUY THE COMPANION STUDY GUIDE

Enhance your understanding of contract management and elevate your professional skills by purchasing the companion workshop and study guide to this book. Designed to complement the practical insights and real-world examples presented in the guide, the workshop and study guide offer a structured and interactive learning experience.

The workshop and study guide provide a deeper dive into key concepts, reinforce your understanding through practice exercises and case studies, and equip you with the tools to apply your knowledge effectively in real-world scenarios. The potential benefits of investing in this valuable resource include:

- Solidified Understanding: Reinforce your grasp of contract fundamentals, terminology, and interpretation principles.
- Enhanced Practical Skills: Develop the ability to draft clear and unambiguous contract documents, manage change orders effectively, and navigate disputes with confidence.
- Improved Risk Management: Learn to identify and mitigate potential risks associated with contract terms and conditions, safeguarding your interests and ensuring project success.

- Boosted Confidence: Gain the confidence to negotiate favorable terms, protect your rights, and make informed decisions in any contractual situation.
- Career Advancement : Enhance your professional expertise and open doors to new opportunities in contract and project management.

It can be purchase on Amazon at https://a.co/d/b2Xe1P8 or in IngramSpark at https://shop.ingramspark.com/b/084?kYfLuK0Uo44SUxBJwfawOfZ4Cs7qdGK0UcvbgjJElcG. Your favorite bookstore may be able to order for you too.

www.ingramcontent.com/pod-product-compliance
Lightning Source LLC
Chambersburg PA
CBHW070748230426
43665CB00017B/2290